SEVENTY-FIVE YEARS

THE STORY OF BEDFORD HIGH SCHOOL

1882-1957

EDITED BY

K. M. WESTAWAY

with an additional chapter edited
by Pearl Hackett

BEDFORD

DIEMER & REYNOLDS LTD

1957

Printed in England

*T*HE first history of Bedford High School, edited by Miss Westaway, appeared in 1932. As we approached our seventy-fifth birthday it was clear that additional chapters must be written, and equally clear that there was one person who could speak with authority of the last twenty-five years, Miss Westaway herself. We were all most grateful, therefore, when she agreed to edit a new history, and in this foreword I wish to record the thanks of the Guild and the School for this book and for all that the Editor has done to make it such a personal and intimate record.

The last chapter, for which the Editor has for obvious reasons taken no responsibility, is added by those who have worked with Miss Westaway during the last thirty years or so and who offer it as an affectionate tribute to a great Head Mistress.

M. G. Watkins.
Bedford High School,
March, 1957.

THE PREFACE of the first history of Bedford High School contained these words :

"It is impossible in one small book to write down all the cherished memories of all the people who have passed through the School and who will, we hope, read the book. It is even impossible to mention all the events, or all the people that should be mentioned. As a history the book is full of shortcomings, and we send it out into the world only too certain of that. But as a waker of memories, as a mirror in which those who know will see reflected all the love and the loyalty, the hard things and the gay things, which during the years have made the School so great, it will meet its welcome and finds its place."

Those words still stand. Twenty-five years have passed since they were written. The School is approaching its seventy-fifth birthday, and a second history is now offered to its past and present members in commemoration of the event.

The first nine chapters of the present version are taken from the first version. Chapter I is exactly as before. The next eight have been subject to a few additions and omissions. The chapters on the Guild and on the boarding houses have been considerably rearranged and added to. The rest of the chapters are new.

My difficulty now, as before, is adequately to express our gratitude to all those who have helped with this work. Miss Watkins' encouragement and thoughtfulness have been a real inspiration. We are greatly indebted to Mr. Edmund Esdaile, a grandson of Mrs. McDowall, for all his help and interest : he still holds many letters and photographs which are a record of a wonderful personality and a stirring period of history. To Dorothy Kitchener and Ruby Prosser for much work behind the scenes, to Miss Pehrson, who designed the dust-wrapper, to Connie Darrington, who made the index, and to Mr. Nightall, representing the firm which has helped us so much through so many years, we offer our most grateful thanks.

And to the School we all say, "A very happy birthday, and many happy returns of the day."

Carlton, Leyburn, Yorkshire.   K. M. WESTAWAY

CONTENTS

CHAPTER I

THE MATRIX (BEFORE 1873)

BY THE REV. C. F. FARRAR

A MATRIX is the die or stamp from which seals and impressions are inscribed upon documents. Such seems the appropriate title of the first chapter of the History of the High School of the Harpur Charity. The matrix was the generous soul of one—in his youth a poor boy of Bedford—who became a prosperous London Merchant Taylor and in 1561 Lord Mayor of London. The latest impression struck from the matrix of that generous soul three hundred and seven years after his benefaction was the founding of the High School under the Scheme of the Harpur Charity in 1873. For the events of those three centuries I must refer the reader to my recent *History of the Harper Trust through Three Centuries,* 1566-1873—centuries with which the School has no connection, save that owing to the marvellous appreciation in value of Harpur's benefaction through those centuries, as from the womb of time the High School was born.

Briefly, in 1566 Sir William Harpur and Dame Alice, his first wife, gave to the Corporation of Bedford 13 acres and 1 rood of land in the Parish of St. Anne's, Holborn, valued at £12 per annum, and other lands situated on the north side of the Ouse at Bedford valued at £28 per annum, in all £40 per annum. His Deed of Gift, dated 22nd April, 1566 (preserved in the Harpur Trust office), defines the intention of his benefaction, *viz.*, the maintenance of a Free School (the Bedford School of today), the giving of marriage portions to poor maidens, and the nourishing and informing of poor boys of the town. Provision for the education of girls evidently did not occur to Harpur, or, if it did, he put the thought aside as an unnecessary thing. History tells us of the erudition of such accomplished ladies as Lady Jane Grey and Queen Elizabeth, but in the sixteenth century the ordinary girl was considered "finished" when she had acquired skill at the hearth and an adept hand in the still-room, while reading and writing were the accomplishments of but few. To

Dame Alice I trace the provision in the Deed of Gift of the marriage portion. She no doubt pointed out to her husband that girls had no part in his benefaction. Possibly both considered female education "a vain thing fondly imagined", but marriage was clearly a girl's *métier*, and in this she should be helped. But even this kind thought was not to be realised for another hundred and fifty years, for I can find no trace of such marriage portions being given until after 1725, and then only of the value of thirty shillings. In fact the value of the benefaction appreciated so slowly that it barely sufficed to carry out the maintenance of the Free School until the Act of Parliament of 1764.

The Holborn Estate, let out as farm land, brought a rental of £50 per annum in 1625 and £99 per annum in 1650. Then the Great Fire of London in 1666, which destroyed some thirteen thousand houses in the City of London and its suburbs, produced a demand for houses, and the 13 acres and 1 rood became a desirable building site. Its early development is due to Dr. Nicholas Barebone, a clever, specious but dishonest building speculator whose history I have written elsewhere. He secured a building lease from the Bedford Corporation in 1686 at £99 per annum from 1686-1709, to be followed by a lease of fifty-one years, 1709-1760, at £149 per annum. Through the dishonest dealings of Dr. Barebone the Corporation ran the risk of losing a great part of the benefaction by an exchange of land proposed to them by Barebone; but fortunately his lease passed into more honest hands, under whose management at its end in 1760 the Holborn Estate produced a rental of £2,274 per annum.

In 1764 an Act of Parliament regulating the Charity was passed. But problems of education would appear to have been beyond the scope of the lay mind of the eighteenth century. Bedford, then a small town of between two and three thousand inhabitants, seems to have found its educational requirements satisfied with a small Grammar School (the Bedford School of today) and the addition of a Writing School in 1764 (the Modern School of today); but girls still remained unprovided for, while the bulk of the Charity as directed by the Act of Parliament was devoted to forty marriage portions of £20 annually, appren-

tice fees for boys and girls with benefactions at the conclusion
of apprenticeship, a resident hospital for poor children, and the
distribution of charitable doles to the poor. The two boys'
schools, receiving but a pittance of the funds, were both insufficient, while the expenditure on the purely eleemosynary
objects practically bankrupted the Trust. An Act of Parliament
in 1794 essayed with little success to regulate the Charity. One
clause of this Act indirectly brings the High School into the
field of local history and enables us to visualise the School in
the past. It ordered the Trustees to build and maintain twenty
almshouses. In 1795 they accordingly purchased for £160 a
plot of ground called Mill Close, now the site of the High School,
whereon in 1800 were built to the design of John Wing—who
built Bedford Bridge in 1811—the twenty almshouses, long
known as the "Best Almshouses" to distinguish them from the
existing almshouses in Dame Alice Street. I remember these
"Best Almshouses" in my youth, a long line of little Georgian
houses standing back some forty yards from Bromham Road,
fronted by broad lawns and bowered in chestnut trees—some of
which survive today—a very charming feature of Bedford until
in 1881 (under the scheme of 1873) they were demolished to
make way for the School buildings. My mother remembered
how in her girlhood there were no houses west of the Barley Mow
Inn, opposite the gaol, and the old people of the almshouses had
an uninterrupted view across the meadows to the river and
beyond to the Ampthill and Ridgmont Hills. Such are memories
of the site of the High School of today. The *History of Bedford
School* tells of the awakening of that school from the lethargy of
centuries by the appointment of Dr. Brereton in 1811, while the
Modern School owes its success to the appointment of John
Moore in 1833. To these two men Bedford owes the beginnings
of higher education in Bedfordshire.

It should be noted here that the free education given at the
Grammar and Commercial Schools (Bedford School and Bedford
Modern School), both prospering under Dr. Brereton and Mr.
Moore, was attracting families to settle in Bedford to take
advantage of the facilities offered. To the influx of the "squat-
ters", as the native Bedfordians called them, is due the con-

struction of such residential quarters as Adelaide Square, Priory Terrace, Victoria Terrace, Albert Terrace, Windsor Terrace, etc.

I must here return to the financial development of the Trust. As already stated, the income in 1760 was £2,274, and by 1794 it showed but a small increase, *viz.*, to £2,918. The income rose to £6,707 in 1806 and to £6,949 in 1826, but by this time the Trust were in debt to the extent of £9,476. The National Society had recently initiated elementary education. The Trustees, after visiting one of the earliest national elementary schools in Baldwin's Gardens, London, built for themselves at a cost of £698 on a site adjoining the hospital for poor children (which occupied the present site of the Modern School) a National School to accommodate 350 boys and 250 girls, and this was opened on 18th January, 1818. Such was the start of elementary education in Bedford, and for the first time the elementary education of girls was carried on by the Trust. The intention was more excellent than the execution, for owing to lack of funds the master was teaching 300 children single-handed. Lives there today an education inspector to credit the fact? In 1833 the Boys' Elementary School had 289 boys and 103 girls, for in this year the girls' section was closed owing to paucity of numbers and irregular attendance. It was not until 1838 that a Girls' Elementary School was restarted, with the addition of an Infants' School (both located in the northern portion of the Modern School buildings which had been erected in 1833) "to fill up that link in the chain of education which has long been deemed desirable". So runs the Minute of the Harpur Trust of 29th December, 1839, in recording the foundation of the Girls' and Infants' Elementary School. It would seem that another very necessary "link in the chain of education" was missing, *viz.*, girls' higher education, but nearly forty years were to elapse before the link was added to by the foundation of the High School.

It may be asked, how did the sisters in these families coming to Bedford secure their education? At some time in the late eighteenth or early nineteenth century the Moravian Community in Bedford established a ladies' school in St. Peter's—the building just beyond the Moravian Chapel—now forming part of Bedford School. It was here that my mother and her sisters were educated

4

in the thirties and forties of the last century. No doubt the curriculum was simple, but, I judge, thorough. "Shakespeare and the musical glasses", English and English literature, French, the piano, hand-embroidery, water colours, calisthenics, and, above all, handwriting. I still remember the handwriting of my eldest aunt—in the Italian style—quite beautiful. This was the only organised girls' school in Bedford in the early part of the nineteenth century. No doubt small private schools were springing up. In my youth in the '60s and '70s I recall the Misses Ray keeping a girls' school on the Bromham Road; a Miss Dixon another, I forget where; while in the 1870s a Madame de Marchot established the French Protestant College in the Crescent, considered at the time a very aristocratic establishment for families who regarded the High School, then in building, as destined to be merely a Higher Educational School. But the French Protestant College was to survive the opening of the High School by only a few years.

But to return to the fate of the Harpur Trust. The income of 1826, *viz.*, £6,949, rose with a phenomenal increase in the next ten years to over £13,000. A third Act of Parliament in 1826 only repeated the error of the two preceding Acts in allotting too small a portion of the funds to its schools and permitting an excessive expenditure on the eleemosynary objects of the Trust. This is evidenced by the Trust accounts of 1831-32, which show the various commitments of the Trust :—

		£	
Grammar School	..	1,433	
Exhibitions	..	480	=£2,735
Commercial School	..	609	Educational
National Schools	..	213	
Almshouses	..	1,993	
Hospital	..	667	
Apprentice Fees and Benefactions	1,423	=£5,010
Marriage Portions	..	427	Eleemosynary
Distribution of Alms	..	500	

Total   £7,745

Enough to point out that the Almshouses cost more than the Grammar School, and the Hospital for twenty-six poor children more than the Commercial (Modern) School, while a sum more than double the cost of the elementary schools was distributed in doles to the poor ! The period of the 1840s was one of much financial stress, of a sinking income and increased educational expenses. It was becoming evident that the Trustees, in giving free higher education to boys and elementary education to boys and girls, with their heavy commitments for charitable purposes, were essaying an impossible task and heading for bankruptcy. A scheme was sanctioned in 1853 by the Court of Chancery which somewhat relieved the financial stress and instituted small fees in the two boys' schools. But in 1866 a Royal Commission was set up to inquire into and report upon Endowed Schools generally. Briefly, the Report advocated locally the abolition of the funds devoted to charitable objects, save the maintenance of the almshouses in Dame Alice Street. These funds were to be devoted to education. The privilege of Bedford-born children to be educated free was to be abolished, and all pupils of higher schools were to pay equal fees ; and admission to these schools, hitherto restricted to Bedford, was to be open to all *urbi et orbi*. The Report advocated the establishment of a High School for Girls with a modern department, which was destined to become the Dame Alice Harpur School of today. The Report led to the formulation of the scheme which now regulates the Trust and which received the Royal Assent on 4th August, 1873. Under the scheme the site of the "Best" Almshouses was to be cleared to make way for the building of the High School of today, a building which in its early years was to harbour both the High School and the Dame Alice Harpur School. So at length the link in the chain of education which the Trustees of 1838 so blindly overlooked and certainly had no money to supply, was at last added.

Such, briefly, is the prehistoric period of the High School—a Pliocene Age—if either term is applicable to the three centuries when the School had no entity, and when no one dreamed of such an institution or even felt the need of it. In these days of the equality of the sexes—I use the phrase with misgiving—it is

6

difficult to realise that the higher education of girls was the latest development in the sphere of education in Bedford. Today (1932) the High School shares, *pari passu*, in the Endowment of Sir William Harpur. The gross income of the Charity today is £34,829. After deduction for the official expenses of the Trust, the residue is divisible into elevenths. Thus four-elevenths are divisible between Bedford School and the High School, four-elevenths between the Modern School and the Dame Alice Harper School, two-elevenths go to elementary education, to give maintenance grants to elementary scholars entering the higher schools, and other assistance. One-eleventh goes to the maintenance of almshouses. Thus today the share of the High School is £2,291, net charges for loans on new buildings, etc., £632.*

The reader must realise, however, that the Endowment of Sir William Harpur, which once sufficed to give free education to many, today provides but a small proportion of the vast expenditure now required by modern education. Today (1932) the cost of the four higher schools amounts to some £86,000 a year, the endowment being supplemented by fees and Government grants. But it must not be forgotten that in any case, apart from such accretions, the endowment is a portion of the increment upon those 13 acres and 1 rood in the Parish of St. Anne's, Holborn, which were once valued at £12 per annum.

---

*The money was not allocated on the principle that girls' needs are as great as those of boys. In the year 1955-6, Bedford School received £7 16s. od. for each boy, and the High School £5 4s. od. for each girl—
EDITOR.

B

CHAPTER II

1873-1882

BY MISS WESTAWAY AND MR. A. H. ALLEN*

THE HISTORY of the Bedford High School really begins on
4th August, 1873, when Queen Victoria signed the Royal Assent
to a scheme for the better regulation of the Bedford Charity or
Harpur Trust. This was the result of a Commission of Inquiry
into Endowed Schools set up in 1866, and the Report of the
Commissioners pointed out that, while the Harpur Trust had
provided higher education for boys and elementary education
for boys and girls, no provision had been made for the higher
education of girls.

Having therefore in view the establishment of girls' higher
schools in Bedford, the Harpur Trust in 1873 appointed certain
members of their body to act as "Governors of the Girls' School",
and these members were directed to elect five ladies to work with
them. It is worth recalling in our book the first meeting of the
Governors of the Girls' School, as it is recorded in the minute
book still in the Harpur Trust Office. The men who were thus
responsible for the School's inception were Mr. Moses Rogers
(Chairman), a retired doctor from India ; Captain Colburne,
previously of the Indian Army ; Mr. Nash ; Mr. Robinson,
Fellow and Tutor of New College, Oxford ; Mr. Scoles, who
built the house called "Pemberley" in Pemberley Avenue, which
later became the School House of Bedford School and was recently
pulled down ; and Dr. Storrar. The last had great influence,
having been one of the Endowed Schools' Commissioners : at
one time he was Chairman of the British Medical Council, and
also held high office in London University. He was a man of
tremendous energy and zeal, and was the chief driving power of
the governing body during the difficult years just then beginning.
The date of this meeting was 19th January, 1874. The only
business accomplished at it was the election of the ladies as

* The information for this period was supplied by Mr. Allen to Miss Westaway, who wrote the chapter in
its present form.

8

required by the new scheme. Of these, Miss Mary Ewart was very well known as one of the pioneers of women's education. She was one of the earliest benefactors of Newnham College, in which she took a great interest, and at Cambridge and at Oxford there are still women's scholarships bearing her name. Mrs. Hillier was the wife of the vicar of Cardington, Mrs. Kilpin was the wife of a well-known Bedford business-man, and Mrs. Hamp was a resident of Bedford. Miss Smith, of Oxford, was another pioneer of women's education, and was the sister of Professor Henry Smith, also of Oxford.

Mrs. Hamp, however, subsequently declined office, and Mrs. George Higgins was elected in her place. Other ladies of note and influence who became Governors during the next few years were Mrs. Phillpotts, the wife of Mr. J. S. Phillpotts, Head Master of Bedford Grammar School; Miss Whitbread, the sister of Mr. Samuel Whitbread (who for over forty years was M.P. for Bedford), and aunt of a former Lord-Lieutenant of Bedfordshire; and Miss Martin, a wonderfully helpful and sympathetic Governor, who later endowed the "Jane Benson Scholarship", to be competed for by girls of the School who wished to go to Bedford College, London.

Dr. Storrar became Chairman in 1876, and at the same time Mr. Allen, who was already Clerk to the Harpur Charity, was made Clerk to the Governing Body of the Girls' Schools. It would be hard to estimate the debt which the schools owed for the next forty-five years to Mr. Allen's brilliant and untiring work for them. (His four daughters, Kittie, Irene, Evelyn and Eleanor, subsequently were pupils at the High School, and the second of these did responsible work on the staff of the Harpur Trust Office for many years.)

The task of the establishment of the two girls' schools proved to be beset with endless delays and difficulties. Indeed, this chapter might almost be entitled "Hill Difficulty", and we who are apt to take the High School so much for granted will remember with honour the names of these pioneers, without whose indomitable zest and courage the School might hardly have existed at all. Already money was accruing to the credit of the schools, but for some years there was insufficient even for a beginning. Meanwhile the Governors were carefully thinking over their plans, and Mr. Allen tells how he was sent by them to visit the North London Collegiate School, and spent a highly-interesting day with Miss Buss, its head mistress, and with her assistant and future successor, Dr. Sophie Bryant. In March, 1878, things really began to move. A committee consisting of Dr. Storrar, Mrs. Phillpotts, Mr. Horsford and Captain Colburne was set up to "inquire and report as to steps which it may be expedient to take with a view to the opening of the Girls' Schools at the earliest possible time".

The Committee made their report in the following month. Referring to the site of the almshouses on the north side of Bromham Road, they recommended that the almshouses should remain untouched, and that on the east half of the open ground in front of them there should be built the Modern School for Girls, for not fewer than 200 girls, at a cost of £3,000, while the west half of the site should be reserved for the future erection of the High School. The reason for this seems to have been that there were in Bedford several private schools attended by girls who, in the alternative, would probably attend the High School, so that their needs were assumed (quite erroneously) not to be urgent. There was no provision in the town for girls who would probably attend the Modern School. The report was accepted, and the Harpur Trust acceded to the request of the Governors to place the desired site at their disposal.

The choice of architect fell on Mr. Basil Champneys, of London. His work was already very well known. At Cambridge in 1875 he had designed "Newnham Hall", which is now known as "Old Hall" at Newnham College. Among his subsequent works were the present Bedford School and the new school buildings at Harrow. He was now asked to send in a design for a Modern School accommodating 200 girls, a High School, accommodating 100, and a central hall for the use of either school, but he was warned that the Governors would probably proceed at first with the building of the Modern School only. Possibly his feeling of success at his election in 1878 was tempered by a little foreboding when it was resolved that his plans "should be circulated among the Governors, to enable

It was now clear that some of the almshouses must after all be removed to make way for the new buildings, and a fresh period of change and uncertainty began for Mr. Champneys. In May he was asked to plan in such a way that the Modern School could hold 300 girls and the High School 200. (It appears that at that time the number of pupils at the Boys' Modern School was greater than that at Bedford School, and it was the general impression that the Girls' Modern School would have more pupils than the High School.) At the same time, Mr. Champneys was to indicate how much of the building could be omitted for the time being if the original figures were adhered to. It must have been rather a feat that in nine days he reappeared with the revised plans. They were not accepted without considerable argument and modification : but when the Governors had eliminated a gymnasium from both schools and the laboratory from the Modern School, and reduced the High School music rooms to one, Mr. Champneys was requested to draw his plans yet again and to obtain tenders for the carrying out of the work. He was given two months for this ; but this time he struck, and was allowed four. His final plans were approved in October, and in the same month Mr. Samuel Foster (whose daughters Ida and Dora were to become pupils at the School, and whose grand-daughter Margaret was head girl, 1927-28) was appointed to carry out the work. The planning suggested in 1878 was reversed, and the High School was built on the east end of the site, and the Modern School on the west.

In due course the almshouses were sold and demolished. An executive committee of the Governors was appointed to deal with details of the business of building, and the minutes of the period make most interesting reading. First Mr. Champneys is in trouble about his supply of bricks, and has to supplement his "Bedford red brick" with Henlow brick of superior price and fame (for use in front). Then he is in trouble about the depths of his foundations (this proved to be a very serious difficulty, partly owing to the presence of an underground stream) ; then about the height of the floor of the hall. The executive committee were certainly busy, visiting the site of the growing building and conferring on all kinds of topics, from the relative values of bells and speaking-tubes to the proper positions of gas-pendants in classrooms. Mr. Hammer submitted a model desk for their approval, and became the contractor for the furniture, thus beginning a connection with the School which was valued for many years. The choice of desks, forms and so on was in the main deferred until there should be a head mistress to deal with it.

In November, 1881, an advertisement was issued, saying that the Governors proposed to open the Schools in May, 1882, and inviting candidates for the office of head mistress of either school to send in their applications to Mr. Allen before 21st December. The two short lists were made at the January meeting, 1882, and the appointments were made at a meeting in London on 2nd February. Of six candidates, Mrs. McDowall was elected head mistress of the High School; and, of another six, Miss Porter, head of Bradford Girls' Grammar School, was elected head mistress of the Modern School. More of Mrs. McDowall will appear in later pages of this book. Suffice it here to say that she was a sister of Archbishop Benson, and before her marriage had started High Schools at Norwich and Oxford. Her husband was secretary of the Girls' Public Day School Company, and during her short tenure of office in Bedford they lived in Lansdowne Road. They had a little daughter, Catherine Ada, who, in time, became Mrs. Esdaile. To her son, Mr. Edmund Esdaile, we are indeed grateful for the following family memories which he has written for this book:

"The first mention known to me of my grandmother Ada McDowall (née Benson, born 27th November, 1840) is in the diary of Crabb Robinson, who years before had been introduced by her father to the Linnæan Society; at that time she was teaching at Queen's College, Harley Street. From 1860 onwards many letters of various dates between her, her sister Eleanor, her brother (later Archbishop), and her sister-in-law survive; that sister-in-law, also a cousin, was Aunt Minnie, whom I knew in her latest years, the Archbishop's widow, and Ada's confidante. Ada, in 1860-61, was in Germany, by 1866 in Surbiton, running a kind of local finishing school (in my mother's phrase) with her sister. 'Detestable Surbiton' (she wrote), and, again, 'I would rather live on my £40 per annum than lead the life I do' (1871). Not all, however, was black : in 1870 she is interested in petitioning the Houses of Parliament ('Sir Sterndale Bennett is giving a lesson as I wish') on behalf of lady doctors, and obtains Minnie's signature, spending also Christmas of that year most happily at Wellington in Minnie's house. In 1872 Eleanor married, as his second wife, Thomas Chauncy Hare, who had been present as Huskisson's secretary at the famous railway accident when Huskisson was killed, and who is best known in connection with proportional representation. In 1874 the future Archbishop, still Master of Wellington writes, 'from the depth of the Councils of the Head Masters of England (you find yourself now on that level !), to congratulate' her upon her election to Norwich : 'you must now let me help you in any way I can'. Thence to Oxford ; but in January, 1879, 'it is heartbreaking', on urgent doctor's orders, she 'must leave England *at once* for some warm or dry place'. Back in Oxford that August she asks her brother's advice about joining a sisterhood, an idea vaguely adumbrated once before (in 1871) ; but, without warning, Andrew McDowall next month unintentionally declares his true feelings. Minnie is the confidante ; marriage ensues, and that same brother officiates at the wedding. Andrew, who, like Ada, had lost when young his father, and had known, like her, suddenly restricted means, had been fortunate in attracting the attention of the first Lord Shuttleworth, an important person in educational and public affairs, who also had become a staunch friend. All is set fair for the newly wed, and in their marriage, love and work they were wonderfully courageous—how else could Ada have nurtured both my infant mother and the infant Bedford High School ? Yet on 11th October, before Ada was 42, shortly after the birth of their son, Stephen, all was over : and on 24th October, 'Found loose in Post Office, Bedford', there was a letter to Andrew McDowall, dated 22nd June, beginning 'I hope, dearest, these [*unidentified*] will reach you safely. . . I do so miss you when you don't come home.'

"Tradition dies hard : for the Archbishop established at Truro a Girls' High School, to which in due course, Miss Dora Coate, went as head mistress from the school at Bedford which Ada had begun."

MRS. MCDOWALL

MR. MCDOWALL, CATHERINE AND STEPHEN

Immense work was done behind the scenes during that spring by the Governors and head mistresses. All the rules regarding the admission of pupils, fees, notice to leave, regulation of boarding houses, and so on, were most carefully thought out and framed. The question of High School boarding houses was referred to Mrs. McDowall; and Mrs. Barker, Miss Rayner and Miss Ray were all licensed to receive boarders. Then there was the question of the domestic staff for the School, and we read how Alfred and Julia Wheatley were solemnly summoned to a Governors' meeting, and informed that they were appointed attendants at the High School at 30s. od. a week, and were to consider themselves the servants of Mrs. McDowall and liable to dismissal by her.

The School was opened on 8th May, 1882, with forty-three pupils, ranging in age from nine to seventeen. The formal opening took place on 20th July, and the preparations for the great event were lengthy and immense. The Harpur Trust minutes relating to that summer are packed with interesting details. First there was the election of a deputation to wait upon the Lady Isabella Whitbread to ask her to perform the opening ceremony: and we can still picture the committee sitting over the compilation of the list of guests, the problem of laying hands on enough chairs, the numbering of the seats, and a score of other arrangements. The Mayor circulated handbills all round the town, expressing his earnest desire that the inhabitants would manifest their interest in the important event by the display of flags, banners and other decorations. The appeal was most effective and the town was well decked out, the climax of course being in the neighbourhood of the Schools, where Venetian masts were put up twined with evergreens and ribbons of red, white and blue: and two arches were erected across the Bromham Road, lavishly ornamented with flowers and rosettes. It was a gay scene, and the weather, after causing acute anxiety during the previous days, was at its best. Before and after the ceremony St. Paul's Church bells pealed forth; and at intervals during the afternoon the Promenade band, stationed in the playground, gave selections of music.

The programme of the ceremony was as follows:

Address by the Lord Lieutenant of the County,
Earl Cowper, K.G.
Declaration of Opening by the Lady Isabella Whitbread
Te Deum (*Stainer*)
Address by Dr. Storrar
(Chairman of the Governors of the Girls' Schools)
Anthem (composed for the occasion)
(*P. H. Diemer*)
Address by Mr. S. Whitbread, M.P.
(Chairman of the Governing Body of the
Harpur Trust)
Hymn : "All people that on earth do dwell"
Vote of thanks to the Lady Isabella Whitbread
Proposed by Mr. C. Magniac, M.P.
Seconded by the Mayor of Bedford
(Mr. J. W. Hill)
God Save the Queen

This chapter would be incomplete without the note of *The Bedfordshire Times* on the proceedings : "These High and Modern Schools for Girls have not merely increased the school accommodation in the town, they have not merely added to the attractions of Bedford as an educational centre, they have conferred upon the town quite a distinctive and exceptional character. There now exists a great endowment which combines features hitherto uncombined, and one of which has only recently existed at all. The Bedford Schools are now the hopes not only of 'Bedford Boys' but of—may we without offence repeat Dr. Storrar's epithet ?—'Bedford Beauties'. This is a new and distinctive feature in the modern revolution in the education of women. Here Bedford leads the van ; and if the work be carried on with the care and judgment with which it has been commenced, we may safely predict great and lasting success to the Bedford High and Modern Schools for Girls."

CHAPTER III

1882-1887

BY MISS M. E. ROBERTS

BEDFORD IN 1882 was a pleasant, old fashioned, country town, its streets leading straight into the country. There were hedgerows all along the Clapham Road and no houses beyond the end of Tavistock Street. Over Bromham Road railway bridge a country road led to Biddenham and Bromham; and from St. Peter's Green fields stretched up to the hill, for there was no park, no De Parys Avenue, and there were no suburbs beyond. The only new road being built was Lansdowne Road; though already a new quarter was being laid out in expectation of people flocking to Bedford for its schools, as indeed they were beginning to do.

Mr. Phillpotts, the head master of the Grammar School, affectionately spoken of by boys and parents as "Chief", had already become a great figure in the life of Bedford. Nothing could daunt his courage and energy, and he was determined to raise the Grammar School to a place in the front rank of public schools. Dr. Poole, on his part, so long the esteemed and loved head master of the Modern School, was widening the scope of the education given to boys, most of whom would leave at fifteen to enter business.

From accounts written of those days it is clear that the Bedford townspeople viewed with some distrust the diverting of endowments for the benefit of the increasing colony of "squatters" round about Ashburnham Road, widows of Army officers and others, who came to share in the benefits of the Harpur endowments. At that time a boy could be educated at the Grammar School for £4 a year.

It was in May, 1882, that both Schools opened; the little town was at its freshest and gayest with lilac and may and laburnum, with chestnut blossom and young green leaves. I remember vividly the morning walk to school from my first lodgings over in Cardington Road, then called "Potter Street", the sycamore tree beside St. Mary's Church against the blue sky, the white stone bridge, the wide gleaming river, the bells of St. Paul's playing *Barbara Allen* and other old tunes—with a halt in the middle of the line and a run down to the end—as I hurried by at nine o'clock, for the girls' schools began at 9.15 so that the boys and girls should not throng the streets at the same time. The boys' schools were side by side, the Grammar School in its old building behind St. Paul's, now used as the Town Hall.

Where the new girls' schools were built there had stood for eighty years some cottage almshouses on a green shaded by the beautiful chestnut and lime trees that still surround the playground. The buildings were planned for two schools, one at each end, with a central hall between. Viewed from without, they were a dignified structure of red brick with stone facings ; but within, it must be owned, the effect was rather forbidding, with the classroom window-sills high above our heads and the walls of bare drab brick. But "the library" (which has never yet been a library) was always a beautiful room with its large bay windows, and in winter there was a cheerful open fire in every room. Upstairs there were six classrooms, two rather small ; the one at the north end of the corridor was called "the art room" and was far too small for the purpose ; the corresponding room at the other end was called the laboratory ; and there was a gymnasium, also too small, reached by crossing a bit of the playground in all weathers. But provision, however inadequate, for art, science and physical exercises did at least indicate ideals which were advanced for those days.

There were 43 girls in attendance that first morning—Monday, 8th May, 1882—and they were placed in four forms. The highest, Form V, was in the gallery room ; the little ones, Forms II and I, were in the next two rooms along the corridor ; and Form III, in the big room at the end, contained all the rest from 12 to 15 years of age. There were four mistresses—Miss Carter, a woman of considerable ability and force of character and always quiet and steadfast, had been second mistress at the Norwich High School ; Miss Olive Harcourt, young, tall, good looking, full of life and efficiency and very popular from the first, had been educated at Miss Buss's "North London Collegiate School" and at Girton College, Cambridge ; Miss Kenny, educated in Germany, had been a junior mistress at the Norwich High School ; and Miss M. E. Roberts had been at Somerville College, Oxford, and afterwards at what is now the Maria Grey Training College. Each mistress had charge of a form, and taught her special subject in other parts of the School. Drawing was taught by Mr. Denyer, head of the Bedford School of Art, a quiet enthusiast of few words, class singing by Mr. Diemer, music by Mr. Ford, and drilling by Sergeant Campbell.

At our first staff meeting before the School began, the head mistress dictated to us a time-table for each form and gave us detailed directions as to arrangements, and when we had been at school a few days it might have been a year, so habitual and regular did the routine of activities seem. The workmen were not out of the building, hammering and singing went on behind the doors of the big hall, and the playground was littered with their material, but there were the blackboards and the time-tables, the bells and the clocks, there were the mistresses on their platforms and the girls in rows at their new single desks, and we really were the Bedford High School.

It would have been a good thing if a woman had been at the planning of the building who was familiar with the daily life of a girls' school, for where were the cloakrooms ? Did they expect girls to hang up a cap and tramp like boys into their classrooms with muddy boots, to be worn all day ? Nothing was provided but two cell-like places under the stairs, entered from the main corridor leading to the hall, and, for the staff, a tiny box of a room beside the hall door. So a big classroom was fitted up with boot-racks and pegs, and there I remember standing on duty the first morning to see that there was no loitering to talk.

How one recalls the fashions of those days, the pigtails and the curls and the long hair beautifully brushed and tied back with ribbons, the pretty freshly-starched frocks, the long black-stockinged legs and the little ones' pinafores—"Don't forget to say we wore pinafores !" said somebody to me at the last Guild meeting ! The elder girls had their hair "up" and their skirts down to the ankle. And then the many-buttoned boots and the eternal quest for button-hooks! "Mary, were you speaking?" "No, Miss A——, I was not speaking, I was only asking for a button-hook!"

A few girls drove in from such outlying places as Kempston and Clapham, for it was another twelve years before bicycles for girls appeared, and a school dinner was prepared in the caretaker's room in the bell-turret. It was served in the library, presided over by the "mistress of the week". What a week that was! The "mistress of the week" was on duty in the cloakroom every day, morning and afternoon, before and after school, for a week, also at "break" in the playground or directing exercises and marching in the gymnasium, and she was also in charge during the dinner hour.

At the end of the term, on Thursday afternoon, 20th July, there was an impressive ceremony and the two schools were formally opened. Each member of the staff received a big gilt-edged card of invitation, a pleasant courtesy we had not expected, as we had assumed that our attendance would be required as a duty.

Gaily-coloured Venetian masts, decked with flags and twined with evergreens, were put up on both sides of Bromham Road for the whole length of the School grounds. The bells of St. Paul's pealed, a band marched through the town, and in the School hall were assembled the girls of the High School and of the Modern School and their parents. The Governors of the Harpur Trust and a number of distinguished visitors were on the platform, and before the speeches began the youngest girl in the School, pretty, curly-headed May Billson, who sat shyly by her mother until the moment came, went forward and presented a bouquet to Lady Isabella Whitbread.

An address was given by Earl Cowper, Lord Lieutenant of the County, and then the schools were formally declared open by Lady Isabella Whitbread and the "Te Deum" was sung.

Afterwards the building was thrown open to the visitors, and one of a group of Modern School girls coming from their end of the building where the afternoon sun was streaming in, and racing through our dim corridors, was heard to exclaim, "A regular dungeon, I call it!" Already school patriotism was dawning! One of the Governors, Miss Eleanor Smith, of Oxford, a well known and formidable old lady, seemed to be lost among the back premises; but when I ignorantly asked if I should show her the way round the buildings she replied severely, "My dear, I have had the putting up of them!" So ended a memorable day, and next morning all broke up for the holidays.

The opportunity amongst us of our first head mistress, Mrs. McDowall (Miss Ada Benson), was all too short for her to be known and appreciated in Bedford as she had been elsewhere, but she laid sure foundations, she held up a great ideal and her work still lives. On that morning in May when we first assembled for school prayers, she read in her reverent, quiet voice those words of St. Paul that we all remember. As a girl I had heard her read those words when she opened her first school, the Norwich High School, and others remember her reading them on the first day at the Oxford High School. She read them without the verses that precede and follow, just those words which claim an allegiance and set forth an ideal to which young hearts will always rise in response:

"Whatsoever things are true, whatsoever things are honest, whatsoever things are just, whatsoever things are pure, whatsoever things are lovely, whatsoever things are of good report; if there be any virtue and if there be any praise, think on these things."

Of her it was indeed true that "in a short time she fulfilled a long time".

Her brother, Dr. Benson (afterwards Archbishop), had been the first head master of Wellington College, and to him she owed much in her ideas and methods. Our classes were "Forms", the highest being the sixth, not, as in most girls' schools of that day, the "First Class". Members of her staff were to be called "Mistresses" and to hold the same sort of position as masters in boys' public schools, for the word "Governess" had lost its dignity. As soon as she had a Sixth Form fit for responsibility, she introduced a prefect system at Oxford. There was never any sort of sentimental affection for her in either of her schools;

and although at Oxford we girls knew she could be delightful out of school, as when occasionally she invited her Sixth Form to tea, for the most part she inspired a loyalty that was coupled with fear of her displeasure if we should fall below what she expected of us. Her rules were strict, but we were an undisciplined lot, fresh from lax private schools and governesses at home, and it was all very bracing for us.

Not long after, she married, and later, when the much talked of Harpur Schools were to be opened, it was hardly surprising that friends sought her out, knowing that no one could lay a better foundation for a great school. London was near enough for Mr. McDowall to go up daily to his office, and this made it possible for her; she was appointed head mistress, and, with a devoted husband who shared her interest in the work, and with a little daughter, she came to Bedford. And then, after her one long interesting summer term it all ended. Early in the autumn term, on 11th October, about ten days after the birth of a son, she died.

The School was carried on until Christmas by Miss Carter, the second mistress, and in December we heard that the Governors had appointed as head mistress Miss Marian Belcher, Vice-Principal of Cheltenham Ladies' College. I must own that there was rather a dread amongst us on the staff of anybody from Cheltenham, for some of us had known enthusiastic young people who talked of "College" and of Miss Beale without making us understand wherein her real greatness lay. But we were soon to learn, for Miss Belcher brought with her the true large spirit of that wonderful place.

Before we re-assembled in January our new head mistress had written a kind personal note to each one of her staff. She met us first at a mistresses' meeting in the library the day before School began, and I never can forget her as she entered the room that day—the beaming kindliness of her face, the simple friendliness of her greeting of each—all our doubts vanished in the warmth of her smile. She made no sudden changes in organisation but was appreciative of all that had been done; and she left, at first, much of the detail to Miss Carter and Miss Harcourt, who were models of orderly precision, while she gave herself

MISS BELCHER

to larger matters and was easy of access to parents, girls and staff. She took a large share in the teaching of the elder girls. How well I remember her thoughtful and quickening lessons on the New Testament, her graphic and interesting history lessons, and some delightful lessons on Chaucer's women—for it was the privilege of one or other of us to go to her lessons and help to correct the note-books.

At Easter, 1883, Miss Carter left on her appointment as head mistress of the Church of England High School at Preston. Her one term of work with Miss Belcher had led to a steadfast friendship which lasted to the end of her short life. She died in 1887 in Miss Belcher's sheltering care at Bedford. She had a spirit that rose above anything selfish and petty to a serenity that came from faith and love, and no one who knew her can ever forget what she was.

Miss Carter was succeeded as second mistress by Miss E. Baker, who had been one of the early students of Girton College.

It was no wonder that, as Miss Belcher became known, the reputation of the School increased, for she won confidence on every side. Already, when she came, the expected limit of 100 girls had been passed, for we re-opened in January, 1883, with 116 on the roll, and before long this number was doubled. For the first year the daily roll of attendance of the whole school was called after prayers in the hall every morning ; but this interesting practice had to cease, and registers were kept in each form after Easter, 1883.

Those were years of very interesting experience in a rapidly-expanding school. Classification had to be elastic and adapted to the needs arising, for, though some girls had been well taught, many came from incredibly bad private schools and from desultory education at home, and had no notion of how to set about work or of the pleasure of it. Yet many were keen and intelligent and, given a chance, were able to make rapid progress. "Coming to the High School was like stepping out into the fresh air" somebody said to me the other day, at the Guild gathering.

Though the general plan was annual promotion, the School year beginning in September, new forms were created as numbers increased and girls were "moved up" when ready. But the names of the forms would puzzle anybody used to the regular grading of today. For instance, Form III grew gradually younger every year! In 1882 Miss Harcourt's original Form III included all the girls below the fifth and above the junior forms, and ranged in age from 15 down to 12 years. In 1883 my IIIA was a form of promising girls, most of whom were 13 and 14 years of age, for Form IV had come into existence. In 1884 Form III was again a year younger and a new form, IVc (13-14), was my big form of quick workers in the room downstairs with the bay windows. The next year this was IVB, and was in the big room with Miss Thomas, and IVc was a small class of rather older girls. But, by 1886, forms had settled down and remained more or less the same, with Bedford's own peculiar naming which lasted on. The series of forms from I to VI was complete. So now Form IIIA contained the girls of about 11 years old, just moved up from Miss Hiatt's Junior Division. They passed up the next year to IVc (12-13), then to IVA (13-14 or 15) (known as the "Junior Oxford Form"), then to VB, which took no outside examinations, then to VA (the "Senior Oxford Form"), and then to Form VI where some read for groups in the Cambridge Higher Local Examination and some for the London Intermediate B.A. Of course, in every yearly grade there were parallel forms, as no classes were allowed to be too large, and, from the first, forms were divided into upper and lower divisions for languages and mathematics.

From the first Miss Belcher took the keenest interest in the music, and soon made it a strong feature of the School. The music staff was increased and music rooms were needed. When two cloakrooms were built, one over the other, entered from the staircase, the classroom used as a cloakroom was set free, and, as it had three windows in a row, it was easily divided up into three music rooms, with a space behind where Mrs. Graham dispensed milk at break.

Originally there had been a marvellous plan described in *The Bedfordshire Times* when the School was opened. A large classroom "is to be utilised for the teaching of music. In it there will be five pianofortes, placed in as many glass cases, so as to enclose the sound and enable pupils to practise simultaneously without interfering with one another." As if, in a big day school, girls could *practise* at school! The absurdity of these glass boxes had to be seen to be believed. I do not remember more than one—or was it two?—of the five ever being actually set up; it stood against the inner walls of the classroom where the grand piano stands and it was just large enough to hold a piano, a master and a pupil. A mistress sitting at a table in the space outside correcting her exercise books would be able to chaperone several masters at once, for such seemed to us to be the idea. But where sound could not get out air could not get in; and the first time Mr. Bond-Andrews saw the glass cubicle he dragged his piano out of it and refused to be suffocated. And that was the end of it.

Class-singing was taught to the upper forms by Mr. Diemer, so long a well-known personality in Bedford, and to the little ones by a young Swiss lady, Mademoiselle Truchet, who had charming ways with classes of children, and a clear bird-like voice.

I remember a day—but it must have been a good many years later—when Miss E. Roberts came out of the hall into the little staff room saying, "Have you heard Helen Nicholls' voice? You *must* come and listen : she is in the front row of the singing class." There she stood, I can see her now, so young and fresh and smiling—she was a new girl then and called "Helen" not "Agnes" at school. How little we knew the really great artist she was to become !

Soon, more classrooms were needed, and a long, low, iron room was put up along the back of the playground where the science building now stands, and in it Miss Hiatt reigned over four or five junior forms, one seated beyond the other. A cheerful crowd they were, and she loved them ! Each class had its own mistress, and the desks were put fender-wise in front of the mistress's desk, while, round the central space so left, called "the well", were benches where the children came to sit for oral lessons; they then went to their desks for written work. It was the Cheltenham plan, and the idea was that young mistresses, beginning under the general supervision of an experienced head, received training and moral support.

There never were any very young children in the School; the age of entry was seven, and there was no preparatory class; for Miss Sim, a pioneer in kindergarten work, had most of the little children in Bedford in her school in The Crescent, which is now the well-known Training College for Teachers.

The hall was only half its present size, and was a long, straight, lofty room, for the whole of that portion entered from the main porch was built out later, and the porch replaced nearer to the road than before. Originally the hall was shared by both the Modern and the High School and was divided by a huge wooden shutter that could be pushed into a recess; but, in a few years, the whole hall was allotted to the growing High School. Miss Belcher's platform stood at the end where the organ gallery is now; there were no galleries then. So crowded were we that, for some time, three or four of the middle-school forms had their desks in the hall at the end next to the Modern School. There were drawbacks to this. I remember a mistress who did not stay very long, whose helpless ways really tempted girls to be naughty. Her girls were always out of their seats, buzzing round her desk with questions; and it was so easy, when sent back to her place, for a girl to catch her foot in the leg of the folding easel—quite by accident, of course—and down came the board with a grand clatter.

On Saturday morning Miss Belcher used to go round to each form to read marks, a wonderful way of keeping in touch with the week's work of every girl. I say *on Saturday morning!* Yes! Soon after she came our dear Miss Belcher took away our free Saturday, and many years passed before she realised the error of her ways and restored it! Accustomed as she had been to school on Saturday at Cheltenham, she regarded the High School plan of a whole free day as a waste of precious hours and she wanted the extra time for her weekly visit to each class. The School morning ended at noon on Saturday and was not interrupted by break; milk was brought round on a tray during lessons.

Miss Belcher's mark-reading was something never to be forgotten. It was not the mere reading of a list in order of merit, for at first no such lists were made and marks were not added up. It was a survey of the whole week's record. As her finger travelled across the wide page following the entries opposite each name, each girl stood up in turn. Nothing escaped her, and all was there to be seen. Work not produced at the appointed time was marked "late", bad work was "refused" and girls had to return to school in the afternoon to do it again under the mistress's eye—and often with explanation and help. Incidentally mark-reading was a survey of the mistress's work too, for, when recurrent refused lessons appeared in any subject, it was clear that something was wrong, and enquiry would be made afterwards. And how quick she was to see anything exceptionally well done and to praise it, and to recognise plodding! She liked the opportunity of drawing a class out in friendly conversation. Once, with a class of little girls, she asked, "Can anybody ask me anything in French?" A small voice volunteered *"Quel âge avez vous?"* To which Miss Belcher benignly replied, *"Je suis plus agée que vous"*.

Regular attendance was insisted upon, leave of absence was only given for urgent cause ; one would think that there would be no chance for "slackers". Few people contrived to sit inert at their desks and let arithmetic roll over their heads. One afternoon Miss Belcher's sister, walking along Bromham Road, heard an indignant girl behind her say to another, "I never knew anything like this High School! If you go there you've *got* to go, and if they tell you to do a thing you've *got* to do it!" No wonder A. writes : "Coming from a private school, it took me about a year to settle down, and I was often in hot water!"

Rules were strict—or rather I should say there was one strict far-reaching and comprehensive rule of silence ; for punctuality, tidiness and good manners hardly went by rule. No talking was allowed anywhere inside the building, except at break, not even before and after school hours, and no loitering in the playground was allowed either. This was an even stricter rule than we had had at the beginning, for originally talking was allowed before morning school. "Eh! What a parrots!" said an old Scotch gardener, when a Girls' High School was pointed out to him, little knowing the peace and quietness that reigned within! "The atmosphere of some girls' schools strikes one as conventlike", said a well-known educationist once to me. Of course he was wrong ; it was nothing of the kind. He forgot that lessons ended at one o'clock and much of a girl's day was lived in the freedom of home. The afternoons were free except for music lessons and drawing, and this was possible in the days when "science" was one botany lesson a week. I think perhaps discipline was *too* strict, and some mistresses were in danger of treating a class as if it were a gang of convicted felons liable to break out at any moment. And people were far too much afraid of letting girls make a noise—and what a noise they do make in these days of freedom !

Miss Henrietta Lloyd has contributed her own memories of school life seventy years ago :—

"I looked up to and admired every member of the staff in those days as being quite above the rest of the world ! How well I remember them all ! Miss White, Miss Holmes, Miss Lee, Miss Poole (afterwards Mrs. Treffry), Miss Trentham, Miss M. E. Roberts, Miss Robbins, the two Miss Irvines, very popular young Scottish mistresses (Miss Amy caused great excitement among us when she married a 'Highland laddie', Mr. Gordon of Perthshire). Then there was Miss Morant, who gave us a different kind of thrill when she left to become a Wantage Sister, and used to come occasionally to visit the School in her nun's habit, and Miss Hiatt, Head of the Junior Department, and Miss Elizabeth Roberts, a Welsh lady, who taught us science. Mr. Denyer used to come once a week to teach drawing to the Upper School. We used to assemble *en bloc* in what was then a large extra classroom. Mr. Denyer used to draw simple pictures or diagrams on a large blackboard and expect us to copy them, but with such numbers it was impossible for him to give proper attention to each one of us. Drawing was not my forte, and so I used to contrive to sit in one of the back rows, thankful that it was very seldom that he could get round to me !

"The whole School used to meet in the hall also for the singing class, which was taken first by a Dr. Steinmetz, a venerable old gentleman with white hair, who, however, taught us well. When he left we had Mr. Diemer, who was younger and much stricter. Music was taught, for beginners, by Miss Robbins and

Mlle Truchet, for more advanced pupils by Miss Muriel, Frau Valero, a German lady who could speak very little English, Mr. Bond-Andrews, and later by Miss Hartley. Our French teachers were Mlle Lutz, who took the junior classes, Mlle Thirion (a very highly certificated person), and Mme de Nolhac. Mlle Thirion was quite a character, very clever and a good teacher, but most eccentric. She used to convulse us with suppressed laughter with her queer broken English, and curious remarks. She suffered from chronic indigestion, poor thing, and would often mutter, when a bad fit was on her, 'I don't like your English food, it makes me seek'. She seemed to look down on poor little Mlle Lutz, a very quiet, retiring little person, for being a Swiss, while she, herself, was a Parisian, and she would sometimes correct our French accent in class with, 'Non, non, spik not so, dat's Suisse, lak Mlle Lutz', with a supreme look of disdain, 'not Parisien'. Mme de Nolhac was a very different personality —she was an aristocrat and had belonged to a very select circle in France, her husband having been a prominent politician under Napoleon III, but when the Emperor was deposed, the de Nolhacs were exiled, and came to England, where shortly afterwards M. de Nolhac died, and his poor widow, late in life, forced to earn her living by teaching French. She was a dear thing— I had private lessons in French conversation from her, and got to know her well.

"Drill was taken in my first term at School by an ex-Army sergeant. He was rather a dragon with us, and very impatient, so we were not sorry when he was succeeded by Miss Stansfeld, who became a general favourite, and who brought the physical culture of the School to a high pitch of excellence. Under her we got a well-fitted gymnasium, and a suitable costume, and we all thoroughly enjoyed her classes. When I first entered B.H.S. there was no good assembly hall, and no organ. Miss Robbins used to play the hymns at prayers on a piano. I remember the thrill and excitement in the School on the two great occasions when the new Great Hall was formally opened, and when the organ was installed and dedicated. The Harpur Trust and the head masters and head mistresses of all the other Bedford schools, attended in full state, in their respective gowns and hoods, our parents were invited, and we were given a holiday, but allowed to attend, and hear the speeches. On one occasion the then Duchess of Bedford presided—she had been an old Cheltenham College girl and taught by Miss Belcher. We thought her a delightful person.

"There were three boarding houses in my day. Mrs. and Miss Barker's in Ashburnham Road, the Misses Burgess's in Linden Road and Mrs. Urquhart's in Lansdowne Road. We had no playing fields then, and no sport of any kind on our agenda. I was only a day girl, but I used to hear of tennis and tea parties and other entertainments got up by these Houses, and used to envy the boarders who always seemed a happy set of girls. When I got into the Sixth Form I found that one of our great privileges was the annual river picnic we gave at the end of the summer term to our teachers. It was an event much looked forward to by us all. We used to start quite early in the afternoon in three of four boats which we rowed ourselves down the river till we found a quiet and shady nook where we unloaded, boiled our kettles, and spread our picnic. We girls used to vie with one another in bringing the most gorgeous and delicious refreshments. I remember today Martie Sampson's lovely snow cake, the enormous bowls of strawberries and clotted cream, and the various 'sticky buns' with different icings supplied by our much patronised confectioners—Mann and Son. On this occasion all formality was dispensed with. Pupils and teachers were all girls together, joking and talking freely together till dusk when we regretfully turned homewards till 'next time'.

"*Alta Petens*—'Seeking High Things', is the motto on our School badge, chosen for us by Miss Belcher, who wanted it to be an inspiration for B.H.S. girls for all time. 'Seeking High Things', not only things of the mind and education, but also things of the spirit and the building up of character, and that is what I feel was the 'good foundation' laid in those old days by the teaching and training we got in the dear Bedford High School."

Miss Roberts continues :

Few events broke the regularity of the daily routine, but I remember the Mayor, Mr. Joshua Hawkins, coming to present

the Medals of the Royal Humane Society to Grace and Ethel
Alderton, two children who had saved a boy's life. Their
mother was sketching on the river bank, and her three girls,
aged about ten, eight and five, were alone in the boat in mid-
stream when a little boy, fishing from the opposite bank, fell in.
Gracie jumped in at once, caught the boy, and both sank. Ethel
jumped in to help her sister; meanwhile the baby girl of five
caught hold of an oar and pulled the boat round, and all got in.
Plucky children!

Sometimes we had interesting visitors. Once Miss Beale
came to visit what was becoming almost a daughter school, and
we were touched to see the love and deference shown towards
her by Miss Belcher, who gathered her staff together to hear an
address from Miss Beale. It was just like her to give us the
opportunity of coming face to face with one who was a great
force in her generation and, withal, so human, with such delightful humour.

Another visitor about 1884 was the wonderful little Swedish
lady, Madame Bergman-Oesterberg, founder of the Dartford
Physical Training College. She had left home and husband in
Sweden to come to London to introduce the Ling system of
physical training to English people. "He has his work and I
have mine," she said to Miss Belcher when she was asked how
she could bear to do it. And so it was that Miss Stansfeld came
to Bedford; she was the ablest of Madame's band of enthusiastic
young students trained by herself to be pioneers in the
work.

In these mobile days how circumscribed our range must
seem, but we did not feel it so. We enjoyed long country walks
round by Bromham and Oakley, and picking cowslips in the
Clapham fields, or blackberries in the autumn. We made parties
to go in a rumbling wagonette to Old Warden "in lilac time",
and we could go by train to the glorious Woburn woods. And
there was always the river and river picnics; after school Miss
Belcher was very fond of rowing up to the Kempston woods
for tea with a party of us.

And then, before we lost our Saturdays, Bedford was near
enough to London for us to go up to a matinée at the Lyceum

and see Irving and Ellen Terry, and near enough to Oxford to go and hear Mr. Ruskin lecture !

Only a certain percentage of boarders was allowed under the Scheme of the Charity Commissioners ; all other girls had to reside with their parents or near relatives. The Boarding Houses conducted by Mrs. Barker (West Wick) and by Miss Baker (The Quantocks), with the sanction of the Governors, were quickly filled, and others were opened later. It does seem to be an ideal arrangement for girls who have to go away from home for education to have the advantage of a large, fully staffed and equipped school, and yet not to be obliged to live in too large a crowd, but to have the individual consideration possible for a group of twenty-five to thirty.

As I look down the list of names in the register of attendance of that first term, entered in Mrs. McDowall's writing, how many faces come vividly to mind. I can see our first head girl, Louie Carter, so tall and staid and thoughtful and with her bright, friendly smile ; and all that Fifth Form group not yet promoted to the dignity of a Sixth Form—Margaret Craig, Janie Handford, Beatrice Hockliffe, Louisa Porter, Edith Scott. What would the Guild have been without those two inspiring people, Mrs. Wragge and Mrs. Wrey ! How they bound the years together by their living affection for the School. And among the younger girls, Ethel Footman, even as a child a person to be relied on, always one "who sweareth to his neighbour and disappointeth him not".

And the little First Form girls were such dears, and many of them people of character too. There was little Frances Craig, so fearless and deliberate, and Kathie Sampson, who spoke such pretty French and careful English, for her parents had left her at school in Switzerland for a time on their way from India. Even at eight years old she had made up her mind to be a missionary. "I shall first teach the people to make a railway," and then, after a pause, no doubt seeing the need of a comrade in the work, she added thoughtfully, "but I must have a husband first." And it all came true. Later on, when her unusual ability for mathematics disclosed itself, we knew she could do brilliantly at Cambridge, but her purpose never swerved ;

she chose to become a qualified medical woman, went out to China, married a medical missionary, and gave the best years of her life to the work.

In September, 1885, Miss Collie came, and with her a new element seemed to enter into the life of the whole School. She had been a pupil of Miss Belcher's at Cheltenham, and had been one of the first women to take a London B.A. degree, for the London University had only recently opened its degrees to women; and she had been on Miss Beale's staff. Soon she became Miss Belcher's right hand in the general affairs of the School.

I had seven more years at Bedford, full and interesting years, but here ends the period allotted to me for these recollections.

CHAPTER IV

1887-1897

BY MISS ETHEL BELCHER

THESE RECOLLECTIONS of the years 1887-1897 are, I am afraid, given from a very one-sided point of view—that of a girl who progressed in a normal way up the School, and whose horizon, though of course it widened each year, was mostly bounded by her own experience and that of other members of her form.

In 1887 the High School buildings consisted of the block at the gaol end of the School, the hall (the top of the present T-shaped room) and an iron room where the science wing now stands. The Girls' Modern School used all the classrooms at the Trinity Church end, and half the passage cloakroom; they had prayers in the gymnasium, and it was always a great excitement to us when we were small, if we caught sight of them going through our part of the cloakroom. There was no library, the room afterwards used as such being then a form room; all the books the School possessed were kept in the Sixth Form room. Form I, under Miss Craig, and another form, lived in the hall, and the rest of the Junior School was in the iron room.

Early in 1888 a large crack appeared in the wall at one end of the hall, and a partition was put up dividing it, as in former years, into two, so that one half might still be used while repairs were going on. During this time the Junior School and Form II had prayers taken by Miss Hiatt in the iron room.

The first extension of the School I remember was a new iron room, divided into form rooms by curtains, and about 1890 the Middle School was housed in that. Soon afterwards the Modern School moved out to the old Grammar School buildings by the river, the Middle School went into the west end of the main building, while the Junior School took over the new iron room, and the old one became an art room. In 1895 the block for the Junior School and art room was opened, and the old iron room became a science room, only a piece of the new one remaining to join the two buildings. That is the last change I remember

34

in this period; the present enlarged hall was not actually in use before I left, though it was in process of building.

In September, 1887, Miss Stansfeld joined the staff. Previously the girls had been drilled by a man of whom I used to hear tales from my friends, though I never came under his tuition myself. Our gymnastic dress at that time was made of heavy thick blue serge with light blue sailor collar or yoke, and sometimes a light blue belt and cuffs; there was no regulation length or pattern, and we must have appeared a very motley crew. Later on it became more uniform and consisted of a dark blue serge dress with pleats put into a yoke, but as we grew taller we never dreamt of wearing it to school without an extra skirt over it, coming well below the knees. The tunic and blouse did not come into use till after 1897, even for gymnastics, and it was not till some years later that they were used for games. There were no school games at that time except the very simple ones played in break and a strange kind of hockey, which was played on Saturday afternoons in the gravel playground near the gaol with a string ball and glorified walking sticks, and was the privilege of the Upper School only. The goal posts were two sticks at one end and the large chestnut tree and a stick at the other; the boundaries were the walls and the privet hedges. We had practically no rules, except that we always changed places after a goal was scored; if the ball went out, whoever reached it first threw it in, and we played with the stick in either hand as we liked, and with the front or the back of it. With the arrival of Miss Lee we began to learn that there were rules, though we must have been extraordinarily difficult to teach, as I remember how keen we were on our own peculiar game.

The other game which, as I went up the School, became very popular was rounders, but there were no opportunities for playing it except in break, or before School, and in that again we made our own rules, which bore very little resemblance to those of the present day.

I believe the first form match ever played was a rounders match between VA and VB in 1892 or 1893, which caused the utmost excitement and interest. VA were urged on to put forth all their efforts by the fact that Miss Collie gave them badges, strips of yellow ribbon with the eagle sewn on.

The first real development in games was made possible by the laying down of an asphalt tennis court at the west end of the School about 1892, and in 1894 the first external match was played against Baker Street High School, at Neasden, the four champions representing the School on that occasion being Lilian Woodcock, Ethel Belcher, Eleanor Norris and Mabel Madden. Baker Street and Oxford High School were our chief opponents for some years, and till 1899, when Oxford won, the School did not lose a match. The silver badges awarded to the first four champions were presented in 1894 by Mr. Alfred Loder, the father of a girl at the Quantocks, and the beautiful House Challenge Cup was given in 1896 by the staff and other friends, on the initiative of Miss Barker (later Mrs. Greville), of West Wick. The Day Girls (not then divided into different houses) held it for several years at the beginning.

On looking back over these early years, I realise what great encouragement was given to girls who were keen, even though the facilities for games were so restricted, and when I think of the mistresses who helped us I know we were extraordinarily fortunate. Miss Belcher used to come often and watch our efforts, Miss Collie and Miss Poole showed their interest in their forms' games, Miss Lee and Miss Spencer gave self-sacrificing attendance at hockey, Miss Jackson often coached us at tennis, and several others took us to play matches. It was, however, necessarily the few who benefited in this way, and the large majority of girls at that time had no games at all in connection with their school life.

It was during these years that bicycling came into fashion for women; the first High School girl who was seen on a bicycle was considered by some to be bringing great disgrace on her school, and the head mistress received a request from a number of parents to make a rule forbidding such behaviour. Wisely, however, she saw that it was an activity to be encouraged, and very soon bicycling became most popular, but it was considered very important to have one's skirts of suitable length, and duly fastened down with elastic to keep one from showing too much of one's legs.

My recollections about work during these years, of course, grow more vivid towards the end. At the beginning arithmetic looms largest in my memory, probably because I came into the lowest form of the Middle School with practically no knowledge except of the very simplest processes. The ambition of everyone was to be in Miss Collie's, Miss Poole's or Miss Irvine's division, and the height of happiness in those days was to be in IVc with Miss Poole and in Miss Collie's arithmetic division.

One had a horrible feeling of trying to avoid growing up when one reached IVA, of which Miss M. E. Roberts, afterwards for many years head mistress of Bradford Girls' Grammar School, was then form mistress, and that perhaps made us difficult to deal with, but I think it was then that I first began to feel the joy of work for work's sake. This may have been due partly to the excitement of working for an external examination, as then we took the Junior Oxford and various subjects in the South Kensington examination; the main attraction, however, about the latter was coming back in the evening to do the papers, and in the former, having tea at School one afternoon. The Senior Oxford was taken from VA, Miss Collie's form, and we certainly worked hard then, though without any brilliant examination results. Many of us played hard too, as far as opportunity allowed, and most of us enjoyed life immensely. The Sixth Form years stand out in my memory still as a thoroughly happy time, and the joy of work, as well as of friendships and games has left a very vivid impression, but I can only give as my own recollections those of work on the London side.

Miss Collie, of course, directed our Latin, and many, many times in after life I have been grateful for her insistence on thoroughness and accuracy in every bit of work we did. I believe her teaching affected our whole outlook and made us realise the paltriness of any slipshod careless work, and the value of thoroughness in all departments of life. Miss Heppel (later Mrs. Purdon) inspired tremendous respect for her own knowledge, and we believed nothing of classical lore to be beyond her range. We enjoyed our Greek lessons immensely, especially when she went off on archæological or mythological side-issues, and showed us how wide was the interest involved in the text we happened to be reading. Fräulein Bunde was a wonderful teacher, and gave me a love for German I have never lost. I remember how the sense of power over language grew under her tuition and how one gradually became less self-conscious in trying to express oneself in speech. I have often since, when travelling, realised my debt to her, as she really did teach us to speak German, as well as to write it and appreciate its literature. Mathematics with Miss Lee and Miss Spencer are also a happy memory : I have always been thankful for the advanced work I did in that subject, and to some, of course, the mathematical periods were the chief interest of the week. In 1897, for the first time, six candidates were sent in from the School for the London External Pass B.A., then a most useful examination on which to get teaching posts.

The work of the Cambridge side was more specialised, and for many years extraordinarily good results were obtained in the old Cambridge Higher Local. The Cambridge Sixth is, I think, in the memories of most Old Girls, bound up with thoughts of Miss Holmes, and the debt the form owed her during the time she presided over it cannot be put into words. From the point of view of work, H. Gnosspelius, a member of this form in the years 1893-96, sent me the following recollections :

"It is pleasant to recall across the years the delight with which one began work for the literature and history groups of the Cambridge Higher Local—an examination which was surely built on less tiresome lines than many, though it had one drawback, the insistence on a pass in arithmetic !

"But the rest of that road to learning was sunny, and there was no sameness in it. For our three guides led us by such varied routes that the dullest must have found breadth of view and elasticity of mind by the way.

"First Miss Holmes, for whom one dared not write more than the prescribed two pages, however full the material she had provided. Such a respect for condensation did she give us that a diffuse author or speaker still fills one with dismay, and the fervent desire that such a one could have come under her firm guidance before it was too late !

"Then Miss Ebbutt, who looked with kindly eyes on many a poor essay, if only it were interesting. And how often does one wish that a certain type of modern novel could be brought under that standard for revision.

"And last, Miss Scott, who, despite that dreary adjective 'Constitutional', so filled the history lessons with colour and life that the uphill struggle to produce something approaching to style was cheered by the interest of the subject itself. Again, what sound educational and literary doctrine showed there.

"True teachers that they were, their road still remains a sunny memory. And though we may often waste words and be tiresome or clumsy, there it still is, and we may climb on to it again if we will."

Miss Belcher's Scripture lessons to the sixth are another lasting memory, and were a real foundation for future study. Those weekly essays for her, which, I suppose, caused some of us more anxiety and more searchings of heart than anything else we did, helped our power of independent thought and judgment far more than any of us realised at the time. Her pleasure at an essay which showed such thought, and any sense, however feeble, of spiritual values, was always an extraordinarily rich reward to the writer.

The music of the School during this period was, of course, not as fully developed as in later years, but the beginning of great things was seen in the appointment of Dr. Harding, and the gradual increase of his influence on all musical activities. The string work owed an enormous amount to Herr Woltmann, who was violin master and conductor of the orchestra for a considerable number of years. The orchestra cannot be mentioned without reference to Miss Davey, who, till her death, gave splendid service as accompanist, and will be remembered with affection by many who perhaps were never in her form, but knew her through music.

I suppose our education would now be considered sadly lacking in some respects, especially on the scientific side. Botany in my day was taught up to an elementary standard, but what a vivid recollection one has of Miss Roberts's lessons and the botany walks and the keenness and interest she roused in that

D

subject ! Chemistry was learnt only by girls who were taking Matriculation, though I suppose a few who might be going to take up science at college did more at School, but the majority did none at all after the age of 14 or 15. No needlework was taught above the Junior School, very little handwork, no domestic science of any kind, although many girls did learn something of these last subjects at home, and certainly life at school was far simpler than it is nowadays with the infinite range of subjects from which choice can be made. The lack of scientific training was certainly a distinct handicap, but perhaps in some cases the loss was counterbalanced by additional opportunities for learning languages.

Several isolated events which took place in these years stand out in memory and must be recorded. When I first went to Bedford we had school on Saturdays, and I remember the day when we were told that Saturday was to be a whole holiday. Miss Belcher seldom spoke to us after prayers, but when she did her words left a great impression. She told us that one of the reasons for the change was that girls ought to learn to make themselves useful at home, and that we must consider Saturday morning as a special time for helping in domestic duties, darning stockings, etc. I remember being much impressed by the fact that it was not to be considered as a holiday for enjoying ourselves.

The first exhibition of needlework and handicraft took place in November, 1894, under the direction of Miss Poole. A large amount of very beautiful work done by past and present members of the School was exhibited, but the recollection that has always remained with me is of Miss Arblaster's carving, Mlle de Nolhac's embroidery, and Miss Collie's bedspread, and of my own surprise that many of the people I respected most for their learning and skill in other ways were also so clever with their hands.

In June, 1897, the Annual Conference of the Association of Head Mistresses was held at the High School, when one hundred and five head mistresses were present, which in those days was considered a large number. A conversazione was held in the large hall on the Friday evening, the meetings on Friday and Saturday took place in the art room, and lunch on Saturday was in the Junior School hall. The Sixth Form felt it a great honour to come on the Saturday to hand round milk and biscuits in the middle of the morning ; I also helped to row several august head mistresses on the river in the afternoon, and was able to do various little things for those who were staying in my aunt's house, such as fastening up the button boots of one ; but Miss Beale refused to accept my services, preferring those of my aunt !

The annual Sixth Form picnic was a tremendous event to us. For a good many years it took the form of a river trip, and I can see now heavily-laden boats starting off from Chetham's. When the use of bicycles came in we changed to an excursion to the Shefford woods, and a carriage was hired for the mistresses who did not ride. Rounders was the popular game at School then, and was always played vigorously by staff and girls on these picnics, while Miss Belcher and the few others who did not play sat on cushions and applauded. I doubt if we ever realised how easily our enthusiasm could have been damped if the staff had not been as they were ; but my recollection is that they appeared to enjoy themselves as much as we did.

CHAPTER V

1898

BY MRS. WRAGGE (MARGARET CRAIG)

.THE LARGE HALL was originally common to both the High and Modern Schools, divided by heavy sliding partitions. After the removal of the Modern School to St. Paul's Square, the hall was used by the High School alone, for purposes of assembly and examinations; but soon, owing to the growth of the School, it became inadequate for these purposes, and its enlargement was decided upon. The work was entrusted to Mr. Henry Young, Architect and Surveyor to the Harpur Trust, whose task it was to preserve the architectural features while extending its size. This he succeeded in doing in the spring of 1898. An extension was thrown out in front, and the original central porch, with its large pair of doors, reinstated for use on great occasions. The extended roof was placed upon wrought-iron trussed girders, and the old and new ceilings were groined. The internal plan of the hall was reversed, and the seating accommodation now arranged from north to south. The length of the central portion of the enlarged hall was 72 feet, and the width 36 feet, with two recesses, covered by overhead galleries across the sides of the north end, 36 feet by 13 feet, the whole giving ample accommodation for 800 persons. Four exits were provided, in addition to the main doorway. Electric light and hot-water radiators were installed throughout. The final result was an immense improvement in cheerful spaciousness.

While the alterations in the hall were proceeding, the opportunity was taken to build the new organ, given by many friends of the School. For this instrument Miss Belcher, twelve months previously, had been encouraged to beg by the generous dying gift of Jessie Hill, a Guild member and one of the first pupils of the School. The specifications were carefully prepared by Dr. Harding, the work was entrusted to Messrs. Norman and Beard, of Norwich, and the Governors of the School voted the sum necessary to provide the hydraulic pressure apparatus for blowing.

THE HALL

The organ, costing £510, was placed in the eastern gallery of the large hall, and, at the time of its building, was one of the most effective two-manual organs in the country; its compass five octaves, its working parts noiseless, with patent tubular pneumatic action applied throughout; the console detached; the tone excellent and enhanced by the fine acoustic properties of the hall. To the joy of Miss Belcher, the whole cost was cleared and the money in the hands of the Hon. Treasurer, Miss Hilda Gnosspelius, before the Guild meeting in July, 1898. The hall and organ together were opened on Tuesday, 21st June, by Mr. Guy Pym, M.P., who was supported on the platform by Mrs. Pym, the Mayor of Bedford, Miss Belcher, Mr. J. S. Phillpotts (Head Master of Bedford Grammar School), and the Rev. Dr. Poole (Head Master of the Boys' Modern School). The hall was filled with friends and pupils. There were speeches by the Mayor, Mr. George Wells, Chairman of the Governing Body, and Mr. Guy Pym, Chairman of the Harpur Trust; an organ recital was given by Dr. Harding; the "Te Deum" was sung by the School choir; and the distribution of School certificates was undertaken by Mrs. Guy Pym. Then Miss Belcher spoke, thanking all who had given the organ to the School; and the whole company joined in singing "Now thank we all our God".

That day, together with the third biennial meeting of the Guild, which happened a fortnight later, may be regarded as the culmination of Miss Belcher's work for the School. It was a time of complete satisfaction and joy in accomplishment—the crown of her sixteen years' work as head mistress. At the Guild meeting (1st-4th July, 1898) upwards of four hundred old scholars rejoiced with her, and the last resolution passed at that business meeting of the Guild was to the effect that the woodcarvers among them should unite to make the head mistress's chair. The School was complete, its traditions were established, its numbers not unworthy of its reputation. Only her throne, if you like to call it so, was lacking—it seemed the zenith of achievement.

But before the year closed, joy was turned into sorrow; the School and the Guild were plunged into mourning. On 15th December the much-loved head mistress passed away. Her earthly life as well as her work finished, she was called to higher service and her great reward.

Those sixteen years during which Miss Belcher was head mistress were the years of the making of the School. Before her time it had hardly begun to exist : all that has happened since has been built upon her foundations. "One of the dreams of my life was to be some day the head of a great school", so she once said, years before she came to Bedford. It is given to few to realise so completely their early ideals. But the School was a small thing when she was appointed on St. Thomas's Day, 1882. It was in its infancy. It was only two terms old.

At the close of Miss Belcher's life there were 579 girls in attendance. The School which she found occupying half a building had overflowed, and the portion previously belonging to the Girls' Modern School had been bought for £5,500. A new Junior School building had sprung up at a cost of £4,500, and the big hall had been enlarged by the outlay of £2,000 more. £12,000 in all had been expended on plant, and the money had been forthcoming from the revenue of the School. Judged merely by the world's standard of success, the growth was very good.

But numbers and statistics are sometimes misleading. This particular success was based upon something less tangible but more potent—upon a personality—upon an ideal. It is not easy perhaps to convey the impression of such a personality to those who did not know her. It was characteristic of Miss Belcher that when she was appointed she tried to preserve as a tradition the history of those two previous terms. Girls then in the Sixth Form remember how the new head mistress called them into her office, and gently drew from them all that they could tell her of the opening of the School, all that was happy in their memory of the first head mistress, every bit of ritual or good custom ; and from her reverence for the past the School soon learned to be proud of its traditions. The fragments that she gathered she treasured with care. The portrait of the first head mistress was hung in an honoured place in the hall. The passage of Scripture which had been read by Mrs. McDowall on the first day that the School opened, became the School motto

44

in the time of her successor. "Whatsoever things are true, pure, honest and of good report"—we had already been taught to "think on these things"; but Miss Belcher's girls associate with her memory those opening verses of the same chapter (Phil. iv) which she first introduced into the lection, always read on the last day of term. "Rejoice in the Lord always. Let your moderation be known unto all men, and the peace of God shall keep your hearts and minds". The sound of her full and gentle voice still echoes through the very words. Joy, moderation, peace, how they sum up her life !

In her relation to her staff, there are many who remember her considerate regard for the feelings of others, her womanly tact, and, what is more rare, her justice—a combination of gifts which won for her a band of fellow workers as loyal as could be found in any school in England. Teaching was to her mind one of the noblest of callings, "not to be taken in hand lightly or inadvisedly" in order to earn a living. It required special and great gifts, and none could excel in it without giving herself entirely to the work. An old pupil who had begun to get restless and dissatisfied with home life once went to ask her help to get an appointment as a teacher. The girl was well qualified by examination ; the head mistress listened patiently, and bit by bit wrung from her the real reason for her desire for work—discontent. Then kindly, but very firmly, she said, "No, I could not think of helping you. That is no motive at all for taking to teaching. Go home and do your duty. Teaching is a vocation".

The girls who were under her at Cheltenham had the best opportunities for remembering her as a teacher. It was always a great regret to her and to her Bedford girls that the administrative work of the growing school claimed her attention more and more. She loved teaching ; and she was never so happy as when giving a lesson in Scripture, history or literature ; and she had the power of arousing the enthusiastic interest of her pupils in whatever subject she taught. "Really, mother, I didn't know that Scripture could be so interesting !" was the naïve confession that was made at home by one honest member of the form.

In the Scripture lessons Miss Belcher's breadth of view in

treating any debatable point was remarkable. She loved to dwell on matters which all held in common rather than on questions of opinion. She remarked one day with genuine pride that the three best books sent in on a difficult lesson came from girls representing entirely different schools of thought. In history, the persons and scenes were made to stand out vividly, for everything she touched was living and real. She was a true lover of poetry, and the literature lessons were often prolonged through break, as the sixth listened enthralled to her readings from the poets. Miss Belcher trained her girls to look for beauty everywhere—beauty of language, of form, of character. She always cared a great deal how an answer was expressed. It would be easy, in these later days of opportunity for women, to find a teacher more learned ; but they are rare indeed who have a greater power than hers of filling a dull subject with interest.

To be sent to Miss Belcher was supposed to be a terrible thing. It was the punishment for insubordination and infringement of School rules. Yet, much as it was dreaded, it is a touching fact that often the greatest devotion to the head mistress began in these interviews.

One writes : "As I look back, it seems wonderful how thoroughly Miss Belcher entered into the feelings of a naughty girl. I remember once being sent to her ; I am rather ashamed to say that it was for being extremely impertinent to my form mistress, with whom at that time I did not get on—my own fault, no doubt. After having, in her own kind way, tried to make me see how badly I had behaved, Miss Belcher said to me, 'I suppose now, C., you don't like being found fault with ?' 'No !' I answered with all my heart, 'I don't.' 'I am sure you don't,' she said, with that charming sunny smile of hers, 'and I know exactly how you feel about it, because I can't bear it myself'."

But let it not be thought that the head mistress was merely gentle and loving in a weak and amiable way. There was an austerity which lay behind, rarely shown, and indeed only called forth in condemnation of anything mean or unworthy. Miss Belcher would not have been so much beloved if she had not also been feared. She believed in people to the very end, but

46

on the rare occasions when her confidence proved to be misplaced, the penalty was severe. Her faith once shaken was not easily restored. Her quiet anger was never aroused by personal or petty considerations, and it was never scornful; but it was a hard thing to face. With great personal humility, she had an inborn dignity that did not need to be constantly asserting itself. It was manifested in the respect which she showed to others, which silently demanded repayment in kind. However intimate the friendship between a subordinate and herself, there was no possibility of forgetting the relative positions, and no reminder in word or act was needed. In the high standard of work and devotion that she demanded from her staff, she was never so severe to others as she was to herself.

School prayers led by Miss Belcher are a memory upon which all her old pupils love to dwell. Many of the girls have said that they never knew how glorious were the Collects of the Book of Common Prayer until they heard them read by her beautiful voice. A new meaning shone through familiar words. The elder girls used always to invite special friends who wished to see the School to "come to prayers", and strangers were deeply impressed by the reverent little service with which the day's work always began. It was no wonder; for there was so much thought and preparation put into each morning's worship; lesson and hymn and prayers all seemed set in harmony, with the purpose of bringing out a special thought or idea. The teaching of the Church's year, with its festivals and fasts, meant so much to the head mistress that gradually her School saw these things through her eyes. Very little was said in the way of doctrinal teaching. The School was, of course, open to all shades of religion, and there was nothing in the School morning service to which any Christian parent could object. But all through the well-known formularies breathes the spirit of God, and the School did not miss the lesson, although it was meant only for those girls who had ears to hear.

And, after all, her life was the best lesson the School ever had, open and clear to be read of all. One of her favourite Psalms for the School service was Psalm xv, the description of the perfect godlike character, "Lord, who shall dwell in Thy Tabernacle or who shall rest upon Thy holy hill ?" And as she sang it she lived it. I do not believe that anyone could tell of her having failed in utter truthfulness ; and when she believed a thing was right, it was done at all costs. No one ever heard an unkind word pass her lips, or an imputation of bad motives to others. She hated back-biting and slander so much that those who talked with her were often silently rebuked by her unfailing and all-embracing charity. Even of those who misjudged her, or who treated her unkindly, she would never say more than "I am so sorry about it"; "Yes, it is a pity"; "I wish she had not done it". And often her gentleness and forbearance turned an enemy into a friend.

Confirmation time was a special opportunity of influence. One who remembers thankfully the help which she received has written as follows : "The classes which she held with us for some six weeks before the Confirmation day were not meant, as she told us, in any way to take the place of those connected with our several churches ; but it seemed to her that, knowing us intimately as she did, and, through her daily contact with us, understanding our special difficulties and special faults, she might be of some help to us at this time of our lives. It was she who taught us to say the 'Veni Creator Spiritus' as a special prayer to be used at this time, and we always began each class by repeating it after her. 'I like to think', she said once, 'how the old knights used to repeat the Creed with swords drawn to show that they were ready, if need be, to fight for their faith'. And week by week, as the hour drew to a close, she made us stand and, her beautiful reverent voice leading us, we said the Creed. As the Confirmation day drew near she saw each of us alone ; and, sitting with her on this occasion, a member of the Fifth Form told her that she feared the feeling of reaction when the excitement of this time should have passed. Her answer was full of bracing helpfulness : 'But then', she said, 'you will fall back on *principle*. These times of feeling are very good, but it would not be well that they should last, and when the reaction follows, your principle must come in ; it is on that and not on feeling that you must lean and rely.' Presently she added, 'But I think it does seem as if we did a great deal for you now, and left you rather too much to yourselves afterwards.' A few days later, when the Confirmation was over, she gathered together all who had been confirmed that year or in the past, and four times during the last weeks of the Spring Term, she talked to us about the coming Easter Communion."

Her humility was extraordinary. It was not until her last illness that she allowed herself to realise how much she was beloved by both past and present members of the School. In her full vigour she so feared unreality of feeling that she rarely allowed demonstrative love. So she laid the foundations of the School the more securely because she based them, not on personal attachment to herself, but on principles of faithfulness, loyalty and duty. In the midst of such work, at the early age of forty-nine, she died.

The inspiring thought of those who took up her work was the earnest desire to make the School, which she loved so much, what they knew she would wish it to be. This kept the staff united, and the Guild of old pupils loyal and true. The tradition remained unbroken and stood the shock of change. It was good that Miss S. M. Collie, who had worked for many years as chief of Miss Belcher's staff, was called upon to succeed her in the office of head mistress.

CHAPTER VI

1899-1914

BY MISS E. ROBERTS

WHEN THE SCHOOL lost Miss Belcher as its Head Mistress we were extremely fortunate in having Miss Collie to take her place and so ensure that there was no break in the continuity of the School tradition, which included all that was best in girls' education at the time. She had the loyal co-operation of the whole Staff, and, with Miss Holmes in charge of the Sixth Form, Miss Hiatt as head of the Junior School, and Miss Poole, postponing her wedding for a term, to keep her position as head of the Middle School, the work went on smoothly without change of any kind. The contribution of Miss Gertrude Stone to the life of the Junior School during these years was enjoyed beyond all words by those privileged to share it. Her charm, her generosity, and her sense of humour enriched the life of all, and there are still many old friends who are enjoying all these when they still visit her at Kempston.

When Miss Poole left, Miss Irvine became head of the Middle School, but kept her old Form IIIAJ, Miss Gane being in charge of IVc until I took it over in 1904, Miss Gane then going to IVAI when Miss Hart Smith left. The School now entered upon a period of great academic success, and in looking through old records, we remark as an outstanding feature the number of scholarships gained and the constantly recurring expressions, "First in the Higher Local Examinations", "First girl in the Senior Oxford Examination". It seems to have been the fashion at this time for the Head Girl to obtain a scholarship to one of the universities, and we have the series of brilliant classical scholars, who, starting their career in Miss Collie's Latin division in IVc and passing through the capable hands of Miss McDougall and Miss Paul, followed one another to Newnham. Two of these later returned to their old School : Miss Edghill, who was Senior Classical Mistress for seven years, and Miss Westaway, who became our head mistress. We may say that a third

Newnham student of this period returned to us, in a way, for later we had an Old Girl on the Governing Body in the person of Lady Jaqueta Williams (Jaqueta Northcote). No less successful were the historical students who passed to Oxford through the hands of Miss Scott, Miss Chambers and Miss Finlay, one of whom, Miss Agnes Sandys, was also on the staff for some time.

But alas! Not all our promising students went to the universities. In 1904 we lost the most brilliant of them in Lettice Hay Shaw. She died when she was only seventeen, but she had already, at fifteen, gained the £30 prize for the highest candidate in all England in the Oxford Senior Examination, and had written a good deal of poetry of great promise—some of the lyrics were set to music by Dr. Harding and are well known to members of the Guild. Lettice was not only a scholar but possessed that charm of manner which endeared her to all who came across her—girls and mistresses alike—and without being in the least a prig she impressed her companions by her innate and simple goodness. I remember being very much struck by this when I had to take temporary charge of Form IIIAJ, of which she was the head girl; it seemed impossible for anything mean or small to take place when Lettice was there.

The science of the School has, paradoxically, suffered from the fact that we possessed a laboratory, of sorts, from the first. (I can even now hear the pride in Miss Belcher's voice as she showed visitors over the School, and opened the door with "and *this* is our laboratory".) This has meant that we had to wait longer than most schools for the erection of an adequate science block.

The present girls will find it difficult to believe that what is now Room XI was for many years the only fitted laboratory, and that it was here that all the practical science work—chemical, physical and biological—was done! It was fitted with benches all round and had a demonstration table at the end, and some of the Old Girls will remember what a crush it was in the days of matriculation chemistry and what difficulties we had in getting enough light for microscopic work. Even so, it was in this old room that a goodly number of flourishing medical practitioners gained their first insight into scientific method!

In 1898, when Professor Armstrong and his "heuristic method" —in which the only text books advocated were Jules Verne's novels—had caused a good deal of fluttering in the scientific dove-cote, it became absolutely necessary to make some provision for individual practical work. One of the old "tin buildings", which had already figured, during the period in which the School was rapidly expanding, first as a Lower School and then as an art room, had now become available by the opening of the new block. This became the "science room", being fitted with tables and a very limited supply of apparatus. At first no water was laid on and we had to manage as best we could with zinc baths and large jugs! Later sinks and taps were fitted, and gradually we acquired more fixtures and apparatus, and it was here that we carried on until the present science block was opened in 1927, at least twenty-five years overdue.

There is no occurrence of such magnitude as a Royal visit to be recorded during these fifteen years, but in 1906 we had what agitated us all nearly as much at the time, and that was our first full inspection by the Board of Education. For a whole week the School was pervaded by an atmosphere of unrest—harassed mistresses trying to shepherd important personages from one form where they had overstayed their time to another one anxiously awaiting them!

On the recreative side of the life of the School there must be recorded the long series of concerts which took place yearly in the Christmas term. At the "Big Concert" we had for many years the great honour of having the Duchess of Bedford to give away the certificates. She was unfailing in her kindness, and later on, when she had to give up her visits, the Lady Ampthill took her place. The grace and charm of these two ladies added greatly to the pleasure of those who received certificates from their hands. Mr. Tanqueray Willaume was another familiar figure on the concert platform; he was one of the School Governors, and for many years used to read the names of those who held certificates.

At these concerts the whole of the Upper School was, with great difficulty, crowded on to the raised platform, with the orchestra in front. The singing was at first conducted by Mr.

Diemer, who had been associated with the School from its earliest days, and after his death in 1910 it was taken on by Dr. Harding. At the "Little Concert" on the Friday morning, the Lower School, and then the Middle School, took their turn. At first they were conducted by Mlle Truchet, who was afterwards Madame Pondepeyre, and, when she left Bedford, Dr. Harding took them on also. When the School Orchestra was started under Herr Woltmann it performed at both concerts.

In 1910 the Field Club came into existence, with E. Askwith, D. Madden and K. Westaway as members of the first committee. The archæological and botanical section were the most flourishing, many expeditions were organised every year, and some very good lantern lectures were given under its auspices. It is to the activities of the Field Club that the School owes the possession of its own lantern.

In the following year the *Aquila* was started, with E. Askwith as its first editor. This has been, and still is, an outstanding feature of the School. It is of immense value, not only in encouraging the art of good writing, but also in keeping a record of all the School activities so that past as well as present members can know what is going on.

To turn now to the physical activities of the School. The gymnastics in Miss Stansfeld's charge had been flourishing ever since she introduced the Swedish system in 1887. She had a gymnasium of a kind, but it had to be entirely re-equipped and was very inadequate for the needs of the increasing numbers. Still it *was* a gymnasium. In 1907 Miss Collie presented the School with two shields for inter-form competitions—one for the Upper School and one for the Lower School—and the following year Miss Stansfeld gave another one for the Middle School, so as to make the sections more even. The first holders of the shields were IVA, IVc and IIB. The competition takes place annually, and the emulation and friendly rivalry helps to keep up interest in the work and to foster form-spirit, especially as the shields are awarded partly on the work done during the year and partly on competition work. Miss Stansfeld judged these competitions for many years and so kept in touch with the gymnastics of the School.

With regard to the games, the question of space became very urgent. We only had the playground, with one asphalt tennis court, for the use of the whole School, so that the need of a field became imperative. Miss Belcher had for some time been looking for a suitable field, and, with two of the Governors, Dr. Burge and Mr. Jackson, had tramped over all possible and impossible sites in and around Bedford. Finally, in 1899, the Governors appointed a committee to arrange for the purchase of eight acres of ground on the Beckett estate—the present field. They further allotted a sum of £300 for fencing, planting and turfing the field, and this was supplemented by a valuable gift of trees and shrubs from the Duke of Bedford. Six tennis courts, a hockey ground and a cricket pitch were available at first, and gradually the other hockey grounds and the rest of the tennis courts were prepared. The old shed, our only shelter, was also provided.

After this start by the Governors, the field was passed over to the School, which became responsible for its future upkeep. Since then it has gone on improving under the affectionate care of Rogers, directed at first by his father, "Old Rogers", who also coached cricket on Saturday mornings for many years. The field was opened in May, 1900, and in 1901 the Guild had its first tennis tournament there—Past *v* Present (E. Belcher, G. Chaldecott, M. Stansfeld and M. Davis playing for the Past).

The funds were a difficulty in the early days, as the children only paid a very small subscription. Mrs. Treffry organised a performance of *The Princess* by some of the Guild members, which brought in the substantial sum of £60, and later on there was a bicycle gymkhana in the field, arranged by Mrs. Treffry, which also swelled the funds. (This, our first gymkhana, was a great delight to the children and a great anxiety to those responsible for their safety. At it, Miss Lee won the prize for the Mistresses' Race, which involved the correct working of a long multiplication sum !)

Thus we went on for many years until the Pavilion was opened on 13th June, 1913—which was indeed a red letter day in the history of the field. For some time Ethel Belcher and some of the Old Girls had been very energetic in raising money to build

MISS COLLIE

a pavilion, and they had collected £300, which would have been enough for a modest one, though nothing like the beautiful building which Mr. T. Rose so generously presented to the School as a memorial to his daughter Nesta, a gifted and beloved member of the first Hockey XI, who had died just after leaving school. The architect of the pavilion was Mr. Frank Anderson, whose daughters Blanche and Christine were both members of the School. At the opening the historic cricket match, Fathers *v* Daughters, was played, in which I am afraid the fathers were the victors, even though they replaced bats with broom sticks !*

The money originally collected was invested and the interest used for the upkeep of the building. Great was our pride in showing off this wonderful building to visiting teams, whom we could now provide with changing rooms, and for whom lunch could be provided on the spot without going down to the School. The Pavilion was fitted with every possible requisite—full lunch and tea sets, kettles and gas stoves—even down to the humble but necessary tea-cloths.

In connection with the early days of the School games, I recall one name particularly, that of Joan Evans, who died at the early age of seventeen in 1908. She was of the best type of English school-girl, full of life and high spirits, looking forward with zest to her life as a physical training student and future games mistress. She was in the First Hockey XI for two years and had been captain for one term when she was taken ill. She had the best of all sporting traditions, "all for the team and not for self", which we hope will always characterise the Bedford High School games. The cup which is held by the captain of the First Hockey XI was presented, in her memory, by her uncle, Mr. Herbert Belcher.

Soon after the field was opened the School gardens were organised. Plots were allotted to three of four girls, who were responsible for keeping them in order. Hilda Gnosspelius very kindly gave prizes for the best gardens. Mrs. Treffry and Miss

---

* The Fathers' team was as follows : Mr. C. W. Kaye (capt.), Mr. Anderson, Mr. Bolton, Mr. Dasent, Dr. Harding, the Rev. R. L. Lacey, Mr. Maltby, Dr. Nash, Mr. Parkinson, Sir Harry Stewart and Capt. Swire. The Girls' captain was B. Singer (later Mrs. Meeson).

Howard acted as judges, and the first prize was won by Molly Evans, Phyllis Belcher and Margaret Milne.

The field has proved of inestimable value to the School, and has always played a large part in its life. It affords ample room for hockey, lacrosse, cricket, tennis, netball and rounders, and Miss Stansfeld arranged that all children could be coached in these games, under the supervision of her staff and students.

Of the many challenge cups now possessed by the School, the first to be presented was the Tennis Doubles Cup. This was suggested by Miss Barker and presented in 1896 by the staff and friends, the first holders being E. Belcher and M. Stansfeld. Then in 1899 the Tennis Singles Cup was given, the first holder being D. Priestley. In 1908 a Junior Singles Cup was presented, and was first held by Bee Ebden. The House Hockey Cup was presented in 1902, and was that year won by the Day Girls, who were not then divided into their houses, as they are now. A little later Miss Irvine presented a Junior House Hockey Cup, but in 1917 this was transferred to Junior Netball, a game which was then just gaining a footing in the School and needing encouragement. The Lacrosse House Cup (from A. Kelynack), the Cricket Cup (from the Old Girls), the Lacrosse Captain's Cup (from B. Watson), Senior Netball Cup (from Miss Hatch), Junior Tennis Cup (from Miss Lloyd), Swimming Cup (from Mrs. Page) and Diving Cup (from Mrs. Jarratt), were all given later than this period. They all form a magnificent array when the presentations are due at the end of each term : but the pride felt in such numbers now cannot be greater than that felt in their few precursors of twenty and thirty years ago.

Mr. Westaway, who knew the School very well in this period, wrote as follows:

"North and South, East and West, we have always heard Bedford High School spoken of as one of the very few really great schools.

"Why ?

"The foundations of the School were well and truly laid by that gifted woman, Miss Belcher, but it was her successor who built up the superstructure, and it was my privilege to know

Miss Collie intimately from the beginning of the century until she completed her task in 1919. Miss Collie would be the very first to note the great debt which the School owes to such prominent members of her old staff as Miss Holmes, Miss Scott, Miss Lee, Miss Roberts, Miss Irvine and many another; but all who have worked with her, staff and girls alike, could unhesitatingly say that the School owes its great reputation to her own personality, ability and sagacity.

"Why, when we (of our generation) are all of us together, are we so conscious of Miss Collie's presence and only half conscious of the presence of others? Who shall say? Perhaps it is that we know we always found her scrupulously just and true. Perhaps we should say that it is the inevitable sign of our deep affection for her. But if the reason is hard to find, the fact itself remains. She knew us all. She knows us all. Insight into character was hers in a pre-eminent degree. Do we not respect her the more because we suspect she knows us better than we know ourselves?

"Behind the formality of lessons girls always felt—though then the feeling was vague and not to be expressed—that they were being taught to cultivate the integrity of our minds and to respond to the call of conscience.

"Character calls forth character. That is the B.H.S. secret."

Miss A. S. Paul, M.A., B.D., who was classical mistress from 1902 to 1906, then head mistress successively of Notting Hill High School and of Clapham High School, contributed the following in 1932:

My official connection with Bedford High School fell within the years 1902-06 only: but as the bond of recollection and attachment has far outlived the short period of my actual work there, I think it may be best not to attempt to be strictly chronological, but to put down in a detached form a few impressions of the general tone and atmosphere of the School as I saw it under Miss Collie's guidance.

I remember those years to this day with complete vividness, and have always thought that the way in which the incidents stand out sharply defined, and have not merged like countless others

into the general welter and surge of a very full life, must have
been due not wholly to the fact of my freshness to the experience
but largely to the individuality and uniqueness of the School.
I had the London VI in the room next to Miss Holmes with her
large Cambridge VI, and, to me, fresh from college and new to
the work, the young women who presented themselves with all
the aplomb and magnificence gathered in their progress to the
top of *The* School seemed at times rather a crushing proposition.
I remember well when I was feeling this rather acutely one day
Miss Collie strolled in and asked how I was getting on, and on
hearing that I felt just about scared stiff, said consolingly, "Well,
my dear, no one would know it, so it doesn't matter". It was a
small instance of that proportion-restoring faculty which was
among Miss Collie's marked gifts. Her clear, balanced judgment, when really brought to bear on any question, was wont
to settle the matter out of hand; and her acute vision could
pierce through a great deal of the conventional lumber which
tends to obscure the issue of a problem and magnify the difficulty
of its solution. She was difficult to deceive, but did not by
any means necessarily *show* that she saw through what she did
see through. She knew the wisdom of leaving people, after a
searching interview, to wrap themselves decently in their
surviving rags of self-respect and retreat in good order.

We had a very distinguished set of girls preparing for scholarships in the sixth just at that time, and when half a dozen assembled in my room for an afternoon coaching, Miss Collie
would drop in, occasionally poking fun at my use of what was
then the "new" Latin pronunciation, and addressing me as
"Miss Powl". Sometimes we expected a reprimand for sounds
of unbecoming merriment penetrating to the office, but, even if
hovering, it generally melted away into her irresistible smile,
for she dearly loved these keen and promising Upper VI girls,
and saw in them still the simple, ingenuous little creatures of
the II Forms; and so indeed they were.

Above all, she was keenly alive to the stir of the life of the
spirit in the individualities under her care, and valued its un-
folding more even than "much fine gold" of intellectual attain-
ment. My instances all seem trivial incidents, yet perhaps I

need not apologize for that, since life is made up of such. For
example, one comes back to me now of how, when a somewhat
over-emotional girl used to bring me more flowers than I thought
she had money to spare for (girls were in those days much more
given to displaying their partialities and affections ingenuously,
and had far fewer critical self-judgments and inhibitions than
now), Miss Collie's comment was "Don't stop her—do her
good—the selfish little thing has never wanted to make sacrifices
before". The spiritual value at once took precedence of the
material in her eyes.

CHAPTER VII

1914-1919

BY MISS E. L. LEE

THE OUTSTANDING EVENT of this period was the Great War, which came upon us with startling suddenness just as we had scattered for the summer holidays in 1914. In the earlier part of the year we all rejoiced to see Miss Collie back again in School after her illness during the winter. The Summer Term proceeded in a normal way, with a biennial meeting of the Old Girls' Guild in July.

Those subscribers to the Fellowship Fund who met in the upper room of the School field pavilion, during the Saturday afternoon of the meeting, little thought that in a few weeks that room would be appropriated as Staff Headquarters for the regiment of the 5th Gordon Highlanders billeted in the School field. Just before the end of the term, Godfrey, the senior porter at the time, who was a Naval reservist, was called up, ostensibly for the usual short period of training, but he never returned to his work at the School, being required for active service.

As soon as war was declared in the first week of August, a Division of Scottish troops, composed of Gordons, Camerons, Seaforths and Argyll and Sutherland Highlanders, was quartered in Bedford and the immediate neighbourhood, this being part of the scheme for the defence of London. The authorities had little time for preparation, and commandeered all available buildings and open spaces. About four hundred men were quartered in the High School, the officers using the mistresses' room and the music rooms, while the men occupied the hall, the Junior School and the art room. Another detachment encamped in the playing field, set up a rifle range for practice in one corner, piled stores into the lower room of the pavilion, and ammunition in the bicycle sheds.

After a few weeks the School building was vacated in order that it might be prepared for the return of the girls, but it was a long time before the playing field and the pavilion were restored to normal use. The girls soon became accustomed to the military occupation of the town (the Scottish Division was followed by a Welsh and then by the Royal Engineers), regarding the loss of their games as one of the small ways in which they could help, and they began their four-year occupation of knitting belts, mittens and scarves, and collecting for the Belgian Relief Fund. They were much thrilled when they were allowed to leave school on 22nd October at 11.30 a.m., on the occasion of the visit of the King to review the 25,000 Scottish troops in a large field near the golf links on the Bromham Road.

Miss Collie fitted up her house in Foster Hill Road as a Soldiers' Club, where the men could read, write letters, buy simple meals, play games and take baths. Her porridge became famous. The oatmeal was procured from Aberdeen by Miss M. E. Thomson, and the cooking was done under Miss Collie's personal and strict supervision. Long afterwards a nephew of Mrs. Treffry encountered a Scottish soldier out in Egypt, who paid a glowing tribute to Miss Collie's porridge. Later on, when the Corn Exchange was used as a canteen for the troops, Miss Collie undertook to organise the workers for at least one night in each week, and various members of the staff gladly became regular helpers. The work done by the former members of the staff and Old Girls ranged over a wide field, but naturally nursing and the care of soldiers enlisted the greatest number of workers, both at home and abroad.

The present girls sent a splendid contribution of silver thimbles, bracelets, bangles and other silver trinkets to the Silver Thimble Ambulance Fund. Weekly collections were made for the Disabled Soldiers' and Sailors' Fund, and lectures were given and entertainments arranged in support of the Red Cross Society and Lord Roberts' Memorial Fund. Perhaps the most interesting and successful of these were the performances of *Alice in Wonderland* given in the Town Hall by girls of the Junior and Middle Schools, with incidental music between the acts by the School orchestra under Dr. Harding. Miss Elsie Nicholls was the stage manager, and she planned the dresses, which were faithful reproductions of Tenniel's illustrations of the book. Those present will long remember the demure and convincing Alice, the fierce, forbidding Duchess, the Knave of Hearts looking like guilt personified, the Mad Tea Party, the Mock Turtle's tears, the smile of the Cheshire Cat and the magnificent dresses of the Pack of Cards. So real was the appreciation shown by the audience that another performance was given the following term, by request, in aid of the Band of Hope Union.

In the summer of 1916, Miss Collie started a War Savings Scheme in the School. Contributions were brought in and certificates bought each week during term time until after the end of the war.

On a previous memorable occasion in 1913, Mr. Cecil Sharp had visited Bedford, with his team of dancers. Miss Stansfeld was responsible for the organisation of the visit, and the display was given in the High School hall. In 1916, when "Baby Week" was celebrated all over the country, the field was the scene of a picturesque entertainment, inspired by the memories of Mr. Sharp's visit, given by the girls from all parts of the School in aid of the Infant Welfare Fund. At the beginning, and at the end, of a series of fourteen country dances which had been arranged by Miss Stansfeld and her staff, there was a march past of all those taking part, which gave everyone present an opportunity of seeing the charming cotton frocks and sunbonnets of the girls, and the sober smocks of their partners with their gay scarves and well-matched stockings.

It was not possible in war-time to hold the usual exhibitions of art, plain and fancy needlework, wood-carving, etc., to which Old Girls used to contribute so largely, but small exhibitions were held of the brushwork and handwork, which became a notable feature of the Junior School after Miss Lockyer joined the staff in 1915.

During the years 1914-1919 there were many changes on the staff, some of the mistresses leaving to take up war work. Miss Edghill, who had been senior classical mistress for seven years, was appointed head mistress of Warwick High School; Miss Ethel Belcher, head mistress of Crediton High School; and Miss Neild, head mistress of Bridgenorth High School, from which she moved four years later to Bury. Miss Chambers, who had been Sixth Form mistress for two years and had given valuable assistance not only to the Field Club, the *Aquila* and the games, but to Miss Collie at the canteen in the Corn Exchange, left to be second mistress at Berkhamsted High School. She was appointed in 1919 to be head mistress of the Girls' Grammar School at Hitchin.

Miss Chambers wrote in 1932 :

"Every girl realised that Miss Collie knew and cared about herself and her progress. The mark-readings with each form brought this home to them, and her extraordinary gift for saying the one word necessary. Offenders were dealt with so practically and often so humorously. The girl who beckoned through the railings to a passing lad and sent him to buy a bun for her lunch was invited to eat that bun—sitting on the sofa in the head mistress's office ! The child who arrived home unpardonably late because she was talking to the cabbies about their horses— the other child who forgot her dinner altogether because a second-hand bookstall was so beguiling, realised the fellow-feeling behind any reproof given. After this it was not difficult to realise also that the head who expected your best of you was neither unreasonable nor remotely inaccessible and austere. These were first impressions. As the years went on, one grew to appreciate Miss Collie's great understanding of matters and of people—her amazing gift for remembering everyone and every-thing about everyone who had ever passed through the School, her wisdom in matters of policy.

"Miss Collie's very serious illness in 1913 came as a great shock to us all. But absence and illness made no difference to her interest in the School, nor to her influence there. The machinery was too well oiled for School to suffer from her absence —but her return brought always a feeling of serenity and security —and of leadership to girls and staff alike."

Miss Brockway succeeded Miss Holmes as English mistress in 1913. After varied experiences as form mistress of Form IIc, Form IVA2, and the Cambridge VI, she resigned her post in order to go to India as lecturer on English language and literature at the Women's Christian College in Madras under Miss McDougall, who was on the staff as classical mistress from 1900-1902.

In 1918, Miss Stansfeld, who had been gymnastic mistress since 1887, and in 1903 had started her Physical Training College in Lansdowne Road, delegated much of her work in the gymnasium to her assistants, Miss Ida Hadley and Miss Colwill.

When Miss Collie decided, in 1918, to allow the introduction of Girl Guides into the School, four mistresses undertook the duties of Guide Officers; these were: Miss M. Millburn (German), Miss M. B. Taylor (mathematics), both from Newnham College, Cambridge; Miss D. Drought (French) and Miss A. M. Sandys (history), from Oxford. The movement proved most popular, and by the end of the year there were two well organised and enthusiastic companies, each consisting of six patrols. The first twelve patrol leaders had the honour of being enrolled by Lady Baden-Powell, who came to address the School on what Girl Guides are, what they do, and how they can make themselves helpful and useful.

Three important events in the history of the School occurred in the year 1918: the London meeting of the Guild, the visit to the School of the King and Queen, and the placing of the School under the Board of Education.

So many Guild members expressed a desire for an opportunity of meeting each other again that Miss Collie sent out a letter suggesting the possibility of a meeting in London during the Christmas holidays. The response was most enthusiastic, particularly on the part of the many members engaged in war work in and around London. Miss Steele, head mistress of the Greycoat School, Westminster, who was a friend of the General Secretary, Mrs. Victor Williams (now Lady Jaqueta Williams) kindly placed her school at our disposal, and through her generosity more than two hundred members were able to spend a most delightful afternoon on 5th January. In the hall of the historic Greycoat Hospital, with its old oak panelling and portraits, we began with prayers at 3 o'clock, followed by the President's address. After reviewing the years since the last meeting, Miss Collie said:

"We cannot tell in the least how or where we shall find ourselves when the war is over, but I think it will be well for each of us to think out some plan which will help to guide her through the difficult years that are coming.... What women have to do now is to show that they can be trusted. They have the openings, they have the work, they must show that they mean to do it thoroughly and efficiently, and that they can be depended upon to go on working with the same zeal when the excitement and novelty have worn off.... We have all suffered together, and we shall miss one of the greatest lessons which this war can teach us if, when peace comes, there is not a greater sympathy and a better understanding between all classes of society."

The meeting then resolved itself into a business meeting, and the General Secretary read selections from the very interesting report, written by Miss Holmes, on the work, and more especially the war work, which members were doing. Before leaving we had an opportunity of seeing Miss Collie's portrait, which had been painted by Mr. Ambrose McEvoy, and was on view to Guild members for the first time.

The visit of the King and Queen in 1918 was the School's supreme honour and joy. Miss Collie herself confessed afterwards to having experienced a feeling of dismay when, less than a week beforehand, she was first warned of the impending visit. She and the School will always owe very great gratitude to Lady Ampthill, who gave unstinted help in the preparations for the great day. It was very satisfactory afterwards to know that their Majesties complimented Miss Collie on the way the girls curtsied, and Dr. Harding on the way they sang "God Save the King". It was a wonderfully happy day. The King and Queen were received at the hall door by Mr. Geoffrey Howard (Chairman of the Girls' Schools Governors) and Miss Collie. The following account of the Royal visit, written by May McKisack, the editor of the School magazine, appeared in the summer number of the *Aquila:*

"Nineteen hundred and eighteen will long be remembered as the year in which the School was honoured by a visit of the King and Queen. A rumour of their coming had been in the air for some time, and as soon as it was known that twenty-five minutes of their time was to be allotted to visiting the High School, the excitement grew steadily, every other topic of conversation sinking, for the time being, into the background. Although the visit was to be unofficial (a message having come from Buckingham Palace requesting that the girls might wear their ordinary clothes), certain preparations had to be made.

"Although no one had to be at School until 10.45 a.m. on Thursday, 27th June, most of us were awake early, anxiously watching the weather, which, though brilliant, kept fine and cool. The whole town had a holiday air ; Union Jacks fluttered from every window and church tower, the High Street being especially gay. The big gates of the School were decorated with wreaths and flags, and by 10.30 a.m. an enthusiastic crowd of onlookers had begun to assemble. Several 'Specials' hovering near the gate gave an official air to the scene. The Junior School buildings had been given over to the Girls' Modern School, and from the door of the milkroom to the entrance of the Junior School an awning had been erected, under which their Majesties were to pass.

"Inside, the rooms were bright with flowers. The arrangement of the hall had been completely altered, the seats having been placed in rising rows facing a broad aisle down the centre. Miss Collie's desk stood on a low platform at the end of this aisle, and was beautifully decorated with a mass of blue delphiniums in copper pots. Below the clock hung Miss Collie's portrait, publicly exhibited to the School for the first time, and beside it was a relief of the founder, Sir William Harpur. Chairs were placed near the platform for the Governors and their wives. Rooms IVc and IIIA, where the Cambridge VIth and IVc were to have literature and geometry lessons, were also gaily decorated with delphiniums and roses. The mistresses' room had been arranged for a brushwork class for IIB, and was charmingly decked out with specimens of the handwork of the Junior School.

"Everyone was in her place soon after 10.45, many Old Girls filling the galleries, while others in V.A.D. uniform formed a Guard of Honour outside, and for the next hour and a half the main objects of interest were the Governors and other officials who followed one another at intervals, and who had, perforce, to undergo the ordeal of walking the whole length of the hall between the rows of cheering and clapping girls. As it got near

66

THE VISIT OF THE KING AND QUEEN

12.25 p.m. the excitement became intense, and when the shouts outside announced the approach of the Royal Party, even the least excitable felt a thrill, which found vent in the tremendous applause as the King and Queen, accompanied by their suite, several important officials, and Miss Collie (who had been presented outside) entered the hall.   When they had taken their places, 'God Save the King' was sung to Dr. Harding's accompaniment on the organ, and then Kathleen Tulloch presented a bouquet of pink carnations, tied with silk, on which Miss Milligan (later Mrs. Paulin) had worked in gold a crown, with the letters 'M.R.' and 'Bedford High School, 27th June, 1918'.

"Mrs. Prothero, Messrs. Tanqueray Willaume, G. C. Walker, W. Palmer and A. H. Allen, Miss Lee and Miss Dolby, were then presented to their Majesties, after which, amid renewed cheering, Miss Collie led the way to IVc room, where the Cambridge VIth were having a lesson with Miss Brockway.   Only those in similar circumstances can appreciate the self-control needed to keep one's attention fixed on Hooker's Ecclesiastical Polity while the above-mentioned proceedings were taking place in the hall. For those of us who were thus situated, however, there was considerable compensation in getting such a very near view of their Majesties, while the King talked to Miss Brockway, and the Queen to Rachel Irving.   Proceeding next to IIIAI room, where IVc1 were having geometry, the King and Queen talked with Miss Taylor for some minutes, and then went to inspect IIB, showing considerable interest in the models of Crusoe's island and the poppy fields, superintended by Miss Lockyer.   The King here talked to Betty Page, Christina Smith and Patsy Little, and the Queen to Kitty Mackenzie and Barbara Weston.

"While the King and Queen made their way to the Girls' Modern School, the three privileged forms rushed back to join the others in the hall, where everyone was awaiting the return of the Royal Party.   After about ten minutes they were seen appearing in the distance, and renewed cheers almost drowned Dr. Harding's performance on the organ.   Their Majesties mounted the platform, and when the cheers had died away, the King said he would like to say how glad the Queen and he were to come to the School.   The School had been long renowned, and now they would take a greater interest in it and its doings because they had been there and seen it. He would ask the authorities if they would grant an extra week's holiday to celebrate the event of their coming, and he hoped they would all enjoy it. A serious breach of etiquette was committed by the interruption at the words 'week's holiday', but, as Miss Collie said afterwards, judging by their smiles, neither he nor the Queen seemed to mind very deeply.

"In spite of sore throats, in many cases, all put their best efforts into the final cheers as the King and Queen walked down the aisle towards the door. Long after they had driven off, and the crowd outside had begun to disperse, the shouts were kept up, showing that the School knew how to appreciate its privileges. The next morning the somewhat 'flat' feeling, resultant from the prospect of renewing the ordinary routine after such an exciting day, was very pleasantly relieved by a letter which Miss Collie read from Colonel Wigram (His Majesty's Assistant Private Secretary) expressing the King and Queen's pleasure at having been able to visit the School, and adding that their Majesties had been very specially struck by 'the bright and cheerful expression of the students'. The School is not likely soon to forget a day on which we were so highly honoured.

"The following is a copy of the letter :

Buckingham Palace,
27th June, 1918.

Dear Miss Collie,

The King and Queen were very glad to be able to visit the High School today, and to have an insight into an institution that bears so high a name in the educational world.

I am to thank you for all the arrangements, and to say how pleased their Majesties were to meet you, the members of your staff and the Old Girls of the School : while the bright and cheerful expression of the present students was a special feature of the visit.

The warm welcome with which they were received will not soon be forgotten by the King and Queen.

Yours sincerely,
(*Signed*) CLIVE WIGRAM.

"A little later their Majesties sent signed portraits of themselves to be hung in the hall as a memorial of their visit."

At the end of May, 1914, the School had undergone for a second time a Board of Education Inspection, when for about a a week seven inspectors all the mornings, and some of the afternoons, attended lessons in all parts of the School—a cause of pleasurable excitement to the girls, but of some trepidation and anxiety to the staff!

The reasons which decided the Governors to place the School under the Board of Education were explained by Miss Collie in a short address at the School concert in the autumn of 1918. When she succeeded Miss Belcher in 1899, the School was heavily in debt. The Junior School and the studio had been built two years previously, the enlargement of the hall was completed during Miss Belcher's last term, and all this building had proved a great drain on the resources of the School. For some years they cherished the hope that by rigid economy in the course of time this debt would be paid off, but twenty years had now gone by, and the debt, though greatly reduced, had not been wiped out—in fact since the war it had begun to increase. Meanwhile the cost of everything was almost double what it was, salaries were going up by leaps and bounds, and if they were to keep their place among the first girls' schools they must build laboratories and provide for a domestic science department. All this necessitated a large increase in the funds. There was a kind of myth in the town that the Harpur Trust was an inexhaustible well of riches, and that the Governors had only to dip in their hands, and funds would be forthcoming sufficient to finance any undertaking. Unfortunately that was not true, and the sum given them each year was far from enough. Last year it had become evident to the Governors and to her that unless they were willing to take the help of the State they could not continue to carry on the School as it ought to be carried on. The raising of the fees would do little more than cover the increase in expenditure due to the war and other causes. They could not compete with the grant-earning schools in buildings or equipment, nor could they hope to keep the present staff or to secure other mistresses with first-rate qualifications unless they could offer higher salaries. After much deliberation they decided to apply to the Board of Education for permission to become a grant-earning school. So far they had found the inconveniences were much outweighed by the advantages. There had been a slight curtailment of their liberty and there had been sheaves of forms and papers to fill up, but they were no longer hampered by want of money. Already this term they had spent more on books and scientific apparatus than in any ten years previously. They had been able to offer the staff somewhat more adequate salaries, and they hoped when the present building restrictions were removed to see a block of buildings rise which would contain up-to-date laboratories, rooms properly equipped for the teaching of domestic science, and a library in which the elder girls could study and find books which they could not obtain elsewhere. Miss Collie expressed a hope that any misgivings at this new departure would pass away and that the School with this fresh impetus would be in a position to do even better work than it had done in the past.

One of the obvious changes caused by the School's going under the Board was the inclusion of the charge for stationery and games subscription in the tuition fees, which were re-arranged so that no increase would be made in the fee paid by a pupil after the age of twelve years, even though she remained till she was nineteen. A small percentage of free places had to be offered each year to pupils from elementary schools. Two advanced courses were begun in the Sixth Form, each covering a period of two years ; one in modern studies included French, history and English literature, and the other in science and mathematics included chemistry, botany, physics, and pure and applied mathematics. Each girl taking an advanced course had to devote a certain amount of time to a "corrective" subject— mathematics, science or drawing for those in the Modern Sixth, and literature or some language for those in the Science Sixth.

One of the results of the war was an increased demand for vacancies in the boarding houses. In 1918, Miss Irvine at Wimborne, Miss Pocock at Westlands, and Mrs. Blackmore at Quantocks had long waiting lists, so in September Miss Windsor and Miss Wynne-Edwards opened a new boarding house at

11 Lansdowne Road for nineteen girls, and called the house "Greenways".

The close of the year 1918 will ever be memorable for the world-wide rejoicing on the occasion of the signing of the Armistice on 11th November. After Miss Collie made the announcement to the School, very little work was done for the rest of the morning. The Sixth Form were allowed to go into the town, and much enjoyed seeing the flags and the general excitement. At break, amid the cheering of the girls, the Union Jack was hoisted, and the whole School was given a half holiday in honour of the great event. Many of the girls ended the day by attending the Thanksgiving Service held at St. Paul's.

In 1919, Miss Collie decided that, in spite of many difficult circumstances in the town resulting from the war, a Guild meeting should once more be held in the School. It was not easy to find accommodation for members who came from a distance, and it was decided to curtail the programme and to confine all the important events of the meeting to Friday and Saturday, so that those members whose friends could take them for one night only should not feel that they were missing anything that really mattered. About three hundred members were present, and they appreciated most thoroughly the preparations undertaken by the local members for their comfort and entertainment.

It was in her address after prayers on the Saturday morning that Miss Collie told the Guild that she was addressing them for the last time as their President, as she had made up her mind to give up at Christmas, and retire to the country. This announcement, which came as a surprise to most of the members, was received with a deep sense of regret, and all were very glad when Mrs. Wragge spoke on behalf of the Guild in reply to Miss Collie's address. Part of what she said may be appropriately quoted here :

"A rumour of this decision reached me many weeks ago, and made me determine that I must attend this Guild meeting. I think if the news had been widespread we should have had a record attendance. There are many who could speak on behalf of the Guild better than I, but few have better right to speak, for

71

I was one of the girls of the School on its first opening day, and I have known its three head mistresses.

"I can remember when Miss Collie first appeared upon its teaching staff, and the first impression she made upon us all—a sense of power with an aloofness that fascinated us.

"I remember how her opportunity came when she was appointed to succeed Miss Belcher. The latent power we had all recognised was set free, but the responsibility called out other things too, the gentleness, the kindness, the motherliness, of which you younger Bedford girls know even better than I.

"I shall always remember the way Miss Collie set herself to carry forward that high spiritual tradition which was Miss Belcher's legacy to the School, while leading it onward into a wider and larger life. How well and faithfully that has been done all of you know.

"It is no light duty to be put in charge of this great School... this 'Garden of Girls', as I always think of it : and

   'Such gardens are not made
     By saying "O ! how beautiful !" and sitting in the shade'.

"There is much that is done out of sight, much strenuous and exhausting work—and now, after twenty years, she is laying down her work. Our love and gratitude will follow her into her retirement.

"Perhaps, after all, Kipling says better for us what we would like to say to Miss Collie today, than we can express in any words of our own :

'So when your work is finished, you can wash your hands and
   pray
For the glory of the Garden that it may not pass away—
And the glory of the Garden, it shall not pass away'."

The Editor of *The Guild Leaflet* throughout this period was Miss Holmes, who retired in July, 1913, and kindly consented in 1914 to undertake a task for the performance of which she was second to none. Part of her last editorial will form a fitting conclusion to this account :

"Our School has been singularly fortunate in escaping a frequent change of head, for since the death of Mrs. McDowall, the first head in 1882, only two have reigned over Bedford

High School. Miss Belcher's brilliant headship was terminated by her death in December, 1898. A blow was then struck at the prosperity of the School which filled with dismay those who had watched its phenomenal progress, and who now dreaded the effect of the removal of Miss Belcher's wise guidance. Happily these forebodings were not justified, and Miss Collie, who had for thirteen years been in Miss Belcher's confidence, and who had carried on the work of head during Miss Belcher's long illness, was appointed to succeed her in the Spring Term of 1899.

"On the foundation so well and truly laid by her predecessor she has built up and strengthened a school second to none in the country. She recognised that a school is no lifeless model of another artificer's work but a living organism, capable of growth and development, plastic and sensitive to a changing environment, so, while keeping the spirit and tradition of the past, Miss Collie has responded to the demands of a new age and has shaped her policy in accordance with modern educational ideals.

"To do this required much courage and sacrifice of personal tastes. In many cases the conservative tendency latent in us all might have led her to stand in the old ways overlong, and to shrink from new and untried paths. No charge of this kind can be brought against Miss Collie. Even a cursory glance at the School curriculum will show how closely it responds to the needs of the present times and how admirably adapted it is to fit the girls for their fuller life in this modern world.

"Miss Collie never despaired of reaching any of her pupils, however stubborn might be their antagonism ; she was the friend of them all, tolerant and understanding, and this belief in the soul of goodness in the most unpromising has its reward in the records of the Old Girls' Guild.

"To many of us the Guild is the finest testimony to Miss Collie's tact and influence. All the older members passed at least some of their school days under Miss Belcher, but their present loyalty is unquestioned. The Guild is a vigorous, living society, the members filled with love and devotion to their old school, carrying into mature life the lessons learnt within its walls. The passing away of the years will take nothing from

CHAPTER VIII

1920-1924

BY MISS M. MILLBURN

WHEN MISS TANNER came to take prayers for the first time as head mistress of Bedford High School, we all sat very expectant, and filled with quiet excitement while she read in her clear and pleasant voice the beautiful words of St. Paul which are the School motto and which we had so often heard Miss Collie read. Then, while we sat down to listen to her first speech, she told us very simply but very dramatically the lovely story of Our Lady's Tumbler, that medieval tale of the poor tumbler who entered a monastery when he was already past his prime and found that he was too old to learn any of the stately arts and crafts, book-learning, illuminating, manuscript-copying, singing and music by which the other monks expressed their praise and their love of God. He could do nothing well except his tumbling, and so the thought came to him to offer that to Our Lady, whose statue was down in the underground crypt, and to perform his feats to her with all the zeal and power that he possessed. The more orthodox monks were shocked when they discovered it, but Our Lady stepped down from her pedestal and showed to the poor tumbler such gracious favour as she had never bestowed on the great prelates and dignitaries of the monasteries. Some of us will never forget the effect of that story. We understood that it was what Miss Tanner wanted for the School; that we should throw ourselves heart and soul into whatever we did and do it well, was the keynote of her ideal for us. The best of our talents, no matter what they were, were the only gifts worthy to bring to God.

Miss Tanner was so full of zest herself, and found life so interesting, that she wanted to pass on some of her own enthusiasm to the School. We felt that she belonged to the great outside world; she kept in touch with it and kept us all in touch with it too. She was ready to discuss any new ideas in education, to hear and to learn about these and to support any of the staff who wanted to try new experiments. She was already a member of the Consultative Committee of the Board of Education. She often went to conferences and meetings, and I well remember how generously she would offer, when she returned from any of her travels, to tell us what other people were thinking and doing and what new educational ideas were in the air, so that the staff meetings were occupied not only with the necessary details of School routine, but developed often into debates on educational matters. We had many staff meetings, and they often lasted several hours, for Miss Tanner believed in the value of our coming together to pool our ideas. The girls, too, came to understand Miss Tanner's wide interests and broad sympathies. In a letter describing a discussion on adult education which she had had with the Sixth Form, one of her Old Girls wrote to me : "It opened up round us new fields of interest, new and pressing problems, a world outside School, in which we should have to play our part."

We found that she was a supporter of all generous, large-hearted and humanitarian schemes, especially those for international co-operation. She helped to found a Bedford Branch of the League of Nations Union, and became its first President. She was glad to find a wide syllabus of international history being taught in the School, and being a history specialist, did all she could to strengthen and support the work on that side. With the elder girls she took some lessons herself. Hearing that I was writing this chapter, one who had once been a head girl, wrote : "I have never enjoyed such useful, informative and interesting—I am almost tempted to say exciting—coachings as those she gave me, once a fortnight, before the Somerville Scholarship examination."

Her time was too fully occupied for her to teach every girl, but as far as she was able she took Scripture lessons in all parts of the School, even down to Form IIA. The girls found these lessons delightful. With the elder girls Miss Tanner encouraged discussion, and she was so easy to talk to that the shyest girls felt her friendly sympathy and responded. Miss Tanner continued Miss Collie's plan of taking special classes for girls who were to be confirmed during the School year, and these talks, too, meant a great deal to the girls.

Bedford High School had always had a high reputation for fine scholarship and academic work, and this side of the School life Miss Tanner did all she could to promote. In the next few years twenty-eight girls went on to universities to continue their studies, seven of these with University and State Scholarships, and the high level of results in the other examinations was maintained.

It was no light task to be at the head of a school with the fine tradition of the Bedford High School in those post-war days. The war had strongly accelerated developments in many ways : ideas of freedom, of personal liberty for women which might have developed slowly, had come upon us with a rush—we all had votes, every girl expected to have a career of some sort when she left school, youth was something rather fine and important in itself, no longer to be seen and not heard but to have its opinions courted and listened to from all sides. Miss Tanner called the attention of her girls to the new responsibilities which were being laid upon them. Speaking on one occasion, she said : "Only by the spirit of service can the social and international troubles of the present time be removed. The world is crying out for a generation of men and women who, forgetful of themselves and of their own ambitions and inclinations, are ready to give themselves whole-heartedly to whatever work needs to be done ; and, in spite of a seeming devotion to pleasure and frivolity, there is deep in the hearts of the young people of today a great longing to be of real use in the world. Formerly, a large number of the girls on leaving school were not under the necessity of earning their own living, though many members of the Guild gave themselves unstintingly to voluntary work at home or abroad for the betterment of the world. Now conditions have changed, and almost all our girls wish, and rightly, to be prepared to earn their own living. Some will still undertake what is generally known as social work, but all work faithfully done is social work, and often the best service one can render to one's fellows is to do one's own work as well as it can be done."

To train the senior girls for their new responsibilities Miss Tanner introduced into the School as large a measure of self-government as was possible. More responsibility was given to the prefects, talking was allowed in the cloakrooms and in the passages. The girls were allowed to elect and choose more of their own officials, such as form prefects and School games captains. Again and again Miss Tanner urged them to remember that they were responsible for themselves, and that care for the welfare of other members of the School—not fear of punishment—should make them want to keep the few School rules that there were. Changes had to come, and Miss Tanner asked that all who had known and loved the School in the past should realise that she made them only where the welfare of the School demanded and not because she did not value its old traditions.

Speaking at the meeting of the Guild in June, 1921, she said: "I want to tell you how much the spirit of the Guild has helped me during the last year and a half. I do not think that there can be any school where the devotion of the Old Girls is greater than it is here. It seems to me rather wonderful that we have here today representatives of both the mistresses and the girls who were in the School the day it was opened more than thirty-nine years ago. Only something truly great in the School itself could have inspired such devotion, and from the time when, on one of my first days here, a member of the Guild, who herself left school perhaps twenty-five years ago, came to see me and told me of what the School had meant, and still did mean, to her, I have been cheered in my most despondent moments by the consciousness of all that must have gone to create that spirit, and to keep it alive, and by the knowledge that these things do not die but remain as living forces to help those of us who are working in the School now.

"I see that in her last address to you Miss Collie referred to the conservatism of the Old Girls or Boys of a school, who cannot bear to see even a desk moved from its accustomed place: I know how strong that feeling is in all of us, but I want to ask you, as your president did two years ago, to realise that it may be better for some child of today that the desk should be put into another position, or perhaps removed altogether, and that if we keep it in its original place, when that has ceased to be the best

DAME EMMELINE TANNER

place, we are failing to live up to the true ideals of the School and its founders.

"There is another fact, too, that we are obliged to recognise— no two people express themselves in their work in the same way, and one's work to be worth anything must be spontaneous and sincere and natural to one's self, not a mere imitation of someone else.

"Consequently with a change in the headship of the School must come certain external changes, some of them made quite unconsciously and unwittingly. I ask the Guild not to be hurt by these changes, but to understand and forgive, where forgiveness is needed.

"But there is always more or less consciously with me the fear of a much more serious danger—that a stranger, not brought up in the tradition of the School, may perhaps destroy something of its true greatness. Your first president once reminded you that if we all realise that our work, however great or however small, is given us to do by One whose love knows no limitations, and if we do it reverently, humbly, fully, gladly, as fellow-workers together with Him, it cannot fail. May that consciousness be ever with us, so that the School of which we are a part may be worthy of those who have made it, and may ever continue to be a great power for good in the land."

The developments within the School, which were demanded by the changing world outside, were made more difficult for Miss Tanner by the fact that whereas the war years had seen a rapid extension in the realms of thought and ideas, they had been years of severe economy and retrenchment as far as School building and equipment were concerned. The School was obliged to raise its fees, but even that did not provide enough money for the improvements which were urgently needed. Women were taking a very much greater share in scientific work than they had ever done before ; science teachers were wanted for the new secondary schools which were being built ; they were wanted in industry and in scientific research, and science appealed to many girls. The School laboratories were small and ill-equipped ; Miss Collie's plans for the building of new ones had been stopped by the war. Helped by her science mistresses, Miss Perrott and Miss Campbell (now Mrs. Osborn), who spent many hours in drawing up plans, Miss Tanner put forward several schemes for a new science block of buildings, but for want of money none of them could be carried out. What it was possible to do was done. In each science room a new bench was installed for practical work ; and in order to provide more accommodation for classes a large demonstration bench was put into the form room next to the rest room. In spite of inadequate accommodation, the science work went on and developed, and several girls won university scholarships. All honour to the science mistresses who carried on the work under such great difficulties and with hope of new laboratories constantly deferred.

Where she was not so hampered she worked to extend and improve the School activities. We had a fine river at Bedford but there were no facilities for the girls to learn to swim—Miss Tanner made them, and nearly every afternoon in the summer arranged for a contingent of girls to go to the baths and to have teaching in swimming and life saving. Lacrosse and netball became School games in addition to hockey, tennis and rounders.

The house system, which Miss Collie had introduced for the day girls, dividing them into East, West and Central houses, according to the geographical area of Bedford in which they lived, became more prominent in the School life when members of the teaching staff were appointed as Day Girl house mistresses, and the houses had their separate cloakrooms, in which the house captains were responsible for order. Each boarding house had worn a different hat band : now the unity of the School was marked by there being one band for all, the different houses being differentiated merely by the varying colours of the stripe in the middle of the band. New School blazers were introduced too.

Miss Tanner was able to have the whole of the School, which had become somewhat dingy and dirty during the war years, completely redecorated. The green woodwork in the hall was painted to resemble old oak, and all the friends of the School, Old and Present Girls, parents and staff, combined to collect enough money to present to the School a permanent oak platform, together with all the extensions and accessories for stage performances and tiered seats for School concerts, an oak refectory table and a chair for the platform and an oak case for the clock, all of which greatly added to the dignity and beauty of the School hall. The total cost of the platform and stage was about £500, and the greater part of it came from Old Girls.

As their share of the special effort being made to raise money for the platform, the staff decided to present a play, and chose Barrie's *Kiss for Cinderella*. They had to perform without scenery and on a temporary platform made up of desks and forms, which sometimes gave way at inconvenient moments, but their performance was so much appreciated and so much enjoyed by the actors themselves that it proved to be the first of a series of four staff plays, in which Miss Colwill (later Mrs. Holroyd), Miss B. J. Fisher (later Mrs. Colson) and, later on, Miss Pike (later Mrs. Hutchins), took the chief parts.

There cannot have been many girls' schools with an abler and more academically distinguished staff than that of the Bedford High School of this time. Miss Lee was there as second mistress, and her love of the School was an inspiration to the rest of us. There was no matter affecting its welfare, small or great, to which she was not ready to attend; and who could grudge any service when she was doing so much? Other members of the staff whose names come at once to mind were Miss M. E. Thomson (to whose brilliant scholarship the classical department owes so much), Miss Cracknell and Miss Arden; Miss Agnes Sandys (later Mrs. Leys), who was awarded a Gilchrist Travelling Scholarship and went to Italy to study the Franciscan movement, and Miss Hudson, who left to get married. Miss Tanner made several notable new appointments, among which were Miss Matson, Miss Davis, Miss Hatch and Miss C. B. Thomson. Later Miss Matson became head mistress of Chichester High School, Miss Davis of Bexhill High School, Miss Hatch of Leamington College for Girls and Miss Naylor of Douglas High School, I.O.M. [*and Miss Millburn herself of Northampton School for Girls.*—EDITOR.]. Miss C. B. Thomson became the greatly loved head of the French department.

The secretarial work had increased so much that it could

no longer be done entirely by Miss Forbes, who was a member of the music staff as well, and Miss Chomley gave up her post as geography mistress to become the head mistress's personal secretary. Her cheery laugh was still to ring through the School, her wit and humour to enliven and amuse us in the staff room. She had been the first woman to travel on the Trans-Siberian Railway, and nothing ever daunted her.

In the spring of 1924 Miss Tanner was asked to apply for the head mistress-ship of Roedean, where the Misses Lawrence were about to lay down their great work. She refused at first to consider the invitation, being unwilling to leave Bedford, but was eventually prevailed upon to accept. Her parting from the School was a very sad one on both sides—particularly as Miss Tanner was taken ill at the beginning of her last and good-bye term and had to undergo a serious operation. Happily she recovered before the end of the term and was able to spend her last few weeks at School.

Her happy relationship with the School never wavered. Life at Roedean held much hard work and anxiety for her, including the evacuation of the school to the Lake District during the war, and her memorable presidency of the Head Mistresses' Association at a difficult period. She was never daunted, and never forgot us. On her retirement soon after the war she was created Dame of the British Empire. Her subsequent travels were amazing and a great joy to Bedford and Roedean. We quote from the *Aquila* of 1948 :

"Dame Emmeline Tanner is having a wonderful tour in South Africa and has met a great many Old Girls. At Madeira Mrs. Blandy (Mildred Edmonds) came on board with her husband, who is British Consul, to greet Princess Alice and the Earl of Athlone, who were on the same ship. Dame Emmeline presented Mrs. Blandy to Princess Alice. At Cape Town she found that Honor Edmonds was acting at the new National Theatre. Dame Emmeline was unable to get seats for the show, but they did have a long telephone conversation.

"She spent almost a week with Mrs. Russell (M. Columbine) at Pietermaritzburg, and was much impressed by all the work she has in hand, especially for the natives. She says she met a lot of interesting people there, including Mrs. Bellenden (Joan Cowley), and she plans to return in July and speak at a Conference of the Natal Teachers' Association. Travelling in the train one day she found herself sitting opposite to Kathleen Byrne, who has a post in the Immigration Office at Cape Town.

"She is doing a good deal of travelling and public speaking, and has been in Rhodesia. Mrs. Honey (Jessie Purland) and Mrs. Aylen (Sally Harris) arranged a combined party of Old Girls of Roedean and Bedford at Mrs. Honey's home in Salisbury, and greetings were exchanged with both schools."

What a journey!

She went again in 1953, and the rejoicings were as great as ever.

She died in January, 1955, and Phyllis Robinson wrote, after her Memorial Service at St. Martin's-in-the-Field: "Dr. Bell outlined her remarkable career, her singular accomplishments, her multifarious activities, and at the end of this glittering record came the question, 'Wherein lay her greatness?' It was a question we could all answer."

CHAPTER IX

1924-1932

THE APPOINTMENT of a new head mistress inaugurates a new phase in the history of a school. But to us the word "new" in connection with the advent of Miss Westaway to Bedford High School in 1924 is misleading. As she herself said to the School when she took prayers for the first time, she was very new once upon a time, when she sat in the front row of the Junior School. That in itself was enough to win our hearts—the thought that she had grown up in our School tradition, and had assimilated all that was best in it, and after passing on to Newnham College, Cambridge, and holding a post as classics mistress at Cheltenham Ladies' College, followed by a lectureship in Royal Holloway College, University of London, had come back to identify herself yet more closely, in her new position, with that tradition. To all that is implied by that tradition, to the people who made it and the circumstances under which it gradually unfolded itself according to their ideals, the earlier chapters of this book bear witness. And if we of that generation had a peculiar pride in Miss Westaway, and were glad, not just that we had an Old Girl for our head mistress, but that the Old Girl should be Miss Westaway, we would say that the years that have elapsed since her appointment afforded the justification of our pride.

"When we were at School, we knew it for a great school, but we guessed little enough of the dreams of those who made it. We understand them better now, but when you look back on it, do you not think that the School became in reality what it was first in the minds of the dreamers? I do believe absolutely that dreams come true if we want them hard enough." When Miss Westaway said that in a speech before the largest Guild meeting then on record some of her dreams must have been connected with building. One soon came true, and the year 1927 is memorable in the School history : I mean the opening of the new wing for science and domestic subjects, which was performed in

MISS WESTAWAY

May of that year by the Duchess of Atholl. We were impressed by the ceremony, but then how exciting had been the building operations which had been begun nearly a year before. Arriving every morning to a transformed playground, littered with bricks, invaded by lorries, and resonant with hammering, we loved it, and the staff bore it nobly, even though teaching under such conditions must have been trying at times. However, under the able direction of Mr. Allen, the architect, and the critical eye of Mrs. Osborn (then Miss Campbell), the building slowly but surely assumed its present proportions. The covered way linked the new wing with the old block, and at the latter end three new music rooms were at the same time erected. As for the new wing itself, I shall not attempt to describe it. Even the unscientific cannot fail to be impressed by the general atmosphere of efficiency which the interior of the laboratories produces, and in which we hope many an illustrious scientist will be produced. The record in 1932 was at any rate gratifying, for out of the eight State scholarships gained by members of the School during the past eight years, six have been won by pupils of Mrs. Osborn for botany.

Domestic science likewise flourished under the direction of Miss H. Millburn, and of the girls who have taken the Sixth Form Domestic Science Course, many have gone on to training colleges in this subject. In connection with domestic science, a stimulus was given to School needlework in 1926 through the gift, by an anonymous donor, of a silver cup, to be competed for by the IIIAs. The subjects set involved needlework of the strictly utilitarian variety—darning and patching. The IIIAs, alas, were found to be far from enthusiastic in these arts, and, with a view to fostering the love of needlework throughout the School, the same donor kindly provided additional cups to be competed for in higher forms.

The new wing proved to be but a part of a scheme for extending the School. No less interesting was the building of a new gymnasium. The date stone of this was laid by Miss Stansfeld on the Monday morning of the 1931 Guild meeting, and on 23rd November she visited the School again and formally opened the new building in the presence of the Governors. This improvement had been ardently desired for many years, and now that it has materialised it makes many of us wish that we were at School again. Miss Hadley and Miss Colwill for years taught us to make the best of a confined space, and despite its shortcomings we had an affection for the old gymnasium. Then we learned that it was to be transformed into the new library. The possession of such a library augurs well for the School's intellectual record; every Speech Day brings its list of successes. To the three Exhibitions of £50 which are offered yearly to members of the School desiring to continue their studies at the universities, and awarded on the result of the Higher Certificate examination, a fourth was added in 1927 by the generosity of the late Mrs. Hilda Mahala Broun, sister of Mr. Geoffrey Howard. This Scholarship falls vacant every three years. Besides the School Leaving Exhibitions, at least one university scholarship and exhibition has been won every year by the Bedford High School. In connection with work we recall the School's third full inspection by the Board of Education in November, 1925. For a week we were joyfully in the hands of an army of inspectors, and well remember being rewarded with a whole day's holiday shortly afterwards.

We owe it to the Governors of the Harpur Trust that the science block and gymnasium stand in sober reality, no longer castles in the air, but the existence of the library is due to tremendous efforts on the part of many people. As soon as a scheme for a library was worked out, it became apparent that it would cost a large sum, and great credit is due to all those who devised new means of extorting money in the interests of the library fund. Not content, moreover, with individual efforts, or rather, realising that in co-operation lay their strength, they resolved to concentrate all their energies on a bazaar. This took place on 17th and 18th October, 1930. And such a bazaar! An eye witness has contributed the following account of it:

"For this, the first bazaar ever held in the School, an army of energetic workers had been preparing for months; yet none could have suspected it, so quietly did normal school life continue until one o'clock on Thursday. But Friday afternoon found the building transfigured. The hall was a miniature

Harrods, where stalls, flaunting house colours, were piled with
wares of every description, each house having undertaken a
different department. There were also an Old Girls' stall,
supplied by gifts from all over the world; a staff stall, which
dealt in all those nondescript articles collectively called "fancy";
and a Junior School stall of the fine arts, where one might buy
hand-made Christmas cards and calendars direct from the artists.
On the platform an orchestra played valiantly amidst the hubbub.

"The Junior School had become a restaurant; the gymnasium
a fun-fair; the art room a theatre, where concert succeeded
concert, and the Guild Dramatic Circle gave a capital one-act
play. The corridor was lined with envelopes, in which pennies
could be placed to form a mile walk of opulence, and the walk
led to a fairy village, which for twopence would light up all its
little houses to reward the generous. In the playground you
could send off a gas balloon and hope that it would go all the
way to Holland, where some little Dutch girl, in white cap and
wooden shoes, would pick it up and win a prize for you and for
herself.

"But the greatest transformation took place in the science
block. On the ground floor a 'freak' golf course was laid out,
where pails of water, bridges, mysterious pits, drain-pipes and
hazards, such as golf secretaries may imagine in a nightmare,
baffled the most expert putter. Upstairs the various 'labs' had
been swallowed up in darkness and you might wander in the
most realistic of haunted houses, where rattling chains and ghostly
moans affrighted the ear, where the floor sank beneath your feet,
or rustled and boomed under the lightest tread, where soft
touches unexpectedly caressed your face, or clammy fingers
met your groping hands, where skulls and corpses and blue lights
were commonplaces, and a ghostly motor-car rushed towards
you in a narrow way, yet never reached its victim. When,
nerve-shattered, you emerged, you found in the domestic science
room a 'quick-snack' bar, where you could restore your
equanimity. One thousand people passed through the haunted
house; it was certainly the most ingenious of side-shows.

"So great was the press of visitors in the hall that serious
buying was difficult, and it was found necessary to open the stalls

G

to customers on Saturday morning, when a steady trade was done. No wonder that on Monday morning Miss Westaway was able to announce that the £1,000 required for the library was safely in the bank. The big wooden 'thermometer', which had so long stood in the hall to register the progress of the fund, was brought to the platform and with a dramatic gesture she drew the red tape up, and over the top, amidst the plaudits of the School.

"Perhaps not the least achievement was that on Monday morning no trace remained, in an orderly and workaday school, of all the wonders of Saturday except two forlorn bran tubs, awaiting removal, outside the passage-cloakroom door."

It is not only in the big achievements, such as the building of the science block, the gymnasium, or the library, that we see the embodiment of the ideals, long cherished in the minds of those who love our School; there are all the activities which go to make up the School curriculum in its widest sense.

There are the games. We differed from many girls' schools in not having compulsory games (except in the Middle School). But the provision of three winter games, run simultaneously under the efficient coaching of the physical training staff and students, with tennis and cricket (and rounders for the Middle School) to follow in the summer, was in itself sufficient inducement for most girls of the School to play games. This plan has, of course, been improved upon from time to time. When Miss Westaway came, lacrosse was on a very insecure footing, but it steadily gained in popularity and stood on a par with hockey. Various schemes were tried to harmonise the working of the winter games, such as devoting one term exclusively to hockey, another to lacrosse, or of playing the two games alternately throughout the term, in periods of three weeks each. These schemes were enterprising, but on the whole the simultaneous plan was found the best.

Swimming was officially recognised as one of the School sports in 1924, when it was decided that colours should be awarded to girls who had obtained the bronze medallion of the Royal Life Saving Society and who had passed certain tests set by the School Committee. As the School had no swimming bath of its own, the Commercial Road baths were given up to its use on three afternoons a week, and the house tests and diving competitions, which every summer call forth much keenness and rivalry, used to take place there. In July, 1930, however, Bedford School became the possessor of their own swimming pool, which they kindly let the High School use on four afternoons a week. Those who remember the old difficulties of the Commercial Road baths will realise with what a sense of gratitude the School now avails itself of this privilege.

In tennis contests with other schools we have reason to be proud of our champions. In 1924 two out of the three possible events were won for the School at the Harpenden Tournament, while in 1928 it was noted that of the ten times we had taken part in the Midland Girls' Schools tournament, the School's first couple had played in the finals seven times, and had won the shield three times. Already Valerie Scott, later of international fame, was noticed for her fine promise. But the School coaches did not only aim at the production of a few good couples; the house matches, the system of grading, whereby ambitious pairs can challenge those of a higher grade, and occasional specially organised tournaments, all helped to maintain the general standard of play.

"Field" suggests to me the Field Club, though there is no connection beyond the fact that primarily the Field Club was started to foster out-of-doors activities apart from athletics. To this main purpose its organisers continued faithful, and the programme was arranged to include expeditions to places of archæological, historical or other interest; for example, both Oxford and Cambridge have been visited. At one stage in its career the club was in danger of becoming too exclusive a body, and might have been threatened with extinction had not the membership been established on more democratic lines. Henceforward, any girl in the Upper School who liked could be a member on payment of a shilling a year; and in case membership should be entered on too lightly, additions were soon after made to the ordinary programme of expeditions and lectures in the form of fortnightly meetings, at which members, chosen by lot, read papers on various subjects.

Then there were the Guides and Cadets, who flourished in four companies under Miss Askwith and Miss D. Madden. Nearly every summer holiday they held a camp, which was exceedingly popular, while Miss Askwith's expedition with the Cadets to Belgium in 1930 was felt to be real pioneering and will be long remembered with joy. They also had many opportunities, and took advantage of them to the full, of doing "good turns" to girls less fortunate than themselves, both in Bedford and further afield.

I know that I cannot mention the School's musical activities without at once recalling to everyone's mind the beloved personality of Dr. Harding, and I like to think of him as one who would value more highly his memorial of affection in people's hearts than the gift we are proud to endow to his memory. Miss Westaway's note, which appeared in *The Times* on 31st October, 1930, two days after his death, gathers up our impressions of him during his long connection with the School:

"Beyond the wide circle of musicians who now mourn the loss of Dr. Harding, there is a very great company who, as his pupils, both boys and girls, during a period of over forty years, have owned him a master of unsurpassable inspiration. Many, better qualified than I, will commemorate him as composer, organist, pianist, accompanist, examiner, organiser, in all these ways greatly gifted. But as I knew him best, as a teacher of choral singing, his was nothing short of genius. He would have a chorus of 200 or 300 boys or girls, and put them through part-singing of the most exacting intricacy, and have them singing and thinking as with a single mind. To discipline these great choruses he was sometimes fearsome, sometimes whimsical, sometimes jovial; and always he was completely accepted and beloved. He insisted on work of meticulous accuracy, and spared neither himself nor his pupils in his pursuit of it, and many memories will be stirring now of thrilling rehearsals that bore witness to this. He had an immense scorn of the sentimental, and he was almost shy in expressing his own love of the beautiful, but it was part of his genius as a teacher that he communicated both these things to his pupils without much talking about either. Among many choirs in the schools and town of

Bedford he leaves a memory of a powerful personality and a mind full of lovely things."

The inauguration of the Bedford branch of the Federation of Music Clubs in 1924 was a landmark in the history of Bedford High School music. With these concerts we associate two names especially, that of Miss K. Eggar, herself an Old Girl, who often lectured on the programme a few days before the concert took place; and that of M. Mangeot, who opened the first season of these concerts held in our hall with his Music Society String Quartet. Further accounts of the School's musical activity will be found in another chapter.

The magnificent platform that is put up for School dramatic functions has not languished in disuse. It was put up for the performance of a play by the Guild every two years, and at the 1931 meeting a highly-successful rendering of *Quality Street* was given by members of the Dramatic Circle. As well as these biennial performances there were two staff plays which were keenly appreciated—*The Knight of the Burning Pestle*, played in June, 1925, and *Trelawney of the Wells*, in February, 1927. Other dramatic performances were given from time to time by pupils of Miss Gowen. There was a very good production of *Iphigenia in Tauris*, in February, 1926, given by members of the Sixth under the direction of Miss B. J. Fisher. The most ambitious of all was the production by members of the School of Gilbert Murray's translation of the *Alcestis*. The keenness that is shown to act Greek plays, even in translation, has no doubt been stimulated by the most enjoyable expeditions that were organised by Miss M. E. Thomson whenever there were performances at Oxford or Cambridge, and were real inspirations to all who went.

A school magazine must in some measure reveal the intimate workings of a school. And term by term the *Aquila* has been reflecting B.H.S. history. For most of us only a small portion of that time was personal experience, and for each generation its own school life has a particular significance. It remains for the Guild, existing as it does to link together the little bits of experience of every member, to find its joy and inspiration in experiences that are not only personal to some, but common to all. Such experiences generally centre in things; that is why mere brick and mortar buildings can have such a halo of association. But the same applies in even greater measure to people. If there are persons so linked with our School tradition that their names rise spontaneously to our lips whenever we think of School, then the name of Miss Lee is especially appropriate on this occasion. It is, of course, impossible to "classify" such a person as Miss Lee. She did so much in the course of her forty years at School; in fact, the question we naturally ask is not so much "What did she do?" as "What did she not do?"—if in anything she could help anyone. We think of her as always busy, but her unique quality was that, no matter how widely diverse were the tasks to which she gave her time and energy, they all received the same unsparing and undivided attention. We who were at School at the time of the retirement of Miss Lee, Miss Windsor, Mr. Nightingale, Miss Manning, Miss Plow-Smith, Miss E. Robbins, could not but be proud that our days had overlapped with those of some who made the School so great in early years.

When we said good-bye, in the summer of 1929, we could not hope for another "Miss Lee"—that was impossible; but those of us who had had the opportunity of appreciating Miss Cracknell's close association with us, were very happy to learn of her appointment. We knew that the interest and sympathy, which she had invariably shown to members of her Sixth Form, would be extended to each and every individual with whom her wider sphere of activities would bring her into contact; and in all the years that have followed, both until her retirement and since, her generous friendship for us all has been one of the richest blessings our School has ever known.

CHAPTER X

1932-1939

BY MISS EVELYN ASKWITH

IN THIS CHAPTER we reach the centre of the School's history so far, the end of one age and the start of another.

In May, 1932, with much gladness and with many festivities, the School celebrated its fiftieth birthday. For a school as well as for each one of us as individuals, a fiftieth birthday is a time of solemnity and heart-searching as well as of rejoicing. Of the events of that week-end, four stand out particularly in my memory. First there was the opening of the new library by Sir Arthur Quiller-Couch. This is in the room which was formerly the gymnasium, the scene for the athletic of many former triumphs, but for others not so gifted, the scene at times of disasters and misery. It had been completely transformed and had been made into a library of which any school could be proud, and for the past twenty-five years it has been the place for study for both staff and elder girls. In 1932 Sir Arthur unlocked the door with these words: "In trust that it will advance good learning in this place and also that happiness which is the sister of good learning, I declare this your library open".

My second memory is of the great Thanksgiving Service in St. Paul's Church, preceded by the great procession of staff and girls, in form order—a procession not of 43 girls and four staff as it would have been in 1882, but of nearly 600 girls and a corresponding increase in staff. The procession was led by two policemen, Miss Burnaby and Form I and was an inspiring sight as it slowly made its way from the School along Harpur Street to St. Paul's Church. Inside the church, seats were found not only for the whole School and the whole staff but also for a certain number of Guild members, for representatives of the Harpur Trust, and for civic officials. The preacher was the Bishop of Barking—and from beginning to end the service was full of praise and thanksgiving.

Thirdly, there was the Old Girls' dinner in the School hall.

With my contemporaries I was seated at a table in the south-west corner, where, free from responsibility, we had great fun, reviving memories of our schooldays. But over all of us there lay a shadow—the absence of Miss Collie and the knowledge of her serious illness. She was just able to write us a letter herself (the handwriting is very shaky), and in return we sent her a message of love, together with some flowers, which we learnt afterwards she greatly appreciated.

MISS COLLIE'S LETTER

Crawley Hall,
Husborne Crawley,
nr. Bletchley.
May, 1932.

When I read the list of those who are taking part in the festivities connected with the Jubilee, I see the names of so many of my dear Old Girls that I feel I may once more address you as "My dear Children".

I cannot tell you what it means to me to be unable to join you in anything. I had hoped to be able to hold a little gathering here on Sunday, but I am not well enough. Meanwhile you will hardly be out of my thoughts, and I hope you will have a very happy time meeting one another again.

God bless you, my dear children.

Your loving old friend,

SUSAN M. COLLIE.

After the dinner itself was over, the younger members of the Guild, for whom there had been no room at the tables in the hall, came from the Junior School and crowded into the hall galleries for the toasts and speeches. After Miss Collie's letter had been read and the loyal toast honoured, toasts were proposed to the Harpur Trust, the staff (past and present), the Guild, the School and the head mistress, all of which were drunk with acclamation by the entire company, representing every generation in the School's life.

Fourthly, I look back at the scene in the staff room on the Monday evening after the Open Day. Every member of the teaching staff, part-time, full-time, young and old, had been summoned

94

to attend. The only absentee was Monsieur Mangeot, who was in London, and the room was crowded to overflowing when Miss Westaway entered and introduced Mrs. Harold Howard. On behalf of the Governing Body, Mrs. Howard presented to each one, individually, a gold brooch with the eagle and the inscription, "B.H.S. Jubilee". This completely unexpected tribute and gift from the Governors was a wonderful conclusion for the staff to a joyous, yet hectic, week-end.

Who were these women who were given a "Jubilee Brooch"? The recipients were simply all those, who at that date, May, 1932, happened to form the teaching staff of the High School. Some were quite young, some near to retiring age. To my older readers they may seem insignificant, not to be compared with the giants of the past. Is that really true ? Academically, the average in 1932 was naturally much higher than in the days of the pioneers. It seems invidious to pick out a few when so many are worthy of mention, but there is only space for a few: Miss Cracknell, Miss Lee's successor as second mistress and also a mathematician ; Miss M. E. Thomson, whose brilliant and clear brain added fresh lustre to the classical department ; Miss C. B. Thomson, disclosing a new vision of the French language and a friendship for the people of France, whom she herself loved so dearly, and of the country of France ; Miss Arden, ably assisted by Miss Wilson, like Miss Holmes in earlier days, opened the treasures of English literature to their classes, and inspired them as well with a respect for the use of good English language ; their methods were different from those of Miss Holmes, but their aims and results were similar ; Miss Lockyer, successor to Miss Stone as Head of the Junior School, carried on very high standards in that department, which were most easily visible in handwork of all kinds ; Miss Osborne and Miss Raley, each in turn later to become head of the Junior School, were working in that department ; Miss D. Madden in the mathematics department, each year helped many girls, old and young, through her very successful and well-run Guide camps ; Miss Gowen, guide and counsellor in all forms of dramatic art ; Miss M. E. F. Madden, for many years both organist and librarian; Miss H. S. Millburn teaching her classes to be really capable in all forms of housewifery and achieving an amazingly high standard in these arts ; in the science department Miss Campbell, that brilliant botanist, now Mrs. Osborn, whose husband recently became Chairman of the Harpur Trust, and Miss Collier, very much to the fore on all dramatic occasions ; Miss Mandville, full of life and vigour in history, in games and in many other activities ; and one young member of the staff, assistant to Miss C. B. Thomson, already known as a "wonderful teacher", must be allowed here to make her first bow to you—Miss Watkins.

Most of the women present in the staff room on 9th May, 1932, have now in their turn given up their places to a still younger generation, but there are ten left, who are hoping to wear their brooches as active staff members through the festivities of the 75th birthday.

It is one of the glories of the School that in every generation there have always been women on the staff, able and willing not only to reveal the treasures of their own particular subject, but also to inspire, mainly without words, the girls of the School with the deeper qualities expressed in our motto—the things that are true, honest, just, pure, lovely and of good report. So the Jubilee brooches, treasured by their possessors, were surely meant to be not merely a tribute to those recipients but also a tribute to all members of the teaching staff from 1882, on past 1932 to the present day and on still further into the future.

So the Jubilee ended, and once again the School settled down to its normal life of work and play. Two apparently minor changes, but with good, far-reaching effects, date from this period.

First, a fourth day-girl "house" was formed, known as "Country House" to include all day-girls who lived outside the Borough of Bedford. Its first house mistress was Miss Arden. For the first time these girls, who of necessity could not always take part in School activities, found themselves in a cohesive unit in School. Even so it took years for Country to find its feet, despite its large numbers, which were growing rapidly with the development of motor transport, but its contribution has increased steadily with the passing of the years, and Country can now take its rightful place alongside the seven other houses.

The second change was the abolition of the auction of lost property on the last day of term. Good as the idea and conduct of it had been originally, conditions had changed, and everyone, staff and girls alike, were greatly relieved at its abolition. Since 1932 lost property has been dealt with in a different way, and for the majority of the School term has ended with the head mistress's goodbye to the School in the hall.

. . . . .

Yet the echoes of our Jubilee rejoicings had hardly died away when we were called upon to mourn the passing from our midst of one to whom the School, past and present, owes a debt beyond all estimating. Five weeks after the Jubilee, on 13th June, Miss Collie died peacefully at her home in Husborne Crawley.

It is impossible for any one person, certainly not myself, adequately to pay tribute to, or even to describe Miss Collie. Very shy, very dignified, very well dressed, with great academic ability and great administrative powers, she was also full of courage, which was displayed clearly in her several serious illnesses as well as in the bearing of the pain of the headaches, from which throughout her life, she frequently suffered. Dealing, as she had to do, with girls in the crowd, she never forgot that each one was an individual with her own personal problems, and she had deep sympathy with and insight into the life of each one. Yet even this is not all. Miss Collie's work and influence were based on love : she loved the School and everyone in it, the naughtiest small girl better than most : the things that are true and lovely had a very deep meaning for her.

Will those of you who never knew Miss Collie, go at the first opportunity you can find and study the enlarged photograph of her that hangs on the wall outside the Country Room in the Susan Collie Wing ? It is a wonderful likeness of her as she was at the time when she retired : one can see the dignity of the well-dressed lady, mellowed by age, and one can see her charm and her love shining in her eyes.

Before her death she had expressed the wish that no money should be collected to erect a memorial to her. Her wish was respected, but her name is kept fresh for every generation in the wing known as the Susan Collie Wing, and her influence lives on in the lives of all those who were fortunate enough to have been girls at School or members of the staff when she was head mistress.

Less than eighteen months later, on 18th October, 1933, another grief befell the School. Miss Lee had gone to stay with her brother, the vicar of Collier Street, a tiny village in Kent, a house and village where she was always happy to go. But she was frail, and her heart was no longer strong, and here one evening, quite suddenly and painlessly, she died. The news of her death came as a great shock to everyone in School, and it was hard to believe that we should not again meet Miss Lee in the School corridors.

Miss Lee was on the High School staff from 1889-1929, forty years in her first and only teaching post. At the time she was appointed she was quite outstanding on the staff for her academic qualifications. She came from Newnham College and she had a very quick and clear mathematical brain, and she was an excellent teacher, most inspiring, patient and painstaking with every member of her class. She was also keen on games, and even today the School hockey players owe a great debt to Miss Lee for all she did so many years ago to get hockey started (on a gravelled playground!) and for her many years of close connection with and care for the field. She was the last of our "pioneer" staff, showing to those who should follow her something of the inspiration, zest, faith, courage and love of the women who had led the movement of higher education for women.

Stern when things went wrong, Miss Lee could invariably reduce any girl or any member of the staff to tears, though she would be found next day going out of her way to do some special kindness to the offender. In her later years, when, as second mistress, she had multitudinous duties to perform, it was always said on the staff that though Miss Lee was seldom in the room with her form, yet her form was the best trained and best behaved of all. This is no small tribute as for many years she had a VBii, a difficult stage. Busy as she was, doing things at running speed (literally) in School, Miss Lee always had time for individuals, and her advice and sympathy were very precious and helpful.

Like Miss Collie, whose right-hand support she was for so many years, their secret power was the same, based as it was on the things that are true and lovely and of good report.

. . . . .

Yet another transformation took place in School during these years. In 1931 the new gymnasium had been built. In 1932 the old gymnasium became the library. In 1935 the old iron passage room between the main block and the Junior School block was demolished, and in its place a new permanent block was erected to bear the proud name of the Susan Collie Wing. The commemoration-stone was laid by Lady Jaqueta Williams. Upstairs it contains the Country Room (for the use of Country House girls) and a modern needlework room. Downstairs there are good cloakrooms for the IVths, IIIAs and IIA Forms : all these improvements were long overdue. As a result the passage cloakroom became, as it had originally been intended to be, merely a passage.

These, too, were the years when, in common with other schools, it became the custom to arrange School expeditions on many different occasions—a visit to the Royal Academy in London, a visit to Cambridge to see a Greek play, another to London for a French play and so on. So it was not surprising that during these years School parties were arranged in the Easter holidays to visit the Continent. The first one of all was a visit to Belgium, arranged in 1930 solely for the Cadet Company. On this trip the party stayed in a convent in Bruges, where the sanitary conditions left a good deal to be desired, but where amongst the sisters they found two well-educated English women, with whom they easily made friends. The company explored Bruges pretty thoroughly and they also visited Ghent and the Belgian coast, where they saw the famous Mole at Zeebrugge. Two coach excursions were also included—one over the Dutch border to Middelburg and the other round Ypres and a good many of the 1914-18 battlefields including Hill 60.

In succeeding years parties visited Paris, the Chateaux Country,

Rome and Roman France (Provence). The last one in 1938 was to Holland, when circumstances prevented the School from carrying out their intention of making a steamer trip up the Rhine. With her own love of travel, it was not surprising that Miss Westaway encouraged wholeheartedly these Continental holidays: she joined completely in two of them, that to Rome and the one to Provence : in the other years she met the party at some prearranged place at least once, usually oftener and always gave the whole party some special treat.

Although no one learned much of the language, whether it was French or Italian, at least everyone had the fun of seeing a little of how other nations lived and of hearing French and Italian spoken. Nearly always the party visited a girls' school in the area and were able to compare a lesson, say, in Paris with a lesson at Bedford ! That was an eye-opener for everyone, including the staff, and so were the pinafores (*tabliers*—pink one week, blue the next) worn by every girl in the school at Tours. Nothing could exceed the kindness with which the party was always received in these schools, and everyone really appreciated it, though their thanks were somewhat stilted and stuttering until Miss C. B. Thomson came to the rescue and said all that should be said.

The retirement of Miss Chomley in 1935 meant the loss of a most cheery, original and witty figure from the community. A year later she was elected to the Bedford Town Council (one of the first women to win that honour), and served it with the greatest cheerfulness and diligence till the end of the war, and the staff followed all her activities there, too, with affectionate and admiring interest.

She was succeeded in the Secretary's office, for a time, by Pamela Orr, and when she, to our disappointment, had to return to London, Dorothy Kitchener was appointed to the post, and her twenty years of distinguished service there are recognised by us all with deepest gratitude.

Thus the years passed, happy and busy in work and play, full of personal joys, successes with some failures and sorrows until 1939 dawned. As the bells rang in that New Year, no one could foresee what lay in front of the School nor indeed of the country. For two more terms life in School proceeded normally, though during the summer term everyone was first measured for and then issued with a gas mask : Miss Westaway was asked by the authorities to see that every girl knew how to put on her mask properly and could wear it for a short period.

At the end of that term, three of us set off by car for a short holiday in Devon : when the luggage was in and we were about to start, one of the party threw on to the back seat of the car a square, cardboard box, containing her gas mask. This gave us rather a shock, though actually she was right, for she was not to return to Bedford for eight weeks, and before she returned, England was once again at war with Germany. But the story of those war years lies outside the scope of this chapter, and you must read the book further to learn what happened next.

CHAPTER XI

1939-1949

BY MISS CATHERINE DAUGHTRY

THE OUTBREAK of war did, of course, bring changes. It brought difficulties and it brought anxieties but we, in Bedford, were very fortunate and the life of the School went on.

The bombing of the London estate was disastrous beyond description. We in Bedford were lucky to know it only in terms of devastated finance. There was one year when the schools received no endowment money at all.

The School buildings were already doing their share when the Autumn Term of 1939 began on 21st September. Woodford County High School had arrived in Bedford earlier in the month. At first it was undecided whether they would go to the Girls' Modern School or come to the High School, and after spending their first morning with us (spending it, very wisely, writing letters home) they went to the G.M.S. However, we did house them for a week or more of each holiday, until they left Bedford in 1941. We were sorry to see them go. The hall was again being used by troops, as in the 1914-18 war. Then, about 400 men were quartered in the School but this time they came to us on Sundays only for military church parades.

In 1940 there was a noticeable drop in the number of girls in the School, the result of many boarders returning to their families overseas. To fall in with the "dispersion" the nation was trying to effect in the early war days, the Junior School and IIAs were evacuated to the four boarding houses at the beginning of the Autumn Term, 1939. Once a week each of the forms would return to School for Prayers and for its gymnastics before returning to its boarding house. Day-girls revelled in the opportunity of seeing the inside of the boarding houses, and any boarder who was lucky enough to remain in her own house was regarded (with not a little respect!) as a veritable Cook's guide! Our (for I was just starting in IIB at the time) arrival at the boarding houses must have caused

great upheavals and many domestic difficulties, but all the house
mistresses and staff concerned coped magnificently and everything went smoothly. As it happened our "dispersion" was an
unnecessary effort. Bedford had no bombs of any kind until
long after these forms returned to the School (some in 1940 and
all by 1941). But who was to know?

Meanwhile air-raid precautions were the order of the day.
Certain windows were bricked up and the inner corridors of the
School shored up. The cloakrooms in the Susan Collie Wing
became positive fortresses with their reinforcements and there
was even a baffle wall in the hall. Our nearest air-raid siren was
on the roof of Langley's garage (later to be an American Red
Cross Centre). At the sound of an "alert" every form trooped
off to its allotted (and reinforced) part of the School and remained
there until the "All Clear" sounded. It was the perfect opportunity to make headway with our home reading books and
I never see *Heidi* without thinking of those hours spent sitting
in the Susan Collie Wing cloakrooms! Is *Heidi* still IIA's first
home reading book?

Bedford was fortunate in having very few bombs, but we did
have scores of "alerts", especially for a year or so, 1940-41, and
many a country girl missed her bus or train when one o'clock
or four o'clock came and the "all clear" had not sounded. This
became such a regular happening that, provided their parents
gave written permission, day-girls were allowed to go home when
there was still a "raid on". These letters of consent were kept
locked in the School safe. Once, though, we did have bombs
during School hours. A large piece of railway sleeper, 27 lb.
in weight, arrived in our playground and made quite a dent,
and has been kept as a souvenir. But the "alert" had not
sounded! At the distribution of certificates in November,
1940, at which Professor Richardson (now Sir Albert Richardson,
lately P.R.A.) was the guest of honour, Miss Westaway, beginning
her speech, remarked that it was a sign of the time that she must
first tell the audience what to do in the event of an air-raid warning!

Of course we took our gas masks to every school session.
Failure to do so meant a journey home to collect it.

H

Mrs. Carling was the first mistress in charge of A.R.P. (Air Raid Precautions) and a most efficient team of staff and Sixth Form girls qualified as School air-raid wardens. They attended First Aid lectures and Miss Fisher was a tower of strength when it came to bandaging. Mrs. Carling was succeeded by Miss Sanders and what she enjoyed most was selling the sand-bags and shovels when peace did come!

Every night for four years a noble band of fire watchers looked after the School for us. Quite a number of Old Girls helped the staff with the fire-watching, and we were grateful to them. Miss Westaway and Miss Osborne did the first night-watch in November, 1940. William Eddy, the caretaker, let them in at 8 p.m., remarking cheerfully, "You're for it, Miss, Jerry has just gone over", and as he spoke the siren went! Nothing fell that night, nothing ever did fall on the School, but fire-watching *was* necessary. The first explosive incendiary bombs that were dropped in England landed on Albert Street, Bedford, so close to the School. In September, 1944, Miss Fisher, Miss Pinhorn (of the King's Warren School staff) and four Old Girls' celebrated the last watch. The milk room was the scene of a glorious midnight feast—lasting most of the night!

The School saved and collected everything we could, from National Savings to nettles (for the County Herb Committee). Miss Osborne was treasurer of our National Savings group for its first two years and during that time the School saved over £1,200. Then Miss Burnip took over and carried on the good work. The total amount saved during the war was £12,046. Miss Fisher helped them both and "attracted" many, many sixpences from Middle School girls as she sat at her table near the library.

There were several "weeks" run in connection with the National Savings movement and "Warship Week" was one of these. The School's goal of £1,000 was exceeded by nearly £700 and every morning there were lengthy queues to buy stamps. Nobody minded seeing *those* queues.

We had sales in aid of good causes. "Hospital Saturday" was, perhaps, the most ambitious of these. Miss Hillyer, Matron of

St. Thomas's Hospital, resplendent in E.M.S. uniform, opened the sale. Several Old Girls were there complete in nursing uniform and helped to create a really impressive atmosphere. We raised over £400 in the one morning.

The mobile canteen was one of our most exciting ventures. We collected money. We had a "Canteen Carnival" (a sale *par excellence*), and we found we had raised too much money! So not only were we able to give a mobile canteen to the County W.V.S. but we also gave an endowment fund to go towards the canteen's maintenance. On 16th February, 1942, the Honourable Pearl Lawson Johnston, on behalf of the W.V.S., accepted the canteen at a handing-over ceremony held in the playground, at which several of the town dignitaries were present. Tea was then served from the canteen by Miss Millburn and members of VI Domestic.

During the previous day the mobile canteen had stood in the playground and form by form we were taken to see it. In our eyes nothing else on four wheels was quite so perfect and that "Presented by Bedford High School" was painted on its side was the finishing touch. We all felt very proud of it and were thrilled if we met it in the town during the coming months. The canteen was used regularly to visit isolated units of the army, air force and home guard in the county. We felt prouder still when we learned that our canteen had gone to Europe to help bring some comfort to the starving peoples there.

The Social Service Committee had never been busier. It was organising the knitting of gloves, scarves and socks for troops and making up parcels for refugees and evacuees. Then the School adopted H.M.S. *Fezenta*, a trawler-minesweeper, with a crew of 22 men. How we enjoyed their letters to us telling about the ship and its doings and thanking us for the parcels of magazines, sweets and cigarettes we used to send them. Oddly enough, the home of their chief correspondent was in Adelaide Square. In 1942 the *Fezenta* was de-commissioned and so ended a short but happy friendship.

". . . 'Tis an ill wind" and amongst the hundreds of evacuees pouring into Bedford, and in particular the B.B.C., whose Religious Broadcasting Department, Symphony Orchestra,

Theatre Orchestra and Chorus came in 1941, the School gained many talented and delightful friends. The B.B.C.'s arrival had a tremendous and invigorating effect upon the musical life of the town. The Bedford Music Club gave way willingly to the orchestras that now gave superb symphony concerts, performed operas and presented the delightful "Tuesday Serenade" in the Corn Exchange and Bedford School hall. The latter was found to have particularly good acoustics and was used a great deal for broadcasting purposes. Those of us who were lucky enough to get passes (or who "braved" the doorkeeper!) spent many a memorable evening at these concerts. Sir Adrian Boult (then the conductor of the B.B.C. Symphony Orchestra) and Dr. Welch (Director of Religious Broadcasting) were the guests of honour at two of our happiest war-time speech days.

King's Warren School, of Plumstead, was evacuated to Bedford in July, 1941. Their first two years of evacuation had been spent in Maidstone but there were too many bombs for it to be a good place of refuge, and the authorities decided that they ought to move further north. So they came to us, 180 strong. Their numbers fluctuated considerably according to the air-raid situation in London. In the mornings K.W.S. used rooms in the town or played games at our field, and from 1.30 p.m. to 5 p.m. took possession of our Middle School Wing and various specialist rooms. It was not an ideal arrangement, either for them or for us, but they were the most considerate and friendly guests we possibly could have had.

They had difficulties beyond the obvious upheavals of evacuation. The double move from Plumstead to Maidstone, and from there to Bedford, proved too much for their head mistress, Miss Summers, and she retired, from ill-health, in 1942. The second mistress, Miss Spratt (still such a good friend to the School) carried on for two terms until the new head mistress, Miss Jewell Hill, came. Relations between the two schools could not have been happier and a memorable performance of 1066—*and All That* given by the staffs of K.W.S. and B.H.S. was a bright spot in those grim war days. We realised how thankful King's Warren School must have been when they were able to return to Plumstead in 1945 but we missed seeing their familiar brown uniforms and the Susan Collie Wing cloakrooms seemed strangely empty without their shoe-bags hanging besides ours.

Rye Grammar School, consisting of both girls and boys, was also evacuated to Bedford. The girls used our buildings for part of the summer holidays of 1940 before taking over a large house in Kimbolton Road. We still saw them, though, as they continued to use our science block, gymnasium and field until they went home late in 1944.

Of course we had our domestic difficulties and crises, but what school did not ? Cleaners became almost impossible to get and their wages soared up and up. Fuel was rationed, soap was rationed and not even a duster could be bought without first filling up forms !

Our junior porter, Charles Bennett, went into the Army at the start of the war (he had always wanted to be a soldier) and his successors were not successes. William Eddy, the caretaker, tried to cope, aided by them, but decided that he would rather be single-handed. To help him we did, of course, make some adjustments in the domestic arrangements, but stoking the boilers was always a problem. Rogers managed to find time to lend a helping hand at School as well as looking after the field, also single-handed. Between them they did wonderful work. Eventually William was called up and went off to the Mediterranean. His frequent letters were tremendously enjoyed. We were thankful to see him return four years later. In the milkroom Mrs. Harris coped cheerfully with shortages of milk, of milk bottles and straws, and buns that got less and less sticky as the war went on.

The Summer Term of 1942 will always be remembered for two happy occasions. On 8th May both Bedford High School and the Girls' Modern School commemorated the sixtieth anniversary of their joint inauguration. The School revelled in having no homework for the whole of its Diamond Jubilee week and the Staff Entertainment, with its irresistible choir, the Puddlecombe Choir, was a great success. The School always loves a Staff Entertainment and this seemed to be an extra special one. On the Saturday afternoon 250 Old Girls came to tea at School. The war, obviously, restricted our celebrations but not our sense of thankfulness for the strength and stability of our School in an uncertain world, and it was with this thought in mind that we all, staff and girls, attended our Diamond Jubilee Thanksgiving Service, held at St. Paul's Church on 9th May, 1942. We were delighted to have the Rev. W. B. Belcher, M.C., M.A. (nephew of Miss Belcher), to preach the sermon.

The second of these occasions was the visit of Her Majesty Queen Marie of Yugoslavia, when she came to Bedford and visited the four schools together with the Harpur Central School. It was the High School's first royal visit for many years (since 1918, when King George V and Queen Mary came to us). Queen Marie's combination of dignity and friendliness could not have failed to impress us all and we will long remember it as a proud and happy day.

Afterwards one of the Governors was heard to remark, "It was wonderful of the School to learn the Yugoslav National Anthem in such a short time—especially in a foreign language". He did not realise that we had sung an English translation!

Queen Marie wrote to the School several times and in those letters told us something of her country's sufferings and heroism. The School collected for the Yugoslav Relief Fund and the ways and means of raising money varied greatly. Some girls gave puppet shows, some went carol singing and Grizel Crichton earned two shillings and sixpence by knitting dishcloths. How many she knitted for this princely sum history does not relate!

One of the distinguishing features of "the modest little school behind the trees" was lost when one of our chestnut trees was pronounced rotten and dangerous and had to be pulled down in 1944. It had stood in front of the "best almshouses", it had probably stood there long before them. Later three more trees had to come down and Miss Elspet Stewart gave us new young chestnuts to replace them. It was a wonderful gift and the trees are flourishing.

The flower beds around the School have been for many years looked after by Miss Fisher. She *must* have green fingers for there is always a colourful display of flowers and this was most noticeable in victory year, 1945.

Victory in Europe Day, 8th May, should have been the first

day of the summer term. So term began two days late. The
Union Jack was hoisted by the main gates on Monday, the 7th,
but disappeared—presumably it was stolen. The Harpur Trust
flag was flying instead on V.E. Day. Japan was still to be
defeated but we were able to remove the baffle walls and ceiling
supports and, to our great joy, the big stage was erected for the
first real Guild meeting since the outbreak of war.

I suppose there are certain parts of the war which have been
stamped so sharply on our memories that we shall never forget
them. It is with joy and pride that we remember the visits to
prayers of Old Girls in the Forces and those of Lady Jaqueta
Williams, a Governor of the Harpur Trust and one of our Old
Girls. Her beautiful home in Shropshire was converted into
a hospital, used first by the Red Cross and then by the Navy.
Despite her many other activities she somehow found time to
come to Bedford and we were always delighted to see her. We
remember the air-raid sirens, gas masks and the difficulties of
School uniform in a land of clothing coupons. But above all
we remember our School, constant in a changing world, essen-
tially a place of learning, whether in war or in peace.

The visit of Field Marshal Viscount Montgomery of Alamein
to the School, coming soon after V.E. Day was, surely, one of
our proudest days.

The date was 28th June, 1945. In the morning Lord Montgomery had been to Bedford School and it was arranged that
Miss Osborne would drive him to us in her car. Imagine
our disappointment when she returned just after 3 p.m. with
an empty car. Was he unable to come after all ? We were not
left wondering for long, for at 3.15 p.m., according to schedule,
Lord Montgomery arrived. A police escort preceded him and
his car bore the flag of the Chief of the Imperial General Staff—
a crown embroidered on the Union Jack. On arrival he in-
spected a guard of honour consisting of Old Girls in the Forces.
He spoke to several of its members including Eva Lancaster,
Q.A., who had been with him in the Middle East. At the East
Porch Miss Westaway welcomed him and conducted him to
the hall and on to the platform, amid loud cheers. Also on the
platform were Lord Montgomery's Aide-de-Camp, Lady Jaqueta

Williams, Sir Richard and Lady Wells, Mrs. Nash, Miss Cracknell and Miss Lomax.

In her speech of welcome Miss Westaway said that she understood that this was Lord Montgomery's first visit to a girls' school and, replying, he told us that his cousin, Lady Jaqueta Williams had insisted that he should come. He added that now he was very glad that he had. With the other guests Lord Montgomery went on a short tour of the School ending in the domestic science room. There, with a broad smile, he accepted a cake made by Miss Millburn, beautifully iced in white with a blue eagle.

Nineteen-forty-five saw our School become independent. A new Education Act came into being. The Governors of the Harpur Trust were faced with decisions affecting the futures of the four schools. They resolved, in May of that year, to notify the Minister of Education of the withdrawal of B.H.S. (and Bedford School) from the Direct Grant list, upon which we had been since 1918. This move had the whole-hearted support of Miss Westaway, and to all those who had the wisdom and foresight to battle for our independence, for acute controversy surrounded the subject, we owe an untold debt of gratitude.

Six months later we were informed that the Minister had definitely agreed to our having the independent status which we had said we desired. At first little change in the School's conditions was discernible (except for slightly higher fees). We still welcomed visits from H.M.I. Mr. Collins so the State was satisfied that we were a good school! We still continued to admit a quota of our number as Free Placers from the State Primary Schools. In 1945 there were nearly twice the number ever admitted in one year before; thus helping the County Council in certain immediate difficulties arising out of the 1945 Education Act.

Miss Westaway wrote:

"But it is not in terms of money or inspection or scholarship regulations that we view our independence. Ours was a great school in the days when it began, and it began without any aid or control from the State at all. Its greatness went on during the years that the State aided us with its "Direct Grant"—its character and its scholarship and its spirit of service remained quite unimpaired. But the old plan of Direct Grant has ceased to be. The conditions of the new scheme are quite different from the old, and henceforth State aid will mean more State control. We have reverted to independence of both, and our task now is to be sure that if the change makes any difference at all, it is even to enhance our greatness."

It is interesting to know that, despite the higher fees, the entrance examination for day girls for the following September which is held each July had, by 1948, to be spread over three afternoons instead of the usual one (admittedly, a very heavy one).

What did Country girls have for their lunches? This may seem an odd question, but there are several answers. During most of the war they either brought their own sandwiches or had a hot lunch, in the Country Room. The British Restaurant supplied the hot lunches but at the end of 1944 said that they could do so no longer. At this point, the Oslo Lunch was introduced. This consisted of hot soup, salad with cold meat, fish or cheese, fresh fruit and a glass of milk. The Country Room's rather small gas cooker made any more cooking impossible and, anyway, the Ministry of Food repeatedly said that such food was so good for us. We did not disbelieve the Ministry but were delighted when Miss Westaway told us on Speech Day, 1945, that Number 3 The Crescent had been bought by the Harpur Trust. It was to be known as O'Maley House, to commemorate the family of Old Girls whose home it had been. The house was for meals and the use of Country House in the lunch hour.

There was much to be done before O'Maley House opened in January, 1948. Miss Hockin coped while builders, gas men and carpenters converted the house so that 120 hot lunches could be served every day. On the top floor was a flat where the cook, Mrs. Jenkins, lived, on the bottom floor the kitchen, complete with an automatic potato peeler, and the two middle floors were dining rooms.

All day-girls whose parents wished it could have hot lunches there twice a week and Country girls could have them every day. The Oslo lunches in the Country Room continued.

We were lucky to have Miss Molly Evans in charge of O'Maley

House and she cheerfully contended with rationing, electricity and gas cuts. I lived only five minutes' walk away from School so, naturally, I always went home for lunch. But there was one exception—when the Misses O'Maley came to lunch and saw their old home in its new guise. I was one of two "waitresses" and well do I remember that delicious boiled ham and parsley sauce !

During the ten years 1939-49, five of our staff left to become head mistresses. The first to go was Miss Chadwick. She went to Petersfield County High School after ten years with us and there she succeeded Miss Emma Lowde, who had been a pupil at B.H.S. Miss Gent, who besides teaching history, took an active interest in the School Cadet Company and the Debating Society, left us in 1942 to become head mistress of Guildford High School. Later that year Miss Baldwin went to Barnsley High School as head mistress. She was missed by everyone and East lost a wonderful house mistress. Five years later Miss Lomax became head mistress of Stamford High School and the next term Miss Ayre head mistress of Jersey College for Girls. Miss Lomax's history lessons will long be remembered and, oh !, those superb drawings she did upon the blackboard ! Miss Ayre had been on the French staff for four years and had been Chairman of the Social Service Committee. She had organised Harvest Sales and parcels to Germany with great skill. However we do not feel that we have quite lost them as "Miss Lomax just slips down the Great North Road" and Miss Ayre is now head mistress of Derby High School.

In what seemed far too short a space of time both Miss Cracknell and Miss Askwith retired. Luckily, though, it was not good-bye as they are both close at hand and we can see them often still. When Miss Osborne reached retiring age one of IIc, unwittingly, expressed to her spirit of perpetual youth a tribute in which we all shared. On hearing that Miss Osborne was leaving she said to her, "We do hope you will be very happy in your next post".

For many years there has been a Holborn Boys' Club, supported by Bedford School and its Old Boys' Club. But nothing was being done for the girls of Holborn, and theirs was a very real need. On 1st November, 1945, the Holborn Girls' Club was started, supported by Bedford High School and the Guild. At first the club was housed in a small room at Coram's Fields, but later moved to Emerald Street to share two huts (one Nissen and the other American Red Cross) with the Holborn Boys' Club. Meanwhile magnificent new club premises are being built in Lamb's Conduit Street, Holborn.

Undeterred by bombed surroundings an active and happy club has grown up. The girls enjoy such activities as handwork, ballet, tap-dancing classes and table tennis. In the summer netball is played regularly in Coram's Fields and Lincoln's Inn Fields. Teams compete in matches against other youth clubs.

Every autumn the School holds a Harvest Sale and the proceeds go to Holborn. They really are wonderful sales and every year they make more money. We feel the cause is a good one, a very good one.

This brings us to the year 1949, the end of this chapter—and the end of an era. Miss Westaway retired after 25 years as head mistress.

In that quarter century the School buildings were enlarged— the music rooms, the science block, the library, the gymnasium, the Susan Collie Wing and O'Maley House were all added during her term of office. The curriculum has been broadened to include such subjects as domestic science, secretarial and pre-nursing courses.* For man years there has been a Sixth Form of over a hundred girls. But it is not in terms of buildings or of syllabuses that we remember her. It is in terms of far greater things.

I may be allowed, perhaps, as her last head girl, to add my own personal tribute of admiration and affection.

---

*The debt of the school to Miss H. S. Millburn, Miss Prosser, and Miss Nicholls for the working out of these courses is immense.—EDITOR.

CHAPTER XII

1949-1957

BY MISS DOROTHY KITCHENER

MISS WATKINS' connection with the School began in 1928, when, after a distinguished career at Oxford, where she held the Clara Evelyn Mordan Scholarship at St. Hugh's College, she joined our French staff under Miss C. B. Thomson. She left in 1937 to become head of the French department at the George Dixon Grammar School for Girls, Birmingham, and, three years later, she became head mistress of Erdington Grammar School, Birmingham.

Her appointment as head mistress of our School in 1949 gave much pleasure, for there were many who had the happiest memories of her in those earlier years as a teacher and a colleague and a Guild member and who welcomed her back with pride and confidence. There was a record attendance at Prayers on the first day of term, and the grace and dignity of her address to the School then, and to the Guild in the following June, had an instant appeal.

It was no easy task that lay ahead. Independence has brought with it added responsibilities, for the School is now entirely dependent on fees and its share of the Harpur Trust endowment to meet all expenses. The Harpur Trust estate in Holborn has been only partially rebuilt as yet, after its destruction in the war, so that the income from the endowment is not large. On the other hand, costs have risen sharply and the first steps towards equal pay for women teachers have been taken. Fees have, therefore, had to be increased. We owe much to our representatives on the Harpur Trust—Mrs. Nash (E. Martin), Mrs. Fensome, and Mrs. Jones (C. Perks), who have successively represented the parents; and to the Lady Jaqueta Williams (J. Northcote), who for twenty-nine years was the staff's representative and who did so much for us during the war years and during the discussions on independence. When she retired in 1955, Miss Watkins and the staff were very proud to elect Miss Westaway as her successor. Her visits to School as a Governor

MISS WATKINS

give the very greatest pleasure. It is good to know that her wisdom is still actively at work for the Harpur Trust and for the School.

Over all these affairs Sir Richard Wells had presided with great distinction and had always taken a great personal interest in the High School. It was sad to hear of his death in November, 1956, only a few weeks after his retirement from the Harpur Trust. He had the affairs of the Trust very much at heart and guided it through times of great difficulty. The appointment of Mr. Osborn to succeed him has given great confidence.

Although we have not been able to embark on any large-scale building schemes, a number of improvements have been made which have added greatly to our comfort. The downstairs cloakroom, the staff cloakroom and the waiting room (Miss Forbes' room) have been enlarged, the corridor behind the hall widened and an annexe has been added to the staff room. The School has been completely rewired and the lighting much improved. In 1950 the hall was redecorated and the garlands removed and last year it was fitted with new velour curtains. It is now almost completely furnished with oak chairs, the gifts of Old Girls.

We have acquired some property in Adelaide Square. In 1953, No. 46 was purchased and the ground floor converted into a junior library with a staff flat above. All but three houses in Adelaide Square behind the science block have also been purchased and for the time being are let to tenants. The entrance in Adelaide Square has been much improved by the provision by new iron gates and by Miss Watkins' gift of six flowering trees which are a great joy in the spring time. The garden round the building is Miss Fisher's special care; daffodils, delphiniums, irises, roses, chrysanthemums and Christmas roses follow each other in gay succession and give infinite pleasure all the year through.

But the strength of a School is not measured in terms of bricks and mortar. It is primarily a place of learning and the academic tradition of the High School is one of its most prized possessions. A steady stream of candidates has gone up to the universities, many of them with State or Open awards, with perhaps a little more emphasis on Oxford than in former years. The academic structure of the School was modified to some extent in 1951, when the General Certificate of Education took the place of the Higher and School Certificate examinations. The new examination is a subject examination and can be taken at three levels—Ordinary, which corresponds to the credit standard of the School Certificate, Advanced, which corresponds to Higher Certificate, and Scholarship, on which scholarships to the university are awarded. Instead of trying to measure a girl's scholastic achievement at school, the new examination is a qualifying examination for her future career, and a girl is encouraged to take only those subjects which are necessary to qualify her for her professional training. The VAs are, therefore, now organised into three groups, each with a particular bias— science and mathematics, classical and modern studies, and practical subjects—but at the same time preserving a general education.

It is at the top of the School that the academic benefits of our independence are perhaps most apparent, for it enables us to have a more generous staffing, and therefore, to offer a wider choice of subjects and smaller classes than is possible in many schools.

But the School still plays its part in the national system and accepts 10 per cent of its entry as free placers each year, and a number of boarders are sponsored by local authorities. All girls of the appropriate age take the eleven plus examination as a kind of insurance, since only a very few of them are assisted if they remain in an independent school.

The place of science and mathematics in the curriculum is becoming increasingly important. This is all the more difficult as there is an acute shortage of teachers of these subjects and the School is extremely fortunate to have such a distinguished body of scientists and mathematicians on the staff. Miss Collier was very much alive to modern needs, and she and her staff have built up a great tradition of scholarship on the science side. This year, Mary Webb brought distinction to the department by gaining a first class in the Cambridge Natural Sciences Tripos, Part II, and a clinical scholarship at Guy's Hospital, for which she was the only woman competitor. Miss Collier's retirement in July, 1956, after thirty-three years on the staff, was a great loss, for she was a real scholar and a wonderful teacher. She was house mistress of Russell House and interested in many facets of the School's life; her wit and clear thinking enlivened many a staff meeting. Miss Nicholls has succeeded her as head of the department and Joan Flood teaches chemistry.

The fame of the mathematics department under Miss Sanders, supported by Miss Batley, has stretched far beyond Bedford, and from time to time, girls have come from other schools for the advanced work in the Sixth Form. But side by side with this, the arts side is strong and vigorous. The classics have been zealously maintained under the scholarly direction of Miss Burnip, and almost every year an open award has been gained at Oxford or Cambridge. The modern languages department has continued to develop under Dr. Fraenkel, and French, German and Spanish are taught; this year three candidates gained State scholarships—a record for one department. Miss Couch and the English department and Miss Lloyd Smith and the history department have kept up a high standard of lively and interesting work. The teaching of geography under Miss Saunders has expanded and there are now two staff and it is taken regularly at both Ordinary and Advanced levels.

Miss Millburn's retirement in 1949 brought to an end a distinguished career in the domestic science department. She was the founder of the course, and established a great tradition of hard and serious work which has been maintained, but the organisation is now somewhat different. Miss Thompson and Miss Harrison have discontinued the course for the Housecraft Certificate of the National Council of Domestic Studies; in its place, cookery and needlework are taken as subjects for the General Certificate of Education. The Secretarial Sixth under Miss Prosser continues to flourish.

Miss Pehrson's reign in the art room will surely be judged as one of the most distinguished phases of the School's history. The House Art Competition is one of the great events of the year and provides an exhibition of a very high standard; more than one adjudicator has expressed himself as "green with envy".

As an off-shoot of the art department, and as well as her work in the preparatory department, Miss Burnaby holds weaving classes at the top of O'Maley House and it is a most interesting and popular course.

Music and drama have a special section of their own in this book but this chapter would be incomplete without mention of Miss Joyce Harding, "the mistress of singing", whose magic inspires any choir she trains, no matter what the age range. Music for speech day and the concert has included some exciting modern works by Benjamin Britten and Vaughan Williams. Her training of the choir for these and for the joint productions with Bedford School of *Acis and Galatea* or of *Messiah* reveal a mastery of choral technique. For Guild members the singing in chapel on Sunday, in particular the closing prayer, "God be in my head and in my understanding" is a cherished memory. And who can ever forget the delight of the Preparatory School singing, with actions, *The Windmill* or *They're changing guard at Buckingham Palace* ?

Miss Norman is head of the music department and has done wonders with the School orchestra. The recorder is very popular, and the flute, clarinet and oboe are taught as well as the 'cello, violin, viola and pianoforte.

There will be few readers of this book who have not some special memory of at least one of Miss Gowen's productions. Her last production, *The Winter's Tale*, was particularly notable for its sensitive interpretation and for the dramatic power and beauty of its execution. Of the Guild plays of this decade, pride of place must go to *Cranford* in 1956. The charm of Miss Matty's drawing-room was most convincing and the characters were well portrayed and beautifully dressed. Patricia Burnaby, as Miss Matty gave one of the best performances of her career and completely captivated her audiences by her gentle, inconsequent charm.

A staff play is always a great event and Miss Garton's production of *Alice in Wonderland* in the spring of 1956 was a spectacular success. The scenery, properties and costumes merited an exhibition of their own and were most ingeniously inspired by Miss Pehrson. Miss Howard as Alice enchanted us all.

Miss Raley retired from the Preparatory School in 1952 after over 30 years in the department, the last four as its head. Her immense vitality and gaiety made her a teacher whose influence was felt throughout the School. Miss Fisher, who has been on the staff since 1924, succeeded her. She is much interested in modern developments; open days are held regularly, lessons on the wireless are sometimes used and a reference library has been built up. A new form has been added at the IIc stage and the wing much improved by the construction of a corridor, so that it is now possible to walk into each room, instead of interrupting all the classes to reach the handwork room.

The retirement of Miss Dorothy Madden in 1954 and of Miss Muriel Madden last year has brought to an end a long association. Old Girls of the School themselves and for over thirty years members of the staff, there is little they do not know about the School and the Guild. Dorothy had a special gift for explaining the intricacies of mathematics or even the simplicities of simple arithmetic to the non-mathematical; she was, too, very much involved in the Guide movement and was captain of a School company as well as county camp adviser. Muriel was, for many years, organist, and was intimately connected with the life of the School through prayers and other special occasions which called for an organ voluntary or the splendour of the National Anthem. In the library, she administered to the academic needs of staff and girls, while, as a coach, she could give that extra help with Latin which often made all the difference to a girl's career. In their younger days they both played hockey for the Midlands, and, in 1922 represented All-England on a tour in Denmark.

One of the major changes in organisation is in the physical training department. In 1952 the Bedford Physical Training College ceased to be an independent college and became the Bedford College of Physical Education, maintained by the local education authority, and our official connection came to an end. The School will always be proud of its long association with Miss Stansfeld and the debt we owe to her and her college can never be put into words. Miss Gibson left the college to be a full-time member of our staff in charge of physical education, with Miss Howard to assist her. The time-table has been radically changed so that some forms now have games in the mornings and others have gymnastics in the afternoons.

We have now six new hard tennis courts at the field. The money for these has been raised in a variety of ways. Miss Gibson has organised sports, an Easter market and a car-cleaning service in aid of the fund, and several fathers have given covenanted subscriptions.

Mention of the field immediately evokes a picture of Rogers, since for over 50 years the two were almost synonymous. He helped his father to prepare and lay out the field, and he tended it with such care until the pitches became almost unique in their perfection in any girls' school. In 1950, we were proud to celebrate a joint Golden Jubilee for Rogers and the field. Miss Westaway presented him with a cheque from the Guild, and the head girl presented him with one from the School. He retired in 1955, after a wonderful life of quiet service and it was sad that he only lived a few weeks to enjoy his well-earned pension.

Meanwhile, at School, in 1953, William Eddy completed twenty-five years of service first as assistant to France, and then, on his retirement, as caretaker. The School was delighted to present him with a clock suitably inscribed to mark the occasion.

The *Aquila* has now reached the respectable age of forty-five. Rising costs of printing have necessitated an increase in price and now it costs two shillings and sixpence a term and derives part of its income from the charges made for advertisements. In 1950 Miss Westaway presented a rose bowl to be held by the editor. The bowl was originally the School's leaving present to Miss Holmes on her retirement; when she died, she left it to Miss Hiatt, and she in turn gave it to Miss Westaway. It embodies a wonderful piece of history.

Gifts from the Guild, forging anew the links between past and present, give very great pleasure. Miss Westaway, before her retirement, endowed a prize for science in memory of her father, for many years H.M. Inspector of Schools and a great friend of the School. In 1955 the Stewart family endowed two prizes, "The Elspet Stewart Prize" is in memory of their sister, who was for so many years a much-loved house mistress of

Westlands; it is to be awarded for work of merit in the Sixth Form for a girl proceeding to a course of professional training. "The Mary Stewart Prize" is for history or English or divinity, and is to be awarded to a girl going to the university, preferably Cambridge or Oxford. Mr. Devitt and his two daughters, Phyllis and Janet, give a prize annually : its terms are wide with a bias towards domestic science, biology, chemistry or speech and drama. An anonymous donor gives a prize for mathematics each year. Miss Betty Hockin presented the School with a sum of money in 1953 to endow a head girl's brooch. It is a most attractive design in silver, incorporating the eagle and "B.H.S.", and will be a permanent memento to each head girl of her term of office. Miss Collier has presented brooches in the house colours to be held by the head of each of the eight houses for her term of office. This term Dr. and Mrs. Bower have endowed a singing scholarship in memory of their daughter, Elizabeth, whose sudden death last year brought great sorrow to a wide circle of friends. Her singing at the 1954 Guild was one of the great joys of that week-end.

From Switzerland Miss Mary Smith sent a gift to the School which has been used to give music lessons to a number of girls whose parents could not afford the extra fee ; from Ireland, Miss Florence Harrison sent a similar gift which will provide lessons on the viola, and Miss Hepworth has given us her own viola.

One of the most striking features of these years has been a growth in the social and corporate life of the School. The war and its aftermath had made evening activities, other than fire-watching, impossible, but in 1951 a host of clubs and societies blossomed forth. The scientists were first in the field with the Eureka Club, and were followed quickly by a revival of the Dramatic Club. The modern linguists formed a French Club, and the historians a Clio Society. The Cecilia Club was formed for those interested in music ; from time to time a Chess Club has flourished while the Film Club has a more general appeal and shows films in the hall three times a term. In addition to talks, lectures and recitals, some interesting expeditions have been made to supersonic wind tunnels, to the opera and theatre as well as occasional joint meetings with Bedford School and Bedford Modern School and each society has a wonderful party at Christmas. The French Club's celebration is a *Mardi Gras* party when a real French meal, complete with wine, is cooked and served in O'Maley House.

Parents' evenings have been held from time to time when a group of parents are invited to meet the staff in the Country Room for coffee and informal discussion.

In 1949 the names of the day houses were changed. West had become so large and unwieldy and Central so small that re-organisation of the system was necessary. New girls are now drafted into the houses on entry, according to age and form, so that the old names became inappropriate. After much thought, it was decided to adopt the names of four famous families of Bedfordshire and the present-day representatives of these families agreed to allow their names to be used ; so East became St. John, West became Mowbray, Central became Beauchamp and Country became Russell.

The Social Service Committee is very active in support of good causes and each term a collection is made at prayers for some particular charity. But the main concern is for the Holborn Girls' Club. A Harvest Sale is arranged in October each year, and this year the record total of £480 was raised. It is a remark-able occasion, undertaken with great enthusiasm by School and Guild and wonderfully supported by the parents. In the summer term the School entertains the Club in Bedford and it is a great day for both hostesses and their guests. After many years in temporary premises, the Governors are now building a permanent home for the Club together with the Holborn Boys' Club in Lambs' Conduit Street. It is hoped that it will be officially opened next year.

Life is certainly busier. A good deal of the pressure is in the domestic sphere. Most members of the staff run their own flats or houses so that School dinner is a boon to many. There is a choice between a hot "O'Maley dinner" or a cold "Oslo lunch". Miss Evans, who had helped Miss Hockin organise and equip O'Maley House just after the war (and in those days of acute shortages this was nothing short of a miracle), retired in

1954. Miss E. Jones is now in charge of the catering, while Miss Nancy Garrett, as bursar, oversees it all, and looks after our physical comfort in sickness and in health. She is S.R.N. and it is not a bit of use trying to malinger in the rest room !

In the boarding houses, the girls help in many ways, especially at the week-end, and it is not unusual to find the house mistress cooking or even stoking in an emergency. Extra help and substitutes of any kind are difficult to find, and if one of the staff is ill, the extra work has to be shared by the department.

As the relationship between parent and child has changed over the years, so has that between teacher and pupil. Discipline is freer, but a look from Miss Batley on speech day still quells the entire hall into silence as the guest of honour approaches. The prefects have a number of special privileges—they may go to the cinema if they wish (a privilege which they use with discretion) and they make their own coffee in the cookery room in break. Once a week a prefect reads the lesson from a Bible which, together with the lectern, was presented to the School by the Parents' Association (which celebrates its twenty-fifth birthday this year). But alongside the changes, the traditional remains—the traditional hymns and psalms for the beginning and end of term, the wedding hymn for the marriage of an Old Girl (the organ played now by Miss Hackett) and the lesson from Romans XII for the first day of term and from Philippians IV for the last day. Parents still come in large numbers at the beginning and end of term, and Old Girls and friends come from time to time.

In November, 1952, the School had a general inspection by the Ministry of Education. For a week a panel of fifteen inspectors visited lessons, talked to staff and girls, breakfasted at a boarding house, lunched at O'Maley House and as far as possible shared the community life of the School. It was a time of intense activity, full of interest and lively discussion.

There have been gay occasions too. The quatercentenary of the granting of the Letters Patent by Edward VI to the Mayor and Corporation of Bedford, which led to the foundation of the Harpur Trust and of Bedford School, was celebrated on 13th June, 1952. A Thanksgiving Service was held in St. Paul's

Church and this preamble was read: "Today assembled in this church are representatives of all those who enjoy benefits from the Letters Patent—the Corporation of Bedford, the Governors of the Harpur Trust, past and present members of Bedford School, Bedford Modern School, Bedford High School, the Dame Alice Harpur School, together with representatives of the Parents' Associations of the Schools and representatives from the alms-houses. Also present are His Worship the Mayor of Holborn, and representatives of the Holborn Boys' and Girls' Clubs."

Two hundred pupils from each of the four schools occupied the nave and aisles ; twenty members of each staff assembled in the Town Hall in academic dress, and led by the choir and clergy, proceeded across to the church through a guard of honour of Bedford Modern School Corps, and followed by the Mayor and Corporation of Bedford together with the Mayor of Holborn. Canon Hilditch conducted the service and the Lord Bishop of Peterborough (The Rt. Rev. Spencer Leeson) preached the sermon which was relayed to an overflow congregation in the Corn Exchange. It was a most impressive service and an in-spiration to all those who were privileged to attend.

Before the service, the Mayor entertained the head masters and head mistresses and the deputy heads to a luncheon in the Council Chamber, the scene of the first Harpur Trust School. Afterwards the staffs and other representatives were entertained to tea in Bedford Modern School hall.

Next day Bedford School had their own celebrations which were honoured by the presence of H.R.H. Princess Margaret. Miss Watkins represented the High School at the luncheon given in her honour.

In view of these greater celebrations to come, the High School's seventieth birthday was commemorated quietly in May of the same year. Special prayers were attended by the officers of the Guild and several former members of the staff and by Lady Jaqueta Williams, who afterwards gave a talk about life at the turn of the century. In the afternoon, the staff gave an entertainment with sketches and scenes of School life from the 1880s to the present day. Miss Evans was in charge of a gymnastic class of the era when formal, disciplined control was the vogue, with plenty of silent marching and the inevitable "bend, stretch". It was a revelation to the present generation, and so was the sight of Miss Spence, their own gymnastic mistress, hanging upside down on the balcony railing at one point! The highlight was undoubtedly Miss Harding's singing class, and those who took part will never forget the tremendous roar which greeted them as they appeared in School uniform, and the applause which followed each song and doubled the length of the item! An enormous birthday cake with seventy candles was marked off in sections for each form, which then retired to its form room to entertain its form mistress and other staff to tea.

We have been fortunate in our Speech Days. The happiest and gayest was Miss Westaway's return in 1954 when she spoke about memory, combining the grave and the gay in her own inimitable way; we remember, too, the charm and friendliness of Mrs. Soames (the daughter of Sir Winston Churchill); our delight in welcoming two Guild husbands, the Lord Bishop of Peterborough and Mrs. Spencer Leeson (C. Lomax) in 1952, and Captain and Mrs. Benstead (M. Collie) in 1955; the inspiration of Dr. J. S. Whale and the clear thinking of Professor M. V. C. Jeffreys.

It has often been said that this School has had a remarkable succession of head mistresses, and that is true. It is equally true of its second mistresses. Miss Batley's brilliance as a mathematical scholar is well known, her kindliness, her quiet powers of discipline and her analytical approach to complicated problems give great strength to the School. In 1950, a new post of deputy second mistress was made to share some of the work; Miss Jones, Miss Addis and Miss Saunders have filled this post with distinction.

But the heart of the matter lies with the head mistress. Those who heard or have read her address to the Guild last June will know that Miss Watkins is one who expects high standards; "steadfastness, constancy and resolution" were the ideals she set before us—ideals that are forged by encounter with difficulty. Her love of the School and its traditions as living attributes is manifest. She gives herself to it unstintingly, sharing gaily in

CHAPTER XIII

THE BOARDING HOUSES

TO EVERY old boarder the history of her own house is a rich and abiding memory, while everyone who has been connected with the School will recognise that the house mistresses and their boarders have, by their full lives, contributed magnificently to the life of the School and carried its name with honour to the farthest parts of the world.

This chapter might easily have become the longest in the book : but it must suffice to give a bare outline of the history of the boarding houses, and to add, as typical of hundreds of contributions that might have been sent, as echoes of hundreds of blessings, realised daily, the tributes of a small number of past boarders to some of the house mistresses of the earlier days.

Before the High School was opened there were a number of private schools for girls in Bedford, and during the years 1881 and 1882 the heads of several of these schools applied to the Governors of the Harper Trust for permission to convert these schools into boarding houses for the new High School. In the spring of 1882 the Governors gave this permission to three ladies, Mrs. Barker, Miss Ray and Miss Rayner, on the understanding that their day-pupils and boarders should be drafted into the High School.

Miss Ray's house was at the corner of Bromham Road and Linden Road. She maintained her connection with the High School for only a short time, and then resumed private school work.

Miss Rayner had a house in Ashburnham Road, next to the present Midland Hotel. She was obliged by ill-health to close her house in 1884.

Mrs. Barker had West Wick in Ashburnham Road. Her husband had been a well-known Bedford doctor. She was left a widow at the age of twenty-five, and took up private school work. During her later years she was helped by her daughter, later Mrs. Greville. West Wick prospered greatly during her long reign over it. She died in 1908. The following year,

Miss Pocock took over the house, until she removed all its boarders and half its name to the new house, Westlands, in 1911.

The Quantocks was begun in 1885 by Miss Baker on the closing of Miss Rayner's house at the end of the previous year. It was known first as Quantock House, and was at 21 Lansdowne Road. It quickly outgrew the accommodation, and in 1888 was transferred to 24 Linden Road, and acquired its present name. Miss Baker remained house mistress till she retired in 1896. She still took the greatest interest in the School, and supplied valuable information for this chapter. Her successors have been Mrs. Aylwin Foster (1896-1910), who died in 1914; Mrs. Blackmore (1910-1919); Mrs. Partridge (1920-1922); Miss Jansson (1922-1929); Mrs. Ashworth (1929-1939); and, since 1939, Miss Thomas, whose inspiration and enterprise are still a joy to old and the new.

The house in Linden Road, which later was known as Lansdowne House, was begun by Mrs. Urquhart. She resigned in 1899, but always maintained a great interest in the School, and was present at the Guild meeting of 1927, only a few months before her death at the age of ninety. She was succeeded at Lansdowne House by Mrs. Dodd, who resigned in 1911. The house was then united with West Wick under Miss Pocock. Lansdowne House was kept, and the name was changed to Westlands. Miss Pocock remained in charge till 1927, when she was succeeded by an Old Girl, Miss Elspet Stewart, who had had previous experience at Sherborne. She guided the house magnificently through peace and war, and retired in 1945. Her second-in-command, Mrs. Howe, succeeded her, but unfortunately had to give up after five years on account of ill-health. The house is now enjoying Mrs. Conway.

Wimborne was begun shortly after Lansdowne House, and was in the hands of Miss Burgess and her sister. Her sister died in 1896, and Miss Burgess retired in 1901, to be succeeded by Miss Irvine and Miss Pocock, and when Miss Pocock went to West Wick in 1911, Miss Irvine carried on alone, but gave up her work on the teaching-staff of the School, to the great sadness of all concerned. She retired in 1928. Then came Mrs. Phillips from Cheltenham Ladies' College, and then Miss Bone from

Sherborne, whose gay courage through the war years will be long remembered. She retired in 1949, and the house is now enjoying Miss Duncan, once a classical student at Royal Holloway College, with interesting experiences at home and abroad.

After the first war, the need was felt for a fourth house, and Miss Windsor, who had been for many years on the teaching staff, and Miss Wynne Edwards from St. Leonard's School, St. Andrews, undertook it together. Their first home was Green-ways, in Lansdowne Road, but they soon moved to Hilbre Grange, at the top of Shakespeare Road. Miss Windsor returned to full-time teaching in January, 1920 (her Scripture teaching was very greatly valued), and Miss Wynne Edwards was left in sole charge. Her somewhat original outlook on life was much enjoyed by all in her charge, but in the spring of 1934 she was suddenly taken very ill and had to retire and Miss Eyton Williams, who had coped gallantly with the crisis, succeeded her until after the war, when, to the house's sorrow, she became Mrs. Tombleson and resigned. The house is now enjoying Mrs. Anderson.

The increase of numbers after the first war was more than even Hilbre Grange could meet, and Mrs. Oldrey was asked to begin the waiting house, at Brumalia in Linden Road. The trouble was that her boarders enjoyed the house so much that they wanted to wait there for all their school lives and not move on to other houses. After Mrs. Oldrey's serious illness in 1932, the pressure had in any case become less, and the waiting house was dispensed with.

WEST WICK

From Miss Connie Malim :

It was to Mrs. Barker that West Wick owed its special character. The girls will remember her indulgent regard for their smallest comforts, and her beaming smile when they made toast at supper time, when there was potted meat for tea, or when it was fine enough to have meals in the garden, or when there was a picnic toward—while her gentle horror at any breach of good manners, or disgrace at School, made it a matter of course that these things did not occur. Her influence was great and wholesome, and the more valued by those who look back, since it was never obtruded.

From four other "Old Barkerites", who insist on remaining anonymous :

What in Mrs. Barker seems to stand out most clearly in our memories is her great kindness of heart and her generous judgment. She was always ready to help us in our difficulties and never failed to put things—our peccadilloes for example—in their right proportion, sometimes even turning a blind eye to a foolish escapade and so making the perpetrator feel foolish indeed. Then, too, she took great pride in the reputation of her house and in the contributions made thereto by individual girls ; she certainly rejoiced with us in our successes and wept with us in our failures, and always put before us a high standard both of life and work. She served the School and its head with an intense personal devotion which never wavered, and she must have helped to kindle in us that loyalty to the School and that love for Miss Belcher which we like to think did really always characterise our house.

LANSDOWNE HOUSE

From Lady Harty (Agnes Nicholls) :

An autocrat of the greatest charm. Such was the impression given me by Mrs. Urquhart, the chatelaine of Lansdowne House, during my sojourn there. It sounds almost an anomaly. A commanding figure, most upright in carriage, belonging to the old school of thought and demeanour—I often wonder what she would have thought of the undisciplined, though attractive, youth of today. She was kindness itself, thoughtful for those in trouble, but a most thorough disciplinarian. Her great creed was that exactitude was necessary in everything—in deed, in word, in thought—but her justice and her kind eyes never made her seem hard. One of her greatest characteristics was her intense power of concentration. I have seen her sit in a room full of chattering girls, writing incessantly and absolutely deaf to the noise ; yet, invariably, if something was said that was unkind or unwise the aristocratic head would turn and the soft voice would say : "Children, children, be careful". Her desire was that all her girls should look upon her fearlessly and with affection ; no matter what untoward incident happened, if you went to her and told her, you were always safe in the knowledge that you would receive the greatest consideration. I think I have never known any people so upright in carriage as Mrs. Urquhart and her daughters. She was constantly impressing this upon her girls. I, for one, always feel I owe her a deep debt of gratitude, for, in my career later on, I found that having been made to sit straight and to walk well was of inestimable help to me. Her affection for her girls never waned, and I am always happy to think that my friendship with her lasted till the end of her long and fine life. It still remains a most happy memory.

QUANTOCKS

From Miss Ella Edghill :

Mrs. Aylwin-Foster came to Quantocks as house mistress in 1895. She had recently lost her husband and there were six children to educate, all, I think, under 12.

I do not suppose that any of us, who were girls in her house at the first, realised at all fully with what courage she took up her two-fold task. Yet perhaps part of her success was due to the fact that her task as house mistress did not present itself to her as very different from that of motherhood. We felt we were regarded as a family, each with a part to play and a share of responsibility ; and though we were ruled firmly, there was no undue degree of organisation. There could never be any question of Mrs. Foster's exceptional fitness for the work she had undertaken. The house prospered and its reputation stood high.

Mrs. Foster was pre-eminently a builder of character. Her quiet dignity, poise and decision made themselves felt at all times ; her entire naturalness, directness and sincerity communicated themselves to those who came into contact with her, so that it was remarkably easy to confide in her. She always spoke to us "as man to man"; indeed, there was nothing official at any time in her relations with anyone. With a real abhorrence of anything second-rate, she combined an increasing tenderness and sympathy.

As we grew older, by her ordering of our lives, and by our intercourse with her, she helped us to put away childish things; for she had a respect for individuality; and a deepening of our sense of the reality and meaning of the life of the spirit was always her primary concern. Her own inner life was so rich and her mind so vigorous that to be with her was in itself an education.

From Mrs. Spencer Leeson (Cecil Lomax):
Mrs. Blackmore was house mistress of Quantocks from 1910 to 1919. Her husband had been head master of the Westminster Choir School for a number of years. She, therefore, brought to her new work the rather broader outlook and understanding of children of one who has passed a large part of her life among the unregenerate male young. We at Quantocks soon learned to love her for her kindness, firmness and common-sense cheerfulness, and prided ourselves on what we considered to be our greater freedom from some of the restrictions of boarding-school life. We look back now with a keen sense of enjoyment on our tramps with her in the country, and on the delightful half-term visits to the skating rink and swimming baths, which she seemed to enjoy just as much as we did. Very enjoyable, too, were those evenings when the select few, who were going in for public examinations, were invited to partake of "hot dinner with her in the Junior study".

From Mrs. Salsbury (Sally Hands):
1932-1957. What a period of change the world has passed through during those twenty-five years, and, in its own small way, how different Quantocks is now.

Before the war the numbers never exceeded thirty, in fact, in 1939 there were no more than twenty-four, including only one Junior, aged nine, who used to be sent to Westlands to play with others of her own age. How surprised we would have been then if we could have looked into 1956 and seen a house of forty-five, with ages varying from seven upwards.

There were spectacular house parties, to which the staff were invited, when there were progressive games, and a wonderful show was presented in the dining-room, where part was used as a stage, and blue, heavy curtains were swung across to hide it.

Everyone wore their best dresses, with the staff usually in evening dress.

But then came the war and her first term as house mistress for Miss Thomas, succeeding much-loved Mrs. Ashworth, and change had to come rapidly. The dining-room was quickly transformed into a gas-proof air-raid shelter, and for months there was a pile of mattresses in the third music room, which were put out at night, and where we had to sleep. Two Seniors had to go round the house each night and see that the windows were blacked out properly. The resident maids went, never to return, and the house turned to and washed up, and did anything else that was asked of them. Blythe, the old man who took the bag cart with our satchels in to School, and who cleaned the shoes, retired, and it became increasingly difficult to replace him, until the bag cart, too, disappeared.

Sunday dresses went, and a second-hand clothes box came into operation to help with the problems of rationing.

Games were severely restricted, and forms I and II had their lessons in the Senior study and the South Wing respectively. This latter was a blessing, as Miss Thomas was allowed to put in tubular heating in the South Wing because of the cold !

And then came the news of victory in Europe, and everybody rejoiced. From somewhere the coloured fairy lights came out all over Bedford, and Quantocks went down the river by launch. In our absence all the lights in the house had been put on in a blaze of glory, so that we should see them as we came up Lansdowne Road, and they would shine a welcome. Alas, that was never to be. It was too much for the wiring ; they fused, and Quantocks returned to candles.

It took a very long time for the effects of the war to wear off, and for life to become properly organised again.

Interests seem to be more shared since the war. How many people remember collecting waste paper in order to save up for the wireless sets ? We realised that anything we wanted had to be bought.

Parties that are given, such as firework and staff ones, are enjoyed even more in the knowledge that one has provided a small share towards the entertainment or the "cleaning-up" squad, and what an enormous amount of good this is doing in preparing us for our future life, either in the home or elsewhere.

Perhaps one of the days that is most looked forward to, from one year to the next, and about which every new girl is told nearly as soon as she arrives, is Quantocks' Christmas Day. This is held on the last Sunday of the Christmas Term, and begins very early in the morning when stockings, filled by the other members of the dormitory, are opened. The Christmas trees and decorations in the studies are given the final finish before church, after which there is a special Christmas dinner, including Christmas pudding with a sprig of holly on the top ! Afterwards everyone goes out to walk off their lunch before returning to tea and Christmas cake. At prayers there is a special carol service in which every member of the house joins. Christmas prayers are read and carols sung, and Miss Thomas reads the lovely story of the birth of Jesus out of *The Friend of Little Children.* Before supper grace is sung in parts, and then everyone settles down to enjoy a hilarious supper, which generally includes ham and tongue and salad, with lemon-squash to drink. Rules are relaxed, and the meal usually finishes with everyone singing.

I feel that in writing of Quantocks from 1932 to 1956 I cannot end without mentioning Mrs. Ashworth (1929-1939) and Miss Thomas (1939-   ), to say how grateful we are to them for all that they did for us while we were at Quantocks, and for the interest that they have always shown when we have either seen or written to them. Nobody could have done more for us than they, helped by Miss Porter (1929-   ), and I am quite sure that when we have left, and look back, our only real memories are happy ones.

WIMBORNE

From Mrs. Line (Dorothy Dimmock) :

During her early years at School the girl looks upon all mistresses as deities aloof and far removed from the real interests which form the centre of the absorbing school life opening before her. They are there to attempt to drum some knowledge into our heads, to chide us when we err. It is only later that the revelation comes, generally through some outstanding personality, that the mistress may be friend as well as guide, that she can understand and sympathise even with our naughtiness, that she enjoys our jokes and respects our confidences.

It was such a revelation as this which came to me when I entered Wimborne in 1911, after being a day-girl for seven years, and came in contact with Miss Irvine in the more intimate life of a boarding house.

Her figure is well known to many succeeding generations of girls. Tall and spare, she held herself erect; her hair was streaked with grey, her nose arched, her mouth straight and firm. She was a disciplinarian, and the heart of even the boldest quaked outside her door when summoned to explain some misdeed— but we always felt that she was absolutely just. Mere high spirits she dealt with gently, but anything mean, deceitful or underhand called forth an anger which lit up startlingly the black and white of motives and actions before blurred and indistinguishable. For any that came to her for help there was a ready sympathy and understanding which reached ahead of stumbling and inarticulate words, which helped to straighten tangled thoughts and gave encouragement to honest endeavour.

It is inevitable that the last years of school life should be richer in proportion than all those which have gone before, and these latter years are bound to leave a stronger mark upon character and development, whether of day-girl or boarder. Nevertheless, for myself I feel that if I had missed these last three years— 1911-1914—as boarder in Wimborne, the loss to me would have been immeasurable.

From Miss Anne Young:

I can remember standing on the platform at St. Pancras in 1943, when I first went to Wimborne. Going to a new school in the middle of the war was exciting in several ways. There was all the strangeness of the girls I did not know, but Miss Bone had arranged for Jean Carr and Tessa Turner to look after me. There was also an unaccustomed visit to London and what seemed to me a large wardrobe of new clothes, although in deference to clothing coupons the clothes list was not very long. I stayed in Wimborne until 1950 and these seven years of crisis and austerity cannot really be described as typical of the School's history, although they laid the foundations for the post-war period and must, in fact, have been very important.

In 1943 the School and house looked very different, with air-raid precautions and blackout, and added inconveniences such as a shortage of domestic help, a sufficient but rather monotonous food supply and the occasional excitement, when there was an air-raid, of going down to the shored-up dining-room in the middle of the night until the all clear went. Throughout these difficulties, both during and after the war, Miss Bone and Miss Duncan managed magnificently. The raw materials may have been monotonous but the food was surprisingly good. We all helped with the washing-up and other domestic tasks.

War had its compensations. There were girls in the house like Lise and Inger Terkelsen from Denmark, whom we should not otherwise have known. The monthly concert given by the B.B.C. Symphony Orchestra helped make up for the lack of excursions and away matches.

There is one thing in which Wimborne is unique. We have our house songs. They are full of allusions that had become meaningless with the passage of time but they are sung with great enjoyment at the end of term and on special occasions. I helped compose a new one which no doubt will soon be as meaningless as the others. Another tradition when I arrived was the annual midnight feast of the Senior study, which no longer, I believe, takes place. There was the famous tale of a feast interrupted by an air-raid, when the diners had to grab the remains and depart hurriedly up the back stairs to appear innocently down the front.

Probably by now my contemporaries and I are fast becoming mere names on the honours boards or, to judge by one's memories, the subject of highly-embellished anecdotes. When we descend on the house for a visit, the inhabitants will find it as difficult as we did to imagine these grown-up females actually sleeping in the most lowly beds of the bedrooms or being dragged out of bed to fetch hot water so that our seniors could wash.

WESTLANDS

From Mrs. Wagner (Dorothy Wise):
When someone has occupied a position for many years, the

very length of time is often brought up against her as a disadvantage. "She was good", the world says, "but, of course, she has old-fashioned ideas". Well, Miss Pocock was "old fashioned", if that implies a proper regard for good manners, and the girls who were under her care have cause to be grateful now for the strict training they received. "Would you do that in your own home?" was a question often put. "No? Then don't do it in anyone else's." An obvious question and answer, one might say, but not easily forgotten.

Miss Pocock's sense of humour never deserted her, and it enabled her to see both sides of any question. No delinquent was ever condemned until she had had a chance to state her case, which was carefully considered before judgment was given.

The success of Miss Pocock as a house mistress was due to her real understanding of girls. She once told the present writer that she would sit in her drawing-room on a Saturday night, listening to the sounds of revelry issuing from the dining-room, and would be able to tell by the way the girls laughed whether they were happy or whether a prefect was exercising her authority a little too freely. She had on occasion two excellent infirmities. She could be both blind and deaf, to the great relief of a high-spirited soul caught in the act of perpetrating some particularly noticeable absurdity.

From Mrs. Macklin (Janet Smallwood):

1927-1945. What wonderful years those were! Miss Stewart was house mistress, Miss Savory matron (1928-1943) and Miss Barbara Harding junior matron (1923-1945), and the combination was wonderful.

Many people passed through the house in those years, yet Miss Stewart remembered the details of every one of them and every one she remembered as an individual. In the house Miss Stewart was respected by Juniors and Seniors alike, but amongst the Juniors it was respect tempered with a little fear, and amongst the Seniors with love. Her kindness, understanding and her wisdom were unlimited and one of her greatest qualities was that however she felt her attitude to those in the house never varied.

The security and purposefulness which she gave to those in the house has reaped benefits throughout their lives. One has only to look through the School records to find the results of her enthusiasm and her ability both to develop the individual and to promote the spirit of success in the house. I doubt if any house has a parallel record both in games and scholastic achievement. Hardly a year passed when the house did not hold at least two cups, and I can most clearly remember her excitement and pride in 1945 when there were ten team or individual trophies in the house.

The difficulties and worries of the war years must have been a tremendous strain on her and yet she took them in her stride. She refused to let us be worried by the war or the air-raid scares and somehow she managed to produce food which was as good as ever. To those whose parents were abroad she became house mistress, mother and friend, and made herself almost wholly responsible for their upbringing.

One has many happy recollections of school days but amongst our happiest are the peace of Sunday evenings when Miss Stewart used to read to each group before bedtime. On re-reading the books I am astonished at her skill in omitting unsuitable passages !

Until 1943 Miss Stewart was most successfully supported by Miss Savory and, until her retirement, by Miss "Bar", who, to the youngest in the house, was the sweetest mother of all trades. She guided our manners, mended our clothes, dried our tears and kept us out of mischief without quelling our natural enthusiasm—and she was loved by every one of us.

Miss Stewart's retirement, after so many years, came as a bitter blow but the wrench would have been greater if her successor had not already been working for two years as matron. Mrs. Howe had the difficult task of following a "great" person and she did this with success until she retired in 1947, for health reasons.

Westlands still keeps its individuality and that can only, I feel, be attributed to the wonderful legacy Miss Stewart left it.

HILBRE GRANGE

From Miss Monica Davison :

When it became evident that their house, "Greenways", was too small, Miss Windsor (who returned to the teaching staff in

1919) and Miss Wynne Edwards, moved in 1918 to Hilbre Grange at the corner of Shakespeare Road and Clapham Road. Thus the house, which must bring back many memories to all those who dwelt there, came into being as the fourth of the boarding houses.

During her term of office Miss Wynne Edwards saw the completion of the new dining-room, which is connected to the Junior study by the covered passage. There were about twenty-five boarders but after 1934 the number was increased to thirty-four. This was when the Harpur Trust bought the deeds of the house and Miss Eyton Williams (now Mrs. Tombleson) very ably stepped into Miss Wynne Edwards' shoes when ill-health forced her to resign.

Miss Wynne Edwards was a keen gardener and will always be remembered with affection as she gardened ". . . upside down in the garden, wearing an incredible hat and apparently able to keep up that uncomfortable position for an unlimited space of time, weeding, pruning and generally looking after the flowers. When thus engaged she was quite oblivious to the passing of time and frequently arrived late for meals". Her enthusiasm spread and some of the boarders were each allocated a small plot of garden and a prize was awarded annually for the best effort. There was much secrecy as to what was going to appear in each little garden, and much scrutinisation of the finished exhibits. There was much activity at the top of the garden! We used the garden a great deal in the fine weather. The lovely big lawn worked overtime summer and winter and all the games' practices put in were amply rewarded.

In the wintertime many a cosy evening has been spent in the lovely large sitting-room, to which our house mistress invited us. Here we were encouraged to develop our hobbies, whether knitting, sewing or stamp collecting. This stood us well for the future—Grange was the very proud first holder of the interhouse arts and crafts cup, which was first awarded in 1946. During those evenings, Miss Wynne Edwards loved to read aloud from the classics and her successors have continued this way of introducing us to the best stories in the English language.

During the war years, Grange was adapted to meet the emergencies that arose. Thirty-six boarders were packed in rather like sardines in a tin. The Senior study was reinforced and used as the air-raid shelter. At night, bedding was brought down from the dormitories and all the boarders slept on mattresses on the floor. Miss Eyton Williams made regular patrols round the house to see that all was well.

In the daytime the dining-room and the Junior study were used as temporary classrooms by two of the Junior School forms, as part of the School's air-raid precautions. All these deviations from the normal routine of the house created excitement and did much to alleviate the stress of those years. It called for careful organisation in which everyone co-operated.

The war years were responsible for introducing classical music into the lives of many members of Hilbre Grange. The B.B.C. Symphony Orchestra was evacuated to Bedford and broadcast regularly from the Corn Exchange and from the Bedford School hall. Miss Eyton Williams knew Sir Adrian Boult and so she was able to take those who were interested to very many concerts including those broadcast to celebrate the end of the war.

Wednesdays, Saturdays and Sundays were red-letter days at Grange. As soon as lunch was finished there was a general exodus towards one particular cupboard in the covered way leading to the Junior study, the sweet cupboard. On these three days the head girl solemnly opened the cupboard and bedlam reigned for a blissful ten to fifteen minutes !

The climax of the School year was, for Hilbre Grange, the last night of the summer term. With great preparations we dressed in our best frocks for house supper. This was an extra special meal complete with fruit squash to drink instead of the usual water. Then followed the distribution of the various house cups and prizes and speeches of appreciation for all that had been done and achieved in the past year.

The highlight of the whole evening then followed, namely, "The Long, Long Trail". This is Grange's tradition. The head girl leading, every member of the house linked hands and, in single file, visited every nook and cranny of the house and garden repeating over and over again the words of the refrain of *The Long, Long Trail.* It must seem unusual to the man in the street but it was our way of bidding farewell to all that Grange had come to mean to us as we left to take our places in the outside world.

CHAPTER XIV

MUSIC, DRAMA AND DANCING

BY MISS PATRICIA BURNABY

A CHAPTER seems too little to convey adequately the development over seventy-five years of even one of the following arts, and so I must start with an apology to all those who are not mentioned, but have contributed towards the very high standard of achievement in all three creative arts which has been our's from the beginning. Some names are like the corner stones in a building, without which there would be no sound structure ; these perforce stand out, but nonetheless each individual brick is absolutely essential to the whole. Each art must be taken separately, but it will be seen how closely the three have been connected in the life of the School.

MUSIC

It is not easy to get any accurate information about music in School during its first years. Even Miss Katherine Eggar, who wrote the chapter in our first book, says : "The authorities who have provided me with materials for this chapter have not been able to reveal anything about our musical doings in those first years". She tells us that "Competition festivals were unknown in those days and examinations for the Associated Board have come into being since that time". However, in December, 1893, the Duchess of Bedford presented the certificates, which included a very creditable list of successes in these examinations. This shows that well before the turn of the century these examinations were well established, and by the number of staff teaching music in the School at that time it must have been considered an important part of a girl's education, even though not included in the general curriculum. In this list of 1893, printed beside the name of each successful pupil, is the name of her teacher. Eight entered pupils for pianoforte that year.

Miss Eggar tells us that "Under Miss Belcher music became part of the School life. I can say from my own experience that

DR. HARDING

she had a great reverence for music, and her attitude to musical girls was sympathetic. She did reckon with a girl's musicality in her estimate of character, and made us realise that the School's prestige might be as well served by good work in music as by good work in history, mathematics, languages or any other subject. Miss Collie, too, whose presence produced an awe unimaginable, save by those who experienced it, had a soft spot for music, and though, of course, bad work was never exonerated, I do believe that the fact that one A—— N—— got up at six to practise the fiddle was weighed against her inability to stand the stinks of chemistry, and that somebody else's coming out first in all England for harmony in the Senior Oxford mitigated scorn for her weakness in arithmetic. Looking back at the records of the 'eighties, one finds names whose reverberations still linger in the minds of the musical—Miss Pleydell-Bouverie, Mr. Bond-Andrews, Mlle Truchet (afterwards Mme Pondepeyre), Mr. Diemer, Mlle de Nolhac (the daughter of Mme de Nolhac), and Dr. Harding. The following is what Mlle de Nolhac wrote about those early days : 'In the early days of the School, the first visiting pianoforte master appointed by Miss Belcher was Mr. Bond Andrews—a very talented pianist and composer, and pupil of Liszt. He held the post for several years, but being under contract to write an opera for Carl Rosa, was unable to attend regularly, and resigned the appointment, being succeeded by Dr. Harding, of whom I need not speak. Mr. Diemer had the singing classes for very many years. I joined the staff in 1890. The other senior members at the time were : Fraulein Zeise, a brilliant pianist, pupil of Liszt ; Miss Macfarlane ; and Miss Muriel, whom I succeeded. Miss Belcher took a very keen interest in the music of the School, and was always very pleased when we suggested giving pupils' recitals. We did remarkably well at examinations, and Mr. Oscar Beringer, who once came for the Associated Board, told me he was particularly pleased with the standard of our work, and considered it next to that of Manchester. In those days pupils did not go in so much for sport and would give more time to practice than they do at present.'

"I held my appointment over twenty-nine years, and only

resigned owing to partial loss of sight. During those years, and especially in the earlier days, I had many excellent pupils, but the best was Ursula Newton, now Mrs. Creighton, who took her degree of L.R.A.M. passing at once as performer and teacher".

Mr. Diemer was actively connected with the earliest activities of the School and took a leading place in the musical life of Bedford as a whole.

He was present at the opening of the High School on 20th June, 1882, when he conducted his own vocal work, "Come, ye children and hearken unto Me", composed for the occasion.

As Mlle de Nolhac herself tell us, she taught here for twenty-nine years and according to Ursula Newton, who took her place for two terms, "Mlle de Nolhac was a much-respected teacher with a very high standard of accuracy and what she called 'style', which meant giving each piece a certain variety, though it seemed very mysterious."

Her memory and that of Miss Plow Smith, a gifted colleague of hers, are perpetuated in two competitions which are competed for annually by music pupils in the School. The de Nolhac Prize was a legacy bequeathed by Mlle de Nolhac herself for memory playing of a piece of classical music and the Plow Smith Bowl was presented by Miss Plow Smith on her retirement in 1925 for sight reading and memory playing for pupils under sixteen. Mlle Truchet (Madam Pondepeyre), who taught the Middle and Junior Schools singing, is remembered by many Old Girls not only for this, but for her lovely voice. "She was a most charming little lady. She taught solo-singing and pianoforte as well as class-singing, and among her pupils was Dolly Lightfoot, who afterwards made a great name for herself on the operatic stage."

It would seem that it was quite an established practice for members of the music staff to take part as we read in the account of the same concert, "The event of the evening was the performance of Grieg's *Sonata for violin and pianoforte* by Herr Woltmann and Dr. Harding, which gave the greatest pleasure to all who heard it."

Herr Woltmann, a very talented musician, was visiting professor, 1893-1914. It was he who formed the School orchestra which met "Every Wednesday afternoon in the art room at 2.30." How hard all must have worked to be able to perform at the concert already mentioned. "All his violin pupils—Mrs. Wells (D. Justice), Florence Harrison, Eileen Holmes, Dorothy Parker and many others—combine to testify to the very high standard he always expected and strove for." Mrs. Wells, who knew him well, being both a distinguished pupil and for five years (1901-06) his assistant at School, wrote the following account in 1932 : "Herr Willy Woltmann was born at Prague, and at the age of five played the violin with unusual talent; however, the rest of his education was by no means neglected for his music, and he went through the 'gymnasium'. He was a very well read and cultured man, and always impressed on his pupils that a general education must go hand in hand with the musical. For a long time he travelled about playing in public, and finally settled in England and became naturalised. He took up teaching, for which he had great talent. Besides working at the High School he taught at Oxford University and had been appointed to the Royal Academy of Music; he had a great number of private pupils in London, and his own excellent orchestra." (It is interesting to note that Joan Watson won the Woltmann Memorial Prize at the Royal College of Music in 1942.)

During the Great War (1914-1918), Miss Willett, who had joined the staff in 1911, taught the violin unassisted until the appointment of Monsieur Mangeot in 1920, with whom she collaborated until her retirement in 1928. During many years she was leader of the School orchestra. With Monsieur Mangeot's appointment a new impetus was given to "strings" in the School—money was a little more plentiful and there were new pupils so that the orchestra, which had been kept alive most gallantly by Dr. Harding, increased its activities with renewed enthusiasm. "In 1926 added zest was given when Mr. and Mrs. Chappel, of Cambridge, presented a silver cup which was to be competed for by the orchestras of Bedford High School, Perse High School and Slepe Hall (St. Ives). Slepe Hall withdrew after one year, but till 1935 there was a competition between the other two schools, held annually at Cambridge and Bedford, and the honours have been about equally divided. Among the judges have been Professor Dent, Dr. Hugh Middleton, and Mr. Bonavia."

One thing for which the School and Bedford have to thank Monsieur Mangeot was the founding of the Bedford Music Club in 1924. The precurser of this was the revival of the chamber concerts which before 1914 Dr. Harding used to arrange to take place in the School hall, and these were wonderfully popular at the time. The executants were mainly Old Girls, and Edith Hawkins, Stella Fyfe and Katherine Eggar frequently performed at them. The first one in July, 1921, must have been delightful when Monsieur Mangeot and Yvonne Arnaud gave a recital preceded by a talk on the history of chamber music given by Dr. Harding. From then on recitals were arranged frequently, and one when Helen Henschel sang "How beautiful they are" from *The Immortal Hour* stands out in my memory. Monsieur Mangeot's contact with a wide circle of musicians of international repute was of immense value. He himself had his own quartet which travelled abroad and, therefore, exchanges were arranged, and so the Music Club heard some of the most famous quartets of the time, among them the Capet, the Budapest, the Poltronieri, the International, the Kolisch, the Pro Arte and many others as well as famous soloists, which included Solomon, Dame Myra Hess and Jelly d'Aranyi. Four concerts were held during the year and two lectures given. For many years these were by Miss Katherine Eggar, who was well known both as a composer, a performer and writer.

Also from the beginning the secretary has been an Old Girl : Miss Diana Butt, Miss Helen Norman and now Miss Doris Wood. All have had their worries and even now Doris Wood heaves a sigh of relief when artists and instruments are safely on the platform at 7.30 p.m. She remembers only too well when only part of a trio arrived ; the occasion when the audience waiting to greet Solomon had to be told that Louis Kentner was there instead owing to the sudden indisposition of the maestro. It is remarkable that in this age of rising prices the subscription has remained the same and great credit is due to the secretary that she has at the same time maintained this tradition of distinguished artists for these concerts.

The forming of an orchestra would seem hardly possible without 'cellists but until 1905 the teaching of this instrument is wrapt in mystery. It was in that year that Miss Bowman was appointed and remained until her marriage in 1914. For one year she was succeeded by Miss Campbell Taylor. Helen Norman gives a brief word picture of her successor Mme Alice Elieson, with whom she learnt for a short time. "She was on the staff of the Royal College of Music and a very able performer herself, who stressed interpretation as coming before technique." One can imagine this somewhat exotic and temperamental artiste being something of a shock in the School where music, though of the highest order, never exceeded the limits of decorum laid down by convention! Miss Dandridge, who came in 1919, trained many of our distinguished Old Girls, among whom was Helen Norman, who has herself been teaching the 'cello here since Miss Dandridge's retirement in 1929.

There are still some names unmentioned whose work started in those early days but who continued to teach through the first quarter of this century and so forge an imperishable link with the past. There are many of us who still remember with affection Miss Hartley, 1890-1918 ; Miss L. Matson, 1892-1922 ; Miss E. M. Robbins, 1899-1930 ; and for me rather especially, Miss Manning, 1893-1926. She was so sympathetic and understanding with a pupil, who loved music and who, in her heart of hearts, would so have liked to achieve a measure of success by being chosen to play at a concert (only the little one, of course), but when the opportunity came was stricken with such an attack of nerves that she could not even face the audition !

Of these men and women who built the musical history of the School in the first forty years there is one outstanding personality, Dr. Harding. Those of us who were privileged to know him count it one of our most treasured memories. His gifts were unique as he combined superb musicianship with an uncanny understanding of the individual and a droll sense of humour, both of which he used to get the best out of his pupils, either *en masse* or in private lessons. My own first recollection is shared by many who, as new girls, were called out to sing alone ! The best I could achieve was a weak and quavering rendering of the National Anthem! His biting comment to the form who stood up, and his charming smile of encouragement as he peered over his glasses and said "You'll do" was typical of many similar incidents. I have the most vivid recollections of the lovely songs we learnt in his classes culminating in the practices for the concerts. What fun they were, as well as hard work. In many ways the choir practices stand out most clearly—his deep sincerity and great knowledge of Church music made these a real inspiration although possibly at the time one was not so aware of the lasting gift he bestowed.

It is impossible to give an adequate account of all that Dr. Harding did for music in Bedford and beyond but some of the notices which were published in the *Guild Leaflet* and the *Aquila* of December, 1930, after his sudden death in the October of that year, will help to show how great a debt is owed to his wisdom and knowledge. "He had been a member of the staff for forty-one years, and it seems impossible to imagine the School and the Guild without him. He was intimately connected with all the developments of our musical life. He was the main inspiration to whom we owe the organ in the hall. He led the enthusiasm which collected the money for it; then he chose it; he played it at its inauguration in 1898; and ever since then he has been most generous in coming to School to play it—and how unforgettable that playing was—on our special occasions, great and small. The last time he did this was at the bazaar on 17th and 18th October.

"As a composer he had a great reputation, and much of this side of his work, too, was connected with the High School. Old Girls will remember how, in 1900, he composed a beautiful Communion Service in memory of Miss Belcher, and this is still very frequently used at St. Paul's Church (it was used at the Memorial Service for the R101 in October, 1929). The songs, dances and incidental music that he composed for the Guild plays before the war—for *Psyche* and *The Egyptian Cinderella*, to mention but two—will always be among our greatest treasures. The last few plays offered him no scope in this way, but at every Guild meeting he has been our master of music— for the play on Saturday night as well as for the service in

Bedford School Chapel on Sunday—while his Monday morning singing classes for past and present girls combined will never be forgotten. His last composition was a little song which the Junior School were to have sung at their concert in December.

"The School was aware and proud of his countless activities outside its walls. He was always a great figure at the Bedford-shire Musical Festival, which, indeed, he founded, and he took a great interest in High School girls' successes there."

Many of the present School, to whom Dr. Harding is a legendary figure, probably do not realise that the organ owes its existence to his enthusiasm.

The organ is so much part of our lives that it is only on the rare occasions when we are without an organist that we realise how much beauty it adds to our services. It seems wonderful to think that in fifty-nine years the School will have had only three organists officially appointed to play for prayers (apart from Dr. Harding). The first, Miss A. M. Robbins, appointed on the staff in 1884, played for prayers "... first on the harmonium, which her skilful touch robbed of half its horrors, and since 1898 on our beautiful organ". In 1922, when she retired, we read "Miss Robbins' place at the organ at prayers is now taken by Miss Muriel Madden". There she has presided ever since except for the brief interlude in 1935 when, owing to a car accident, she had the great misfortune to lose an arm. The courage and fortitude which enabled her to renew her playing, after some months, has been a daily example to us all. It was only in 1955 that, being the musician she is, she realised that the increasing rheumatism in her one arm was preventing her main-taining the high standard of performance she had always set herself. The memory of her daily rendering of the familiar hymns, the carols at Christmas and her ever-changing repertoire of voluntaries remains for ever with those of us who have been connected with School for the past thirty-odd years. The School is indeed blessed to have in Miss Hackett, one of the English staff, someone who is able to carry on this great tradition, and who gives up many of her leisure hours in preparing for each day's requirements. We must not forget that Mrs. Parbury, who originally joined the music staff as Miss

Sale in 1928 (many of whose pupils have been so successful in the world of music), played the organ during Miss Madden's illness and has always been willing to step in when necessity demanded. We now have Dr. Braggins, an eminent Old Girl, who though not one of our permanent staff has for the past year played the organ on occasions and taken over singing classes for Miss J. Harding.

With the passing of Dr. Harding, and Monsieur Mangeot's resignation in 1932, one feared that the loss of such a team would make a break in the great tradition, but no, the foundations were too well laid. Dr. Harding could never be replaced and so his work was divided. Mr. Harold Craxton taught some of his outstanding pupils; the senior singing classes were taught by Miss Edith Clegg, formerly of the Royal Opera House, Covent Garden, a friend of Lady Harty (Agnes Nicholls).

The following tribute was written by Miss Watkins for *The Bedfordshire Times* when we heard of her death in October, 1955.

"Miss Edith Clegg, who died at her home in Seaford on 28th September, was a member of Bedford High School staff from 1931 to 1943. She had studied music at the Guildhall School of Music, and privately in Paris, London and Germany, and had later become known as a prima donna of great distinction at the Royal Opera House, Covent Garden. In later years she was appointed to the staff of the Royal Academy of Music and in addition to her visits to Bedford, she taught at St. Paul's Girls' School.

"Her lessons both for classes and private pupils were memorable. She inspired a real love of singing and nobody who met her could fail to recognise the richness and colour of her personality. It was a real experience to meet her in the staff room or to see her mount the platform on Speech Day. She brought with her a graciousness of manner, dignity and real artistic depth which enriched the lives of all of us.

"Miss Clegg took a great interest in Bedford High School and in her pupils, an interest which was alive and real right up to the time of her death."

On her retirement Miss Joyce Harding became responsible for all the class singing and the training of the choir. For a little while the solo singing was taught by Miss Carrie Tubb, who for many years had been well known to the School Guides, as she had often been a visitor to the School camps with her great friend Miss Edith Baron ; how many times, I wonder, did their caravan rest in the corner of the School's camp site. Camp fires were memorable when she was present—her rendering of *The Trampling of the Lilies* is to me quite unforgettable. Her short connection with the School was a great inspiration and we shall ever be grateful for her generosity in the giving of a singing scholarship when she left Bedford in 1946.

From then on Miss Harding has been in sole charge and how lucky we are. She is very much her father's daughter, one can hardly give her higher praise. It is difficult to pick out any one occasion on which to comment—there are the many times when the School choir has joined with Bedford School in renderings of *The Messiah;* the outstanding performance with them of *Acis and Galatea* ; the lovely anthems at Guild Services ; the School concerts when each time one feels "That is the best we have heard them sing", whether it be Benjamin Britten or Bach, or as this year selections from Vaughan Williams *Sir John in Love.* The intonation and diction are always superb. How little she has allowed the results of her accident to interfere with her work —who would have thought as she conducted this difficult composition what a race against time the rehearsals had been and that the following week she was to enter hospital for an operation to her leg. We hope that by the time this is published she will be completely recovered.

One cannot end without a word about the "Juniors", who adore her. Her way with "ghosties", who almost feel more important than the singers by the time she has finished is typical of her relationship with the children, but not for one minute will she tolerate a voice that is out of tune and how quick she is to hear. They sing everything from memory, all of which she teaches them by word of mouth. To many the "Little Concert" is still the highlight of the year.

In spite of the high standard she sets that does not mean she is without a sense of fun—the School have been electrified on occasions when they have seen her "play the fool" as when

L

she conducted "the Puddlecombe Players" at our 60th birthday celebrations or the staff singing class at our 70th—to quote from an *Aquila* of 1942, "We had guessed it would be funny, but I don't think any of us realised that we should laugh till we cried". I only know that as a member of the Puddlecombe choir it was almost my undoing to see her mount the platform as Madame —— in that hat and feather boa ! She mis-directed us superbly ! There are many Old Girls too, who, like Mme Hentsch, consider the climax of the Guild is always the singing class given by Miss Harding on Monday morning. "It is unique and its mistress inimitable."

Singing then is in safe hands, and the School has been equally fortunate as regards the rest of the music. Monsieur Mangeot was succeeded by Mr. Blofield, who taught the violin and trained the orchestra for barely four years, as in 1936 he was compelled to resign owing to ill-health. In the short time he was at School he made his personality felt and certainly concerts for those sitting on the platform became quite a lively affair. However, it is significant of his calibre when one remembers that it was at his first "Big Concert" in December, 1933, when perhaps one of its most ambitious performances was given by the orchestra, with Jewel Evans playing the allegro from Bach's Concerto. (Jewel has since made a name for herself as "Mary Madden" and is often heard today on the wireless and television. It is not so long since she and her partner, Olive Rees, gave a recital for two pianos at one of the concerts included in the Music Club's programme). It was also during Mr. Blofield's time that wood wind was introduced and we find that "Mr. Elvin, band-master at Radley College, teaches once a week in Room 16". Since when a series of flautists and clarinettists have taught in the School, the most celebrated being Mr. Frederick Thurston.

After he left the orchestra was, and, in fact, still is, conducted by Miss Norman, and the teaching of the violin was continued by Miss Brown, who already taught some of the Juniors and led the orchestra. In 1946 she was succeeded by Mrs. Double-day, whose place was taken by Miss Croxford in 1950. Both these ladies were performers in their own right and we read of delightful recitals given by them—in 1947 Mrs. Doubleday, together with Miss L. Jones, Miss Norman and Miss Wood; December, 1951, Eileen Croxford, traditional songs on the 'cello. Miss Croxford resigned in 1952 in order to have more time for playing. She was already a member of the Hallé Orchestra and she also wanted to do more chamber music with her sisters. The violin teaching is now in the hands of Miss Susan Baker, A.R.C.M., who combines exceptional talent with great attraction. She is so alive and vital that it is not surprising that "strings" are flourishing. She has a number of pupils in the Preparatory School, one or two already taking their place in the orchestra which augurs well for the future.

In tracing the history of singing and the orchestra one has momentarily lost touch with all those talented women who, throughout the last 25 to 30 years have been teaching "music" meaning pianoforte, to countless girls of promise, and not so much promise. Some have not stayed with us long but there are two names that stand out as being corner-stones in this structure—Miss Jones and Mrs. Parbury.

Mrs. Parbury, who as Miss Sale was appointed in 1928, retired in July, 1950. One of her pupils wrote in the *Aquila*: ". . . All who have had contact with her will know how much the School is losing. Her unfailing readiness to co-operate and her untiring energy expended on anything she undertakes have won the admiration of many. Her capacity to run a career and a home with complete efficiency is a revelation. Added to that she displays an extremely lively interest in every pupil who goes to her, whether she is in Form I or VIA. Nothing is ever too much trouble if she can help in the advancement of any one of them. . . ."

Miss Jones joined the staff in 1922. She retired in 1950 but it is sad that she only lived four years to enjoy her well-earned leisure. The following from the *Guild Leaflet*, 1954, shows very clearly all she did for the School: ". . . She retired from the School in April, 1950, after 28 years as a member of the music staff, including 15 years in charge of the music department, but she kept in touch by returning on Speech Days and for Guild week-ends. Many piano pupils will gratefully remember her patience and perseverance in teaching them, and the high standard she

set, and her continued interest in them after they left the School.
By nature reserved, she did not make friends easily, but those who
really knew her admired her unselfishness and good judgment,
and her readiness to talk over problems and give kindly help.
She never spared herself and did her utmost to promote the
cause of music in the School. She was an excellent musician
and had specialised in aural training. In this she did most
valuable work in the Preparatory School classes."

Music in School today is being carried forward by worthy
successors, four who carry the torch are Old Girls who started
their musical education within these walls—Miss Helen Norman,
who is now head of the department, teaching violoncello and
pianoforte, is also responsible for much of the advanced paper
work taken by many girls ; Miss Doris Wood and Miss Findlay,
the latter taking much of the aural training and percussion as
well as recorder ; Miss Martin who has been many years with
us, and Miss Morris, whose talent as a pianist was very apparent
when she accompanied the School at the Speech Day rendering
of *Sir John in Love*, conducted by Miss Harding (our fourth
Old Girl).

These four who have brought back to the School their talent,
are representatives of an ever-increasing number of pupils who
have learnt over the years. Some have used their music, as
these have, to teach others, some have become professionals and
have given their gifts to the public, and heading this illustrious
list is, of course, Lady Harty (Agnes Nicholls), that "Sweet
singer of the Guild", who was Dr. Harding's most outstanding
pupil. I repeat what Miss Eggar has said of her : ". . . She had
singing lessons from him while she was at School. She then
passed on to the Royal College of Music as a student of the
violin, and soon gained a scholarship for singing, and held it
for five years under Albert Visetti. She made a great name for
herself even while at the college and afterwards sang in opera
and in concerts all over the world. She did magnificent war-
work, both in canteens and in entertainments for soldiers, and
her immense circle of friends were delighted when she was
awarded the C.B.E. in recognition of her work. She has been
extraordinarily generous to her old school, in sparing time out

of an extremely busy life to come back to it and sing to both past members (on the occasion of the Guild meetings) and present. No one who has heard her will ever forget that beautiful voice : and no one has encountered her vivid and attractive personality without feeling the richer and the gayer for it. . . ." I only wish it were possible for the present School to have the good fortune to hear her—she has always taken a tremendous interest in the School, and when the house music competition first started she often came to judge them. Her comments and advice were very stimulating. How much she has given us—in those early years when she took part in the Guild plays, and the memorable occasions when she sang for us. Somehow she stands alone in our minds, and dominates, as does her portrait hanging in the organ gallery where she graciously looks down on the ever-changing scene.

There have been, and still are, many other names who have made their mark in the world of music : Ruth Weld, Gladys Haig, Dolly Lightfoot, Gertrude King, Grace Hawkins (Torrens), who was accompanist to Dame Clara Butt (her daughter Fraye St. George Kirke inherited her talent and would probably have made a great name for herself but for the fact that she married very young, and the increasing ties of a large family and the duties of a house-master's wife at one of our large public schools prevented her from pursuing music as a career), Kathleen Dunn-Davies, Josephine Lester, Josephine Scott. Of those who have left more recently : Sylvia Cleaver, who has played with the Boyd Neal Orchestra and Ernest Element String Quartet ; Nancy Neild, who has been a member of the Covent Garden Orchestra ; Sheila McShee, who is making a name for herself as a singer ; Thea King, now Mrs. Frederick Thurston, as a pianist and clarinettist. She, with Elizabeth Bower delighted the Guild with their playing and singing in 1954. We shall never know how far Elizabeth might have gone for she died just over a year later of poliomyelitis, mourned by all who knew her. "With all her gifts she had humility and true dignity. She loved the School and came back on many occasions, at one time to take singing classes during Miss Joyce Harding's absence, at others to help with the Guides, always with cheerful and

unselfish devotion. We have lost a very rare personality".
Dr. and Mrs. Bower have recently endowed a singing scholarship
in her memory.

No mention has been made of all those who could have chosen
music as a career but have devoted their lives to what they felt
would be of more lasting value to humanity : the organists in
the little churches ; those who sing to sleep their own babies
and others ; those who play for youth clubs and dancing classes ;
but each of them owes something to the galaxy of gifted and
patient teachers who have made and are making the musical
history of this school.

In writing about music in the School one cannot ignore the
impact of the B.B.C. This may at first seem unnecessary, as it
must have made a considerable difference to all schools in this
progressive age, but for us it has had a special significance. We
count among our personal friends many of the best-known
names : Sir Adrian Boult, Clarence Raybould, Paul Beard,
Sidonie Goosens, Kathleen Washbourne, Frederick Thurston,
the Sievekings and many others. From 1941-45 the symphony
concerts broadcast from a "hall in the south" were relayed from
our Corn Exchange. Some concerts were given from our
own hall and many, including "Proms", from Bedford School.
Many of the members sent their daughters to the School,
Elizabeth Thurston and the Sievekings were among those
who came. The *Aquila* of those years is full of references to
our contacts : in January, 1942, Sir Adrian Boult presented
the certificates at the Music Pupils' Concert ; in July of that
year Kathleen Washbourne arranged a concert in our hall for
the Red Cross, to mention only two of many occasions.
Apart from these more personal links we shared with the
town the luxury of the best music available and the fortnightly symphony concerts were a great joy as well as
a unique opportunity for widening the musical experience of
the School as a whole. Many of us were also lucky enough
sometimes to get passes for broadcasts which were not open to
the public. I remember going to *The Barber of Seville* and being
hypnotised by the organised chaos, and fascinated by the effects
which produced such convincing sounds when one sat at home

and listened. We shared very closely the sorrow of the nation when Sir Henry Wood died, for he was here conducting the Promenade Concerts from Bedford School when he was taken ill. Many of us were present at some of the rehearsals and have vivid recollections of him striding about in his shirt sleeves impatiently waiting for Phyllis Sellick, who was to take Irene Scharrer's place at the last moment.

Those four years not only enriched our music but gave us a relaxation of immeasurable value at a time when nerves were stretched to capacity.

DRAMA

Considering how obscure seem the beginnings of any interest in drama as a subject to be taught in the High School it is interesting that the urge to act, latent in most human beings, quickly developed among girls who had left School. Amateur theatricals were presumably considered harmless, in fact even desirable as a form of entertainment, so that by the biennial meeting in 1895 we read of the "successful performance, by old pupils only, of a dramatised version of Tennyson's *Princess* at the Town Hall on Saturday evening." This production, like many that followed, was managed most ably by Miss Poole (later Mrs. Treffry), who significantly enough taught mathematics and, therefore, could by no stretch of imagination be considered a professional!

I have been told by the editor that I cannot avoid mentioning Guild plays, but that my main theme is the School not the Guild. Of course I cannot help it—no matter who I ask about drama in those early days immediately says, "Oh! There were the Guild plays". But when you try to delve further they can tell you nothing. "Oh no! We *never* did plays in School."

However, Vera Newton and Daisy (Mrs. Perkins) vaguely remember the arrival of a new elocution mistress: "Dark and slender and *very* smart with a wasp waist". At some recital or concert she recited "Old Man Kangaroo" and other poems, which impressed them both vastly. It seems to have been the first approach in the dramatic presentation of poetry, and as far as I can tell it was Miss Estelle Hawson, appointed in 1900 as a visiting mistress to teach elocution. She apparently gave recitals in the hall to members of the School at the end of Friday mornings, which inspired girls to learn.

Daisy herself longed to become a pupil but her ambition was not achieved. After she left School she took lessons from Mr. Rowland Hill, and must have attracted attention by the recitals she arranged and gave during the 1914-18 war, as by the time I first knew her she had built up a big connection here in Bedford. Her career is interesting as she is one who early became interested in speech therapy and was one of the first of a growing number of Old Girls to use their dramatic talent for this purpose, and she has for many years now done wonderful work at the West End Hospital for Nervous Diseases, where she qualified and became an L.C.S.T.

A letter from Miss Nancy Roberts (known to many as "Gran" of the Grove Family) gives us another recollection: ". . . There was absolutely no interest taken in drama when I was at B.H.S. Any suggestion of going on the stage was severely frowned on —there were School concerts—purely singing, in which I never took part as I could not sing in tune—so to my huge delight I did extra gym. instead of singing. I do remember Mabel Playfair visiting the theatre with some play. I went on the stage very much as a second choice. My ambition was to be a lawyer and then a barrister. My father, himself a lawyer, would not hear of it (though he regretted that decision very much later on). In those far-off days women at the bar were almost unheard of. I then said I'd go on the stage—in a sort of desperation my parents agreed but said I must do it on my own. I did. I answered every advertisement in *The Stage* and eventually got with a famous melodrama management—then "stock" ("repertory" now) and the Compton Comedy Company—and learnt my job the hard way, and I venture to think the *best* way. . . ."

Miss Hawson left in 1903 and one can only suppose that no further official recognition of elocution or speech training as a special subject was considered until 1911 when Miss Elsie Nicholls was appointed. She herself was by now famous for her appearances in Guild plays, and had outstanding talent. It was with her coming that elocution, though an extra, became part of the curriculum. At the same time it would appear that at least in the Junior forms, she must have found that acting had some place, as we read in the first number of the *Aquila* that: "On 2nd December, 1910, Miss Hart and some pupils of IIIA (Junior) gave an entertainment lasting from 12 noon to 1 p.m., taking the form of recitation with some acting from fairy scenes of *A Midsummer Night's Dream* and Bottom's company rehearsing their play. (Bottom and Puck wore gymnasium tunics, being presumably the nearest approach to Athenian dress; while the fairies, *including* Oberon, wore white frocks.) The choir assisted with the music, and the scenery was simple, consisting of such screens as could be collected with a judicious arrangement of trails of greenery." (How little things have changed—this could almost be a description of a form play today!) This production is particularly interesting as the part of Oberon was played by Dorothy Tetley, who later took up the stage as a career and played many leading parts in the West End, and was one of Elsie Nicholl's outstanding pupils. The cast also included Frances Castens (Mrs. Willson) who all her life has taken an interest in amateur theatricals, and was for many years a member of the Guild Dramatic Circle. After she settled in Canada people there soon found that she was a most valuable member of their community and one hears from her of how busy she still is producing and acting.

The changing attitude towards drama and dancing was shown by Miss Collie in her speech to the parents at the School concert of December, 1916, when she recommended as a career, music, dancing and elocution, for those with a special aptitude which was discernible. Miss E. Nicholls' production of *Alice in Wonderland* has already been recorded in Chapter VII. Such impetus was given that each year an increasing number of dramatic entertainments took place: *Eagerheart* by the Guides; *Quality Street* and a French play, produced by Miss Wilson and Miss Naylor; a joint production of *Le Bourgeois Gentilhomme* with Bedford School in 1921; and in 1922 VIBg did *The Rivals*, the beginning of several memorable Sixth Form efforts.

It was not until 1921 that tradition was broken and a recitation was given at a School concert when Beryl Oldrey recited "Sherwood", and then not again until 1925, when Phyllis fforde gave three! But by then Miss Nicholls was no longer there to hear—she died after a long illness, heroically borne, on 21st September, 1924. "She was one of our best and most gifted, and what we shall remember, even above the great gifts themselves, is the wonderful way in which she used them for the help and delight of those about her. After Mrs. Treffry gave up the management of our Guild plays, Miss Nicholls took on the work and the responsibility of managing the later ones. Her love of beauty and her power of evoking it from the most unpromising material were shown in the most memorable way." The lovely oak seat under the gallery was given by the Guild in her memory.

Her place was taken for a short time by Mrs. Mackenzie (Molly Dickson), who had been one of her pupils and, as far as one can tell from records, the first Old Girl to gain an L.R.A.M. for elocution. During her brief sojourn she produced a staff play, *The Knight of the Burning Pestle*; *Pygmalion and Galatea* for the Guild, in which she herself played Cynisca to Dorothy Tanqueray Willaume's Pygmalion and Miss Colwill was Galatea, giving a memorable performance as the statue that came to life. It was during this period that the first Greek play was staged when Miss B. Fisher, together with Miss Colwill and Miss Pike, produced *Iphigenia in Tauris*. The dresses were made by the actors with Miss Beck's help on Greek designs. This success achieved, was by the Sixth Form group, forerunners of the productions which have become renowned as "School plays", which are perhaps one of the outstanding features of the era which began with Miss Winifred Gowen's appointment in 1926.

She came when elocution had its established place as an extra, requiring a specialist to visit the School twice a week. The numbers warranted an assistant and for some time her friend, Miss Dorothy Shadwell, also came, but by degrees it became apparent that there was enough work for one person to teach full-time. Miss Gowen, before she left, not only taught pupils individually or in small groups, but also did a great deal of verse speaking and dramatic work with forms as part of their regular English course. So much interest resulted that finally a

Dramatic Society was founded and is now a flourishing club of over 60 members. Her achievements over 30 years, both personal, and through the successes of her pupils, have been quite remarkable. It is interesting to note that Miss Collie's proviso "Showing a special aptitude" has in all cases shown itself early—one can trace the name of Joyce Redman from the time she passed Grade II with hon. mention until she gained the Lady Gilbert's Prize and Diploma at R.A.D.A., and then on through the years as she has made her name in the theatre. There are many others which include Susan Otto, tragically killed by enemy action, Pat Pleasance, June Bell, Eleanor Rochester, Dagmar Sharples, Valerie Samuel, Phyllis Salmond, Elizabeth Mann, Audrey Meeson, Joyce Rawlins, who was in the film "The Red Shoes", and most recently of all Jennifer Bryant, who is still training. I have left Elwyn Edgecombe to the end, as it is she who has succeeded Miss Gowen and is one of the band of Old Girls to bring back to School those gifts she has developed and perfected. She has her own school of speech and drama at Northampton. We find her name as giving a memorable performance as Shylock when Miss Gowen's pupils presented scenes from *The Merchant of Venice* to the Upper School in December, 1926, and from then on her name figures frequently in lists of successes.

These scenes were the first of those memorable productions and recitals given by Miss Gowen and her pupils, excluding anything she did with the Guild and staff. The introduction of dramatic scenes at a concert seem first to have taken place as a substitute when Dr. Harding was ill in 1929, and no concert as such took place. The year of his death there was no singing at Speech Day and Miss Gowen's pupils gave a nativity play, and since then elocution has always had some part in the programme.

Heading the list of these large productions is *The Alcestis of Euripides* in 1930, when Miss Gowen played Alcestis and Miss Shadwell Admetus with Pixie Bennetts as Heracles. The singing and orchestra were under the direction of Dr. Harding and the chorus (movement and dance) were trained by Miss Colwill. In 1938 came *Macbeth*, in 1940 *Helen* and in 1943

Iphigenia in Taurus for the Aid to Greece Fund, and in 1948 *The Birds of Aristophanes*. What a production, with over 70 in the cast! Only those who saw it or who were in any way connected with it, can know what an achievement this was. The fact that the head mistress was a classical scholar and, therefore, had a particular interest certainly helped, as, for about three weeks prior to the performances, "the Birds" took precedence over everything else in School. The repercussions were even felt in the Junior School as every art class was mass-producing birds' heads in the last week. A crisis had arisen owing to the fact that only six heads had come with the costumes being lent us. Miss Gowen's request to me to make a few heads ended in nearer forty, and the Juniors had to act as models while heads were painted on them by anyone who was free, under my direction.

Miss Gibson, who had only been in School one term, thought everyone mad, her senior in particular, and had no conception of what was required when told by Miss Feaver to teach the storks a dance or blackbirds to fly! The art room under Miss Pehrson was given over to yards and yards of hessian, which finally turned into wings. When one considers that it took well over two hours to get the cast dressed and made up, and that the performances began on time, that in itself was an achievement worth recording. Never do I remember a performance of any play produced by Miss Gowen starting late.

In 1950 came *Twelfth Night*, a lovely production, but to many *A Winter's Tale* in 1953 is considered the most outstanding. The proceeds from this were used to give the School its own lighting equipment and it was, in fact, actually used for this production. It completed what the Treffry Memorial had begun in giving the School a steel superstructure for the acting stage, so that now it is possible to plan a production with the knowledge that one has got the basic equipment for getting the effects one hopes for. One salutes with the greatest admiration all those who have in the past produced such wonderful results with a makeshift stage and lighting equipment.

Miss Gowen's own performances in plays and recitals did much to stimulate an interest in drama. She was herself a superb actress as well as an inspired teacher, and was as well able to make you weep, as laugh. It was a revelation to many new-comers to the Guild to see her depict each character in turn as she tried to make the cast come to life in any play she was produc-ing.

Her contribution to the School's history is a magnificent achievement of preservation and creation. She welded together all the work started by Miss Nicholls so that drama has become a vital part of the School's life and she has left it now in the capable hands of one of her most outstanding pupils.

DANCING

In the earliest days of the School's history attendance at a dancing class was recognised as the normal routine for a girl, and the time-table was so arranged that afternoons were free for these extras, although no classes were actually held in the School. Pupils were taught by Madame and Monsieur Demery at their rooms near the County Theatre, or by Mrs. and Miss Shaw, whose first classes were held in the Harpur Institute (familiar to many of us until recently as the County Library, and shortly to become the home of the Boys' Modern School Junior Department). Mrs. Shaw's classes were so popular and successful that she subsequently bought Crofton House and built the original Crofton Room, with its beautiful floor laid on chains. Molly Evans remembers very vividly the sight of the Mammas almost bouncing as they sat round watching their respective daughters twisting and swirling as they learnt the intricacies of the waltz. (I rather gather that it was the exuberance of the Polka and the Washington Post, which really produced such involuntary movement amongst the audience !). When the Shaws left Bedford Miss Stewart took over Crofton Rooms and in spite of the fact that a visiting mistress had been ap-pointed to take classes at School many continued to attend these outside ones.

We know that from the first, dancing was an integral part of the Guild plays, and always the music was specially composed by Dr. Harding, which is proof enough that the Old Girls taking part must have learnt to dance first. This then is perhaps the moment to speak of Miss Forbes, whose name is so fundamentally associated with these plays in connection with the dancing. There are still some who remember her grace and imagination as she danced herself, but many more who remember her for the beautiful dances she arranged and taught them for these Guild plays. Hers was a natural gift as she had no special training— she did, in fact, teach Nancy Harding as a private pupil until she was fourteen. Her connection with the School was a long one, for she came as a girl in 1888 and in 1900 became Miss Collie's secretary. By the time she retired in 1935 she was the person to whom everyone went to get their problems solved whether it concerned music time-tables, seating in the hall or milk tickets. She taught music and dealt with the domestic arrangements of the School with the same touch of imagination that made whatever she did seem a little different. Her lovely flower arrangements for the hall and staff room come to mind, the little unobtrusive kindnesses, her own charming but individual way of dressing, all somehow created an atmosphere in School which vanished with her. The Forbes Bowl is the tangible evidence we have of her special love and interest— dancing. She gave it on her retirement to be awarded to the girl who had made the most progress in dancing each year. (We now have two other cups, the Parrish Cup and the Parkington Cup. The first is for the Intermediate Group and was given by Mr. and Mrs. Parrish, whose daughter is still at Quantocks. The latter is for the Juniors and was given by Miss Harding in memory of Muriel Parkington, who was her pianist for eighteen years. This partnership was unique, and her sympathetic playing made dancing so much easier. She will long be remembered for her brilliant accompanying at all the classes, and the way her eyes were always watching Miss Harding or the children, seemingly never the music or the keyboard, and so was alive to every need.)

In 1900, Miss Moon, who was a pupil of that famous trainer Mrs. Wordsworth, visited the School twice a week and continued her classes until 1922 when Miss Nancy Harding was appointed —the latter had, in fact, begun to take the Friday evening class a year earlier as Miss Moon found that she could not manage the journey more than once. (Miss Harding had been a member of the general class from the age of fourteen until she left School to take up her training.)

To learn dancing was considered an important part of one's education in a world that still counted grace of movement and poise a necessary accomplishment in a woman, apart from the fact that the ballroom dancing of the late Victorian and Edwardian period certainly required considerable skill and knowledge. Not only were the dances themselves complicated but a knowledge of the etiquette and formalities concerned with attending a ball was essential if one was not to remain a "wallflower" or make some unforgiveable *faux pas*. All the necessary exercises and techniques, including deportment, were taught at these general classes and how valuable they were. (This aspect was still partially true of the early twenties as I can remember very clearly Miss Harding trying valiantly to impart some of the social graces among the gauche and shy of that time. We owe her a great deal.)

To learn and teach dancing was, therefore, a recognised career, but anything that savoured of the stage was somehow regarded as different. Our outlook has changed! We are very proud now to record that Peggy Ward Tamplin (now Peggy White) is on the staff of the Royal Academy of Dancing and is a children's examiner. Since then others have made a name apart from teaching, among them being Daisy Dalzell, Sheila Dudeney (Mrs. Milman) who trained under Madam Judith Espinosa. She now has her own school of dancing at Frinton ; Elizabeth Slack, who was for several years with the Ballet Jooss ; Patricia Grant, who danced with the Sadlers Wells ; and Dolores Brabin Smith, who was with Dolsky's London Ballet Company. Among teachers of dancing the number of Old Girls who have risen high in the profession is great. Perhaps heading the list is Miss Jill Argyll (known at School as Muriel Campbell). It has been a privilege to have her visit the School to judge the dancing competitions from time to time. There is Marian Lombard, who has a large connection round Chichester and trains students for the stage and the teaching of dancing. Joyce Parker (Mrs. Walters) is teaching in Cornwall, and there are many abroad like June Simmonds in India and Elizabeth Ritchie in South Africa, but the best known to us is, of course, Nancy Harding herself.

By the time this book is published she will have given us at School thirty-five years of her creative genius which remains as bright as ever, probably due to the fact that all this time she has never stopped learning. She continues to keep abreast of modern thought and technique but always based on the classical tradition. She trained under Madam Judith Espinosa and Madam Volkova, the celebrated Russian teacher in England. Under Miss Josephine Bradley she gained her ballroom dancing qualifications. She is herself an A.R.A.D. (Advanced Teacher's Certificate), and on the staff of the Royal Academy of Dancing's Teachers' Training Course, as well as being a member of their education committee. Bedford is indeed lucky. She has for many years now owned Crofton House and it was a devastating blow when, on Christmas Eve, 1948, the lovely ballroom was destroyed by fire. For some time her classes were taken in various halls in the town and many took place in our own gymnasium. As soon as building became less difficult the new ballroom was built and still the Mammas sit and watch, but now on a dais built for the purpose and *they* do not bounce !

As one reads the *Aquilas* since her appointment one realises the influence she has had. Before that, dancing figured only as a social event. By 1911 the Sixth Form Dance is described as an annual affair, and from then on one reads of various functions such as the hockey dance, and the boarders' dance. Gradually one reads of displays, the first I think was given in aid of the Platform Fund in 1922. In 1923 the *Guild Leaflet* tells of *A Miniature Ballet* and then follows that succession of enchanting tales depicted through the medium of dance which we look for every two years. *Pixie Led, The Fairy Doll, A Spring Evening, The Princess and the Rabbit, The Stolen Princess, The Golden Hoop* and this year (1956) *The Little Mermaid,* to mention but a few. The stories are all written by herself and danced to music specially composed by her father. Since his death she has continued to use only his music by taking excerpts from his compositions.

Her work for the Guild is perhaps another story but she has given us on so many occasions infinite pleasure and often by her own dancing, and those of her pupils, inspired the School that one cannot avoid mentioning it here. A member of the Junior School wrote in 1939, after seeing *Berkeley Square*, "I liked Miss Harding's dancing, especially the arm movements—the dancing was so tidy with no pushing at all". Sometimes the dances have been arranged as part of the play and sometimes they have taken the form of an introduction or interlude but always they have reflected the mood or period. Whatever has been required she has always given herself unsparingly out of time which is non-existent when you analyse her average day.

School classes in many ways have altered very little over the years except in size, and one is transported back as one watches the children today doing the classic steps—all hoping, as one did oneself, to hear Miss Harding say "By yourself, M——". The classes are now held in the gymnasium instead of the art room and perhaps lose something by the vastness—how cosy those roaring fires looked when one took ones place on a Friday evening. Boarders may now attend the ballroom class at Crofton Rooms on Saturdays after tea, to which the boys also go. The value of dancing, though not an integral part of the curriculum, is still recognised and so the School classes continue and in spite of the ever-increasing demands of the academic time-table there are those "with special aptitude" who dance after School and on Saturdays as well. History was certainly made this year when at the Sixth Form party a ballet was presented as part of the entertainment. Jill Mackness, who was responsible for the choreography and training of the dancers, has been a pupil of Miss Harding since she was a little girl, and the joy of both dancers and spectators was great.

. . . . .

This story of the creative arts during three-quarters of a century leaves one amazed. When one considers that the tradition of this great School is pre-eminently academic, one is filled with pride that the opportunity has also been given to those others whose talents were of a different calibre. One also realises that

M

CHAPTER XV

THE BEDFORD HIGH SCHOOL GUILD

EDITED BY

MRS. GORDON (ELIZABETH KAYE)

Contents:

I.   The origin, purposes, and methods of the B.H.S.G.
     By Mrs. Wragge (Margaret Craig)

II. The corporate work of the B.H.S.G.
  1. The Girls' Evening Club
     By Mrs. Wragge (Margaret Craig)
  2. The Holborn Girls' Club
     By Mrs. Lawe (Marjorie Edwards)
  3. Guild Missionaries
     By Miss Winifred Hardy
  4. The Dramatic Circle
     By Mrs. Barford (Vena Bennett)
  5. Other Societies of the Guild
     By Mrs. Wray (Janie Handford) and Miss Westaway

III. Memories of Guild plays
     By Miss Hilda Gnosspelius and Miss Mary Pigg

IV. The Guild during two wars
     By Lady Jaqueta Williams (Jaqueta Northcote)

V.   Rule XII: Then and now
     By Mrs. Gordon

THE CHAPTER on the Guild in the 1932 volume was edited by Mrs. Gordon, who at that time was still Elizabeth Kaye and was in England. The chapter has had to be enlarged to cover the multitude of activities of the last twenty-five years, and Mrs. Gordon is now (January, 1957) in Cyprus, where she and her husband are doing magnificent work and are very, very busy. But her beginning and ending to the chapter still stand, and we reprint them with great pride and pleasure.

The story of the youth of the Guild is told in the following pages by Old Girls whose memory of those vivid days is still fresh and keen : other Old Girls have carried on the tale through the war years and the complex times that have followed, so that now, at this great landmark of our history we can pause and survey in their entirety the accomplishment and activities of our Guild. A great deal of labour and much research have gone to the making of this chapter, and we all owe most sincere thanks to those whose public spirit led them to undertake the task. Volunteers did not flock forward by the hundred ; quite the contrary ! Each member of the Guild who was approached had the profoundest conviction that in the matter of memory there could be no more inaccurate member than she—in the matter of literary skill none so incapable of lifting a pen. These obstacles at length defeated, a valiant little band led with much determination by Mrs. Wragge (the first general secretary, whose enthusiasm and industry were quite invaluable), set to work to produce the pages which follow ; and they offer them in this year as a small tribute to the School which reared them.

I. THE ORIGIN, PURPOSE AND METHODS OF THE B.H.S.G.

The School was just ten years old in the summer term of 1892, when seventy Old Girls met on 7th July, to give it a birthday present—a picture. Miss Belcher presided, and received the gift. A resolution was then proposed, seconded, and, after discussion, unanimously adopted, to the effect "That a Bedford High School Guild should be formed on the lines followed in other public schools." It was natural that Cheltenham Ladies' College should provide the model, because Miss Belcher and several of her staff were members of the Cheltenham Guild, and so had practical experience of its successful methods. In the discussion which arose upon the resolution, the purposes of the Guild were clearly put before those present, i.e., "To promote a feeling of fellowship", and "By co-operation to help its members in self-improvement and in work for others". These objects were to be achieved by a biennial general meeting of members, and by a personal report to be sent to the general secretary of the Guild by each member, every second year, telling of her work, interests and service. These reports were to form the link between the individual and the whole body of old school-fellows. The biennial meeting would be the focus of the social, philanthropic and religious life of the Guild.

This outline commended itself to the meeting, and before it broke up a provisional committee was appointed, with Margaret Craig as its provisional secretary. It was instructed to communicate with all Old Girls over 19 years of age, who had left from the Upper School, inviting their support. By the end of September, 1892, the first list was complete and one hundred and sixty-eight Old Girls had joined the Guild. By the end of October in the same year the first elected committee set to work, elected its officers, drafted rules and constitution, drew up its first register, and dispatched copies of these documents to all the Guild members.

The following spring found the committee very busy, arranging for the first biennial meeting, which was held on Friday, 30th June to Monday, 3rd July, 1893, and by this time the Guild had grown to a membership of two hundred and thirty-five.

The lines laid down for that happy first reunion have been followed in the series of subsequent biennial meetings, each seeming more happy than the last. There is always the opening conversazione in the large hall on the Friday night, when the Guild is welcomed by its president, the head mistress. The scene is as gay as flowers and colour and music can make it; the best of all is the joy of meeting old friends, seeing happy faces and hearing familiar voices.

On the Saturday morning the general committee meets at 10 a.m., preparatory to the general meeting for business in the large hall at 10.30 a.m. This latter event was regarded from the beginning as the most important part of the biennial meeting. The joyous note of the previous evening passes simply and naturally into a deeper tone, with the opening prayers and the address by the president. The general secretary gives her report, full of personal interest, telling, without names, of the work done by old school-fellows: it is a document full of inspiration and encouragement, which, year by year, expands in scope and variety, yet retains its original depth of purpose and loftiness of aim. The local secretary follows with business details, and the treasurer gives an account of finances. Then the meeting is open for discussion, for proposed developments, and for reports of subsidiary societies.

The afternoon of the Saturday is occupied with the garden party and cricket and tennis matches : and the evening with one of the series of dramatic performances, organised by Guild members and presented in the School hall. On the Sunday afternoon there is a special service, and a special preacher : and in the evening a meeting of the Guild Missionary Circle. On the Monday morning at 9 o'clock the Guild assembles with the present pupils at School prayers—a privilege which is highly valued. The inspiration of the future is added to the memory of the past as "Bedford girls" of all ages join in the familiar prayers and psalms and hymns, and the president uses the opportunity of her parting address to the Guild to "knit the generations each to each". It is a real and great tradition which is being transmitted. Looking back over the years, we are conscious that the School owes as much to the Guild as the Guild owes to the School. Both have played their part in keeping the torch alight, and in handing it on : and both owe more than they can say to the successive head mistresses, who, as presidents of the Guild, have kept alive the contact between the present and the past.

II. THE CORPORATE WORK OF THE B.H.S.G.
I. THE GIRLS' EVENING CLUB

At the time when the Guild was founded there was a widespread enthusiasm for social service. Settlements had sprung up in various poor districts in London, inspired by the first pioneers at Toynbee Hall, Whitechapel. Colleges and boys' schools became individually responsible for their own "Mission" ; and the girls' schools followed the example. Cheltenham College started its St. Hilda's Mission in Bethnal Green, to which Miss Belcher pointed as an ideal for corporate social service for our own Bedford Guild. But the cost of maintaining such an enterprise was prohibitive, and the expense involved to individual residents, and railway fares to occasional helpers, made a London school mission impossible. Miss Belcher also realised that there will always be at any given time a larger number of old school-fellows living in the town of Bedford than elsewhere.

For these reasons she gave her warm support to the suggestion made at the first Guild meeting (1893) that the Guild should give its united social service to the town of Bedford, and that it should adopt the already existing Girls' Evening Club in Tavistock Street as the Guild mission. This club had been worked for five years previously by a small group of Old High School Girls, with Margaret Craig as honorary secretary. It was a recreative club, open every evening for working girls chiefly in daily employment, rough but warm-hearted, much in need of guidance and friendship. The club was unattached to any religious body, but the workers were, for the most part, Anglicans.

After several months' consideration, and negotiations with the former committee, the Evening Club was formally handed over to the High School Guild in February, 1894. A new committee, consisting of twelve Guild members, was appointed. Miss Belcher became its president, Ethel Footman its manager and treasurer, and Frances Craig and Mabel Wells its joint secretaries. At once the Evening Club made a great leap forward. Fifteen volunteers took charge of the various classes; by the end of the following year twenty-one local members of the Guild were fellow workers there, and the club membership reached one hundred. The Bedfordshire County Council gave its support by granting six free cookery lessons to twelve keen members of the club.

In the year 1898 the Girls' Evening Club outgrew its old quarters, and moved into larger premises in Bromham Road, opposite the School. The membership had grown to one hundred and thirty, and there were twenty-seven Guild members doing regular evening work, in charge of various educational classes. At the Guild meeting of the same year, Miss Belcher, in her last presidential address, made a strong appeal for the Guild mission. The following year there were two valuable gifts—a large iron room for bigger meetings and classes, built in the garden of the mission in memory of Mrs. Poynder; and a clock from Miss Hiatt and Miss Holmes, in memory of Miss Belcher. The faithful workers held on, Miss Lee always helping them; and in 1903, when Ethel Footman resigned the position of manager, there were two hundred club members and twenty Guild members as workers. Mabel Wells succeeded to the post of manager, and kept it throughout the whole period during which the Guild continued to recognise the club as its mission. The Needlework Society, led by Louie Campion, remained equally faithful.

The Great War, more than anything else, brought the B.H.S. mission to an end, in spite of the fact that the club continued its work in Guild hands until 1924. The war swept both workers and club members into a changed world, and when peace came old methods had become obsolete. New times called for new measures, social work took fresh forms, and in 1924 the connection between the Guild and the Girls' Evening Club was severed. Yet, while it lasted, the club, as the High School mission, was for thirty years a useful and much-valued link between the School and the town, and gave, in many cases, a preliminary training for much future and responsible social service.

The enthusiasm which inspired the Girls' Evening Club was carried to distant parts of the world. Mrs. Halliley (Margaret Darling) ran one in Durban, S. Africa, many years ago for coloured girls. They were lent an old mule stable (with accompanying perfume). They sang, they sewed, they did drama, they evolved a wonderful variety of badminton (but the mangers did get in the way) and when they sat quiet the rats came out and scuttled along the edge of the mangers. But they did have fun (she said), and though it was down in the docks area and supposed to be very rowdy with non-Europeans, she never had the least annoyance. (And that, surely, is a great tribute to a great personality.)

2. THE HOLBORN GIRLS' CLUB

Of the constructive work of the Guild and the School none ranks higher than that example of social service known as the

Holborn Girls' Club. It is surely of great importance that the members of the School should be warm-hearted towards their "under-privileged" sisters ; and the club has brought to a drab, bomb-shattered section of London, not only some evidence of human kindness and interest, but also a sound and healthy influence on young lives.

Further, the foundation of the club was in a sense a graceful acknowledgment of a debt, since the School itself has drawn revenues through the Harpur Trust from Holborn rents. Moreover, the association is historically much older : large parts of Holborn were included in the great parks which surrounded the Duke of Bedford's London mansion.

Bedford School was already running a club for the boys, and its committee expressed the view very strongly that a female counterpart would be a very great help.

So, in February, 1946, the new venture started in the band room at Coram's Field, one-time London home of the Foundling Hospital. From its inception it prospered. It could hardly be otherwise when one examines the list of names—all of them well known for service to the School—who formed its first committee. There were Miss Westaway, Miss J. Dawes, Miss J. Harding, Miss C. Lucas, Miss L. Jones, Miss C. Messinger, Miss Spafford, Miss Belcher, Miss Sanders and Mrs. Stonebanks.

Under the very able chairmanship of Miss Spafford, devoted work was done by this committee. After her retirement Mrs. Whyte (M. Page) became chairman, and with Mrs. Lawe (M. Edwards) secretary since 1947, has carried most of the responsibility ever since. Other members have retired and new ones have come forward to replace them. One name, however, has remained on the committee list ever since the first meeting—that of a distinguished Old Girl who has given freely of her time and of her sound advice and help, Miss C. Lucas. Another name deserves grateful mention, that of Miss Sanders, who served as treasurer for ten years. The committee, too, has always had a member of the staff and also a senior girl to represent the present generation at the School, and this has been a valuable asset and link.

In 1947 the club had to move, and by invitation it shared the huts of the boys' club in Emerald Street. It moved again in 1951 and was fortunate in getting the use of the Social room in Blemondbury House, one of the great new blocks of working-class flats in Holborn.

Early in 1957 it is to have quarters of its own provided by the Harpur Trust in a new building in Lamb's Conduit Street, a worthy example of the generosity of the Trust. This will allow a large increase in the present membership of 100.

The club leader, Miss Wright, has served since 1947 and under her devoted care (and that of her many voluntary helpers) a club spirit has developed of which the Guild and the School can be proud. The club hours are given to activities which develop physique, interests and morale. Amongst the present activities are gymnastics (including a fine netball team), music, needlework, handicrafts and dancing ; and to these will be added in the new premises, cooking, play-acting and other subjects.

None of this excellent work would have been possible without the enthusiastic support of the Guild and the School. The financial success of the Harvest Sales has been outstanding and forms a shining example of what the School can do when its heart is enlisted in a good cause. In addition, there have been all along generous subscriptions and donations of equipment by members of the Guild and School. But willing and selfless personal service by many friends of the club has perhaps an even deeper meaning in placing the club in its permanent setting as part of the life of a great school.

3. GUILD MISSIONARIES

"Go ye into all the world and preach the gospel." Many members of the Bedford High School Guild have heard that command and obeyed it. They have trained at home as doctors, teachers, and nurses, and have gone abroad to preach the gospel through the ministries of healing and teaching. Often they have been confronted with tasks which they would have declared themselves unable to do at home, yet because there was no one else they have undertaken them and have triumphed over impossibilities.

In the 1932 edition of the history, Mrs. Wragge wrote : "At the third meeting of the Guild in 1898, the subject of mission work overseas was brought before the members, and it was agreed to form a Missionary Study Circle for the dual purpose of increasing knowledge of Christian effort abroad, and strengthening by sympathy those old schoolfellows who should from time to time offer themselves for this service". So early the interest began, and through the years the Guild has been kept informed of the activities of missionary members by means of a report at the biennial meeting and a summary of the letters received in the Leaflet. A meeting of the Missionary Circle, addressed whenever possible by a Guild missionary on furlough, has a regular place in the week-end programme of the biennial meeting.

Some of our members went out as pioneer missionaries, starting schools, laying the foundations of teacher-training ; struggling against primitive conditions and superstitious fear in dispensaries and hospitals, building up a nursing service worthy of the name from most unpromising material. Now, in addition to smaller institutions, we hear of schools giving secondary education in modern buildings, teacher-training institutions and universities ; and well-equipped hospitals with recognised medical schools.

In both Asia and Africa the emergence of nationalist movements, with their inevitable political changes, have affected the life and work of missionaries. No one knows more about the effect of politics on missionary work than Winifred Coate, who for twenty-five years served as principal of the Jerusalem Girls' College and since her retirement in 1948 has spent eight years in appealing for help for Arab refugees in Jordan and in teaching them to help themselves. Recent events have made it necessary for her to leave, and it seems unlikely that missionaries will be able to work there again. From China, too, missionaries like Kathleen Lamb have come home, leaving behind cherished work and friends. Those in other countries have a growing sense of urgency in their work as they foresee the time when they too may have to leave.

It is not possible to mention the work of all who have served abroad as missionaries. Those who have been named remind us of the many Guild members whom they represent. Still the witness continues, for this year, which saw the retirement of Grace Apthorpe after many years in Tanganyika, saw also the appointment of a new Guild missionary. They are of many denominations, they serve in almost every part of the world, their work is as varied as the places in which they find themselves, yet they are one in their devotion to the Lord whom they serve. We do well to remember and honour them.

4. THE DRAMATIC CIRCLE

How many happy hours the Guild members of the Dramatic Circle of today owe to those past members of the Guild, who in far-off years, going back to 1895, began to present plays to the Guild meeting, can never be counted. To those brave women who wrote and produced plays under the most fantastic conditions we really owe our foundation.

It was at the meeting in 1929, after three short plays had been presented to the Guild, that Mrs. D. Perkins (née Newton) and Miss Lee had the happy thought that a Dramatic Circle of Guild members interested in play producing be formed. The object being to give an opportunity for meeting between the biennial reunion, and by the reading of plays to find one suitable for production, always, of course, subject to the approval of the Guild committee.

The idea was greeted with enthusiasm, and the first president to be elected was Mrs. Treffry, a past member of the staff, who as Miss Poole, was responsible for the staging, and managing, of most of the early Guild plays. Mrs. Treffry only missed two meetings and chaired all the general meetings until her death in 1946. The Treffry Memorial is the steel structure for the stage now in use and was first utilised in the production of *Lord Richard in the Pantry*.

The first vice-presidents were Lady Playfair (who, as Mabel Platts, took many leading parts in Guild plays) and Mrs. Purdon, who had been a member of the staff, and wrote many of the old plays, including *Undine*.

The fact that these eminent members of the early Guild productions were so closely connected with the formation of the Circle gave all of us a living link with the old traditions.

The Dramatic Circle have staged the following :

1931—*Quality Street.* Producer, Winifred Gowen.

1933—*If I were King.* A stupendous production with a cast of 59, which incorporated all the arts. Producer, Winifred Gowen.

1935—*A Hundred Years Old.* Producer, Winifred Gowen.

1937—*Pride and Prejudice.* Producer, Winifred Gowen, who also played Darcy.

1939—*Berkeley Square.* Producers, Mrs. Gaye and Mrs. Perkins. Miss Gowen took the part of Peter Standish in this production and gave an outstanding performance.

During the war years all thoughts of plays were abandoned, and it was only in 1945, after six years of war, the Dramatic Circle began to function again.

It was at the 1946 meeting that Dorothy Tanqueray Willaume's resignation was received, and to the deepest sorrow and regret of all members of the Circle she passed away in August of the same year. Dorothy Tanqueray Willaume was one of the original members and she was connected with many Guild plays before the Circle was founded. Those who knew and played with her indeed lost a friend.

In the following years the Dramatic Circle produced :

1948—*Quiet Week-end.* Producer, Winifred Gowen.

1950—*Lord Richard in the Pantry.* Producer, Judy Barford (née Bennet).

In 1952, the Circle desperately seeking a full-length play for the Jubilee year suggested *Undine* to the Guild committee. This was an original play written by Mrs. Purdon, and first presented to the Guild in 1914. This choice was received with acclamation.

It was as well perhaps that no one in the audience ever knew what went on behind the scenes ; perhaps in this production most of all, those concerned in the stage management caught a breath of the fever of the past, and most unbelievable and fantastic things took place.

The original flats were brought to light, and what a glow of joy they created in the breast of the stage manager when she beheld the beautiful sea, with sea-weed, lovely rocks and fishes ; these were not defaced in the slightest by their long stay in darkness.

The flats in the first act were held up by four living bodies so that they could be removed from the stage quickly. The river rushes used in the play, on the last night, were fetched from a fishmonger's slab, as they had been forgotten. It is better to forget the remarks of some people, when they smelt fish. The gauze curtain in the original production was not used on this occasion owing to its frailty and to the very strong stage lights which might have caused it to burn.

What the stage managers thought when they heard a voice from the ranks of the Guild members say, after the performance to the Guild, "It was all right, but what about the gauze curtain we used in 1914 ?", cannot be written.

In 1954 a programme of plays and music was given and much enjoyed.

In 1956, *Cranford* was produced by Winifred Gowen. To the great regret of the Guild and Circle, this is reputed to be her last production.

Perhaps when one is always mixed up in the Dramatic Circle, and the presentation of plays, one is apt to overlook the "power behind the throne", who gives guidance and help when needed, but who is never actually in the picture—this, I think, applies well to our president, Lady Jaqueta Williams. We of the Circle have known always since she became our president that in her we have a tower of strength, and always a fount of wisdom, and to mention last, but not least, her unfailing interest in us. Long may she remain in office.

Another personality most dearly loved by us all is Winifred Gowen. Those of us who have worked with her these last 25 years have indeed been fortunate. "What wisdom, what fire, what sarcasm"—how we all loved it, knowing that in her hands, be the play what it may, it would come "alive", and live as it was meant by the author to live, in her capable hands.

In our last production, *Cranford*, I think the fact that we all knew it was probably Winifred Gowen's last production of a Guild play, inspired us. We really felt we must become members of the Cranford community, so that our producer could go away happy in the thought that down the years she had not laboured in vain, and that as regards acting her disciples had really justified themselves in this beautiful old English story.

A tribute must be paid to Mrs. Doris Glunicke (née Miller), who became a vice-president of the Circle in 1948. Her keen interest in all what goes on, and her constant attendance at meetings, is a sheer delight, and we feel that she is indeed carrying the torch which was lit in 1895.

5. OTHER SOCIETIES OF THE B.H.S.G.

The story of our Guild would not be complete without some account of various societies which have been started within it from time to time. The first of these to spring to life were the Literary and Needlework Societies.

The Literary Society was launched at the first biennial meeting in 1893, at the suggestion of Henrietta Lloyd and Beatrix Vere, and began with the writing of essays on given subjects. These were passed round to the members for remarks and votes— Beatrix Vere acting as secretary and Miss Holmes giving valuable help in criticisms and suggestions. I am afraid members were not always as regular as was hoped in contributing essays, for we notice that the society grew passing rich on the fines imposed for non-fulfilment of this obligation! Still, some excellent essays were chosen out of those sent in, and these were published in the Guild chronicle. It seems, perhaps, a pity that in the growing stress of busier days this essay writing was dropped. However, until 1900 the secretary continued to issue lists of books with suggestions for reading and study, which were published regularly in the Leaflets. Then for some years Miss Holmes contributed literary notes, which gave most helpful advice in the choice of books and guidance in current literature— illuminating, as it were, the passing events of the day, especially during the war years.

Another outcome of the biennial meeting of 1893 was the Needlework Society, of which Elsie Urquhart was the first secretary. Each member subscribed one shilling yearly and undertook to make two garments suitable for the equipment of young girls taking up domestic service. This was run in connection with the Girls' Evening Club during the thirty years of its adoption as the B.H.S.G. mission, and for twenty-eight of these it was successfully carried on by the regular work so devotedly given to it by Louie Campion as secretary.

In 1897 the Guild Musical Society was started, with glee singing under Dr. Harding, and the orchestra conducted by Annie Hawkins; both of these held weekly practices at the School. The following year a Choral Society was begun; a series of chamber concerts, organised by Dr. Harding and Edith Hawkins, was given and the orchestra, also under their leadership, has provided the beautiful music of all our biennial meetings.

Here we would like to pay tribute to the inestimable services of Dr. Harding to the musical life of our Guild, from its foundation until his death in October, 1930; we owe him an immeasurable debt of gratitude for all he gave us of his time and of his genius.

We cannot leave the subject of Guild music without mention of our pride in two of our very gifted musicians : Agnes Nicholls, our "sweet singer", and Katherine Eggar, our composer and pianist. Both these artists have frequently given their services to their old School, greatly to its delight.

And lastly there is our Fellowship Fund—started as the result of a resolution proposed by Jaqueta Northcote (Lady Jaqueta Williams) and Violet Apthorpe at the meeting of 1907, that "a fund be started, to be supported by members of the Guild and given to the head mistress, to be used at her discretion for aiding pupils to continue their education". The resolution was discussed and carried unanimously; and for fifty years this fund has come to the help of some who, through stress of circumstances, would otherwise have been unable to complete their school careers. It is a link of fellowship between past and present. It offers to us of the past an opportunity to show our appreciation of our School in a practical way. It is an expression of our love and loyalty, of our grateful memory of all that the School has meant to us in our lives, and as such it has the very strongest claim on the support of every member of the Guild. In 1949 the fund was taken over by its present secretary, Betty Hockin, and its value in the School's life grows constantly.

III. MEMORIES OF GUILD PLAYS

1. My recollections of the early days of the Guild centre in our first play—*The Princess* in 1895. The delight of it we shall never forget. It was all so fresh and exciting. You see, we were still at School, and even the make-ups were thrilling. I remember how much we admired the stout-heartedness, if not the artistic effect, of one member of the caste, who steadfastly refused to have any paint on her face! We loved it all. I am sure that the charm of the performance was not only a happy memory but a real achievement.

And who that had seen her could forget Mrs. Treffry as stage manager? Undaunted, cheerful, always kind—though firm—with the erring, with a natural eye for effect and a grasp of the details of staging which was unique—she was the perfect trainer of our very raw material. She painted the scenery, too! And during a visit to her home at Penarwyn, one of many excitements was to watch, with awestruck admiration, her tackling of what seemed to lesser spirits a most daunting job.

Then came the moment when I undertook to write a play—having no more notion than the proverbial babe unborn how to set about it. But again Mrs. Treffry's grasp of the layout and technical possibilities made one feel that after all, with her behind one, anything might be done. *St. George and the Dragon* (1901) was our theme. The embodiment of the villain presented some difficulties until Mrs. Treffry found that Mr. Walter Crane possessed the requisite reptile. Accordingly she enlisted his kindly interest and finally bore off a lovely dragon, in triumph, on top of a four-wheeled cab. The staging was suggested by Burne-Jones' pictures. So realistic was the pathos of the scene in which the princess, having bidden farewell to her maidens, is left alone, bound to her tree, that—on the School night—some of the Junior School children burst into tears! Realism indeed, must have been our strong point. At the dress rehearsal Jessie

N

Willaume, who was understudying St. George for Ethel Belcher, was so appalled by the onslaught of the dragon's immense jaws, that she gave one wild shriek and fled from the stage ! Ethel Belcher herself, on the other hand, determined to be more valiant, thrust at the enemy's head so fiercely with her sword that she put out the electric light which illumined his eye, and was immediately overcome by horror lest she should really have exterminated Rhoda James, who was manipulating the dragon's anatomy !

Then in 1903 we did *Frithiof and Ingeborg*, an adaptation of the fine old Icelandic saga. One remembers Elsie Nicholl's most sympathetic playing of Frithiof, and the lovely heroine that Di Justice made.

Dr. Harding composed the music for the songs and dances of all these early plays : and the incidental music. He taught the singers, trained the orchestra, attended the rehearsals night after night, and was a tower of strength at the performances.

We marvelled at the enthusiasm, skill and devotion to most exacting work that Dr. Harding and Mrs. Treffry together gave. They both said it was their pleasure to give it. That was why it made ours.

2. For the younger parts of the School, as opposed to those in the Upper School who attend the service in Bedford School Chapel, the highlight of the Guild Week-end is the Play, with a capital P. In fact, after nine years, the only thing I can clearly remember of my first year is the production of *Quiet Week-end*. This was a play of the kind of humour that appeals to people of all ages, and even if we, in the Junior School, could not fully understand why all these Old Girls had come back to act a play for us, yet our interest was aroused in the magic word "Guild".

Although we gradually came to realise that other things happened at the biennial meetings, the play remained one of their outstanding features. We learned to expect a most entertaining evening, on which the most frequent comment would be, "It was *just* as good as last time !" We got to recognise the members of the cast, so that when we saw them later at the field they were like old friends instead of part of a crowd of strangers, though the others, too, grew less strange each year. We also discovered hidden talents behind the everyday exteriors of people like Miss Dorothy Madden and Miss Gowen, and that Miss Burnaby would always accomplish the difficult task, for a woman, of playing a man convincingly.

The 1956 performance of *Cranford*, however, is chiefly memorable for the very feminine grace and quiet dignity that she brought to the part of Miss Matty. In a play with only two male parts, which is thus ideally suited to an all-female cast, she was well supported, though never over-shadowed, by the others, particularly by the sympathetic portrayals of the older and younger Mrs. Gaskell by Miss Collier and Miss Thompson respectively, and by the fireworks of Miss Hill in the part of Miss Pole. It would be impossible to say, from the narrow experience of only five Guild meetings, especially when they include a revival of *Undine*, that this was the best play ever produced by the Guild, but it does deserve the highest praise the School can bestow : "It was even better than last time !"

IV. THE GUILD DURING TWO WARS
The living God will see to it that war constantly returns as a dreadful medicine for the human race.—Treitschke.

I have been asked to write a short account of the B.H.S. Guild during the two wars, and while I do not believe that God sends us war, yet war may be a dreadful and necessary medicine and it is as well to examine how we react to it ; and to ask whether we were "a cold, soft, lazy and pleasure-seeking generation". The traditions of the High School were to imbue the pupils with loyalty to all that is best in life, and to further a sense of comradeship.

As general secretary to the Guild in the first war, I should have known more of the Old Girls and their work during this period, but we are a reticent nation, and, unfortunately, there were many devoted workers about whom little is known, indeed, we have records of less than half our members.

The largest number of us took up nursing in all its forms :

we were commandants, sisters in charge, staff nurses, quarter-masters, V.A.D.s, masseuses, ward maids, cooks and almoners. Mrs. Hilda Chibnall was given the Royal Red Cross for her work under fire in Gallipoli. Mrs. Lawrence Dale and Mrs. Hewlett Johnson also received the Royal Red Cross for their work in Africa and Manchester. Miss Evelyn Faulder received the Military Medal for gallantry when an ammunition dump was destroyed by a bomb. Mrs. Beatty was made a C.B.E. for her remarkable work to the Green Cross.

Dr. Maud Forrester Brown did work never before done by women.

There were clerical workers in all the Government offices. Factory workers, who did highly-skilled work for munitions, aeroplanes, tanks and dynamos. There were those who set men free for the services by being chauffeurs, cashiers, farm workers and teachers on the staffs of boys' schools and in the universities.

Many people worked hard for the Y.M.C.A. and canteens, and among these we find Miss Collie and the staff. Endless part-time work of all sorts was done by busy housewives.

In all a wonderful and interesting record.

The second world war found the nation less unprepared. We find folk not only as determined to help, but also more highly skilled, and it has been said that during that war people worked with wonderful serenity and lightness of heart.

There were more doctors, including such grand people as Dr. Maud Forrester Brown, Dr. Joyce Wenham, Dr. Sylvia Gadsden and Dr. Alison Wareham. A large number of the nurses were Q.A.s, there were masseuses, radiographers, speech-therapists, dispensers and V.A.D.s. They were sent to all parts of the world, Malta, Alexandria, India, Syria, Rhodesia, Australia and to the great hospitals in the big towns where they often suffered grievously from bombing.

Many of the Old Girls joined all branches of the forces and some became gunners and pilots. Others yet entered Government offices, worked for the W.V.S. and Y.M.C.A., collected war savings and, perhaps with the greatest self-sacrifice, coped with evacuees.

Mrs. Symonds (M. Askwith) was awarded the M.B.E. for her work with the W.V.S., Lady Hartwell (M. Church) and E. Lancaster for their work as Q.A.s, and Margaret Hurst as a member of the A.T.S.

The High School became a hostess school and shared the building with King's Warren School, Plumstead.

Staff, besides other part-time work, did fire-watching at night, which must have been a terrible strain after a hard day's work. The teachers in the Guild were a most dauntless crowd and the new generation cannot possibly estimate the greatness of their work during the war.

Let me end with a quotation from Swinburne which may explain why such comparatively ordinary folk as we were could do so much :

> "I am in thee to save thee,
> As my soul in thee saith,
> Give thou as I gave thee,
> Thy life-blood and breath."

V. RULE XII: THEN AND NOW

The history of the Guild in the years since its foundation is the history in miniature of the latter part of the women's movement in England.

The opening of our own School in 1882 was a sign of newly-won freedom, although to post-war generations of school-girls the High School appears as one of those established facts which must have existed almost from the beginning of things. We take it all so much for granted : and it certainly requires a mental effort for us to realise how short a time separates our own day and our own order of things from the days of the pioneers of the higher education of women. Was not our own Miss Collie the first pupil of the Cheltenham Ladies' College to take a degree of London University ? And was she not, on that account, called forward and shown to visitors by the great Miss Beale as an example of what a modern girl (and incidentally, no doubt, the ladies' college !) *could* do when once the barriers of prejudice were down and opportunities of learning given to her as well as to her brothers ? But the audacity and originality required even to wish to sit for a university examination would have caused intense and unaffected horror in the breasts of nearly all parents of a generation earlier.

We all remember that Rule XII classes the work which members are likely to report upon under three main headings : teaching, nursing, domestic. It is true that for the sake of comprehensiveness the words "and other" are added, but we may believe that no very great variety was envisaged when the rule was drawn up. In the general secretary's report for 1901—a document that was printed in the first number of the *Guild Leaflet*—we read that "There are apparently several new professions by which women can earn a living and enjoy doing so". Examination reveals these to be poultry farming and professional gardening ! The report of 1903 has this entry : "The most original of this year's reports is written from 'an old oak tea-room' at Glasgow". All honour to this pioneer ; she may have been the first to be surprised at the number of gentlewomen who, a quarter of a century later, hoped (often against hope, it may be feared) to keep by this method the wolf from the door. Two years later we find mention for the first time of physical training, "At what we should like to call, if Miss Stansfeld will let us, our own physical training college". It is on this occasion, too, that we find the first reference to medical training, solely, it appears, from the point of view of missionary work. Soon after this, secretarial work makes its appearance in the reports. In 1907 we find this significant entry : "I have taken up work with the Independent Labour Party and am helping to organise the Birmingham tailoresses with the hope of improving their conditions." The horizon, we can see, is widening : and it will soon be a far cry back to the days when the following report could be sent in : "I am a governess and there is no chance of rising higher. A governess's life is so lonely in many families. The evenings are so long, and a governess has generally no opportunity of making friends. . . . The system is wrong : that is all". Nowadays no woman need take up the work unless her inclination and her abilities lead her to it : our release from that bondage is due to the many pioneers of education for women, not least among them being the founders and early heads of our School.

The story of the early days is told on a previous page : it is for us to trace here the sequel to that story. Yet it hardly needs re-telling. We have only to recall any of the reports that have appeared in the Leaflet during the last ten years to prove how far easier it now is to give a list of what women may *not* do than what they may ! Teachers we still have, home workers and nurses—is it not one of the glories of the Guild that King George V was nursed throughout his dangerous illness by one of its members (M. Purdie) ? We cannot put into words the importance of the work done by those who teach and those who make homes : over sixty per cent. of the Guild's workers, says a recent report, are in one form or another dealing with children. If this does not give a chance of building Jerusalem in England's green and pleasant land, nothing else can. The religious life of the Guild has already been touched upon : we know it is there even though little is said about it. For the rest, we are sugar brokers and actuaries ; actresses and pianists and speakers at festivals of the poetry of living poets ; we are painters and metal workers and map-designers ; we breed dogs, rabbits, hens, pigs, canaries ; we wrestle with market gardens at home, with locusts by the myriad in outposts of the Empire ; we do every kind of medical work ; we are cooks, opticians, bankers, insurance agents, engineers (electrical and other) ; we are experts at winter sports ; we deal in furs and gowns and corsets ; we are authors, playwrights and journalists. And when we have digested this list, we suddenly become aware that we have not even mentioned the army of social workers, salaried and voluntary, who run half the parishes and quite three-quarters of the Guide and Brownie packs of England : nor yet again those who sit upon benches and administer punishment to England's delinquents, or upon town councils and county councils, in order to tar our roads, vaccinate our children, license our dogs and our motor-cars, devastate our beauty-spots, and in general carry on the business that keeps the country from rack and ruin. In fact, almost the only thing that Guild members, so far, do not sit on, or in, is Parliament.

We have surveyed the past and the present : what of the future ? Of one thing we may be sure. The conditions of life are changing beneath our eyes with such rapidity that the events of one year are hardly grasped before the next year sweeps us to an entirely new angle of vision—but whatever changes may come, we need only hold fast to the mottoes of the Guild and of the School to find our feet upon a sure rock from which we cannot be swept away. "Seek high things", counselled our founders ; "Love that which is lovely and of good report". Upon these foundations the Guild has built for sixty-five years a record of steady work and service. If we need encouragement or inspiration let us turn for a moment to those old reports, and let us note the devotion of many of these lives, in surroundings monotonous as well as novel, in quiet corners at home as well as in wide spaces overseas. It is for present and coming generations to see to it that they also build.

A house was building . . . mid the rise and fall
Of golden trowels tinkling in the hands
Of builders gathered wide from all the lands.
Is the house finished ? Nay, come help to build.

———————

During all these years of difficulty and change, the practical administration of a Guild of nearly two thousand members, scattered all over the world, was indeed a heavy and exacting task : and what the Guild feels it owes to Joyce Harding (local secretary), Ruby Prosser (assistant secretary) and Molly Evans (treasurer) for years of wonderful help, can never be expressed in words, but we do hope they realise our affection and gratitude.

CHAPTER XVI

1957

THIS IS a story which can never be complete. Many who read it will be reminded of other people and other events unrecorded, or they may wish to alter the emphasis here and there, for the School means something different to each one of us, and each one of us guards jealously her own vision of it; but however varied the pattern in the personal outlook may be, there is a golden thread of continuity running through the history which all would acknowledge. Not many schools can look backward with such certainty and affection to the past. One or two present Guild members entered the School in Mrs. McDowall's time; more can remember Miss Belcher as head mistress and her nieces keep in close touch with us; one of Miss Collie's pupils early in the century was Kate Westaway, who inherited the traditions begun in the first twenty years; and when Miss Tanner resigned her headship here in order to move to Roedean, Miss Westaway returned as head mistress and to begin twenty-five years of magnificent work; in her retirement she continues it with undiminished zest as vice-president of the Guild, editor of the *Guild Leaflet* (and a prolific correspondent with its members, near and far), and as a Governor of the Harpur Trust.

The continuity is provided, too, by the staff, some of whom can remember the years before our fiftieth birthday. We have always been happy in the choice of mistresses, some making a long stay with us and providing a steady example of wisdom and experience, while the fresh outlook and ideas of newcomers have enriched and broadened our work. By the staff our tradition of scholarship is maintained, and our purpose to prepare girls to be of service to their generation in many and varied ways. We are doing our share in meeting the present demand for scientists and mathematicians; there are now girls in the School who hope to do aeronautical research or to become nuclear physicists ; nursing, teaching, medicine and its ancillary services, political work, the arts, social service, journalism and good home-making are represented among the ambitions of our girls as well as in the records of Guild members. But we believe that it is not the career which is of the first importance ; what matters is the kind of person who undertakes it and her understanding of those fundamental values which we try to teach.

The School is fortunate in its Governors. Some, with knowledge of the financial world and management of property have restored the Holborn estate after its war-time losses, and the income from the endowment is steadily increasing. Let us hope that in the years to come, whatever political and economic developments there may be, the deliberations of the Trust will continue to be free from political bias and for the continuing good of the schools.

Independence has, of course, brought its financial problems, but in spite of the fact that fees have now become an important item in the family budget, sufficient parents believe that what we have to offer is worth while for the School to be full and for there to be a constant demand for places ; and how delightful and heartening it is to have the waiting list increased by the entries of School grandchildren or great-grandchildren. Age last birthday ? "One day" or "one month".

Through the years we have lost many things—open fireplaces, for instance, and the welcome diversion of France's entry into a classroom with more coal for the fire, the "garlands" in the hall, limited afternoon school, "trotters", the bag-men, who carried the boarders' and sometimes the mistresses' books on their little hand-carts to and from School, "sandwiching" for examinations in the hall—all these belonged to their time and have no place in ours. And what have we gained ? The advantages of modern developments on the material plane, with a centralised heating system controlled with great competence by William ; creature comforts which fifty years ago would have been thought pampering in the extreme ; school dinners in comparatively spacious surroundings instead of in a dark huddle under the big gallery—and so we might continue. But we do not live on the material plane alone, and we can count with sober pride the store of treasured associations which year by year increases. How rich they must have felt in 1882, rich in promise and hope, rich in people who were ready to cherish and serve this new school! How much richer are we with our store of traditions and memories!

Here we stand at the gateway leading to the last twenty-five years of our first century. As we look back we can see the faith, the purpose and the ideals which have brought us to this point in our story. As we look forward we must resolve not only to keep faith with the past but to live courageously in our own time, to hold fast to the things of enduring worth, to prize the traditions which we have inherited and to hand them on vital and shining, so that in 1982 our successors may feel the same gratitude and joy that we express on completing our seventy-fifth year.

EPILOGUE

IN NOVEMBER, 1956, Mrs. Macnamara (Frances Craig), who entered the School in May, 1882, wrote from New Zealand:

"I remember that first day of the School, when I entered at the age of nine. I entered by the door (on the prison side of the school—the High School) with a big porch. I was told to go to the cloakroom, up stone steps, and take off my coat and hat, and change my shoes—in silence. That rule was to be obeyed always after passing through the swing door of the porch. Then I had to go to the First Form room, where other little girls were sitting at their desks, with Miss Lily Roberts on the platform facing them. Then we went down to prayers in the (now) Sixth Form room—there were only forty of us, so the hall was too large (and so dark with brown paint).

"Mrs. McDowall's personality was so quiet and so gentle that it took away all fear from a child's mind. She read that lesson :

'Whatsoever things are true . . .'

which through all the years has influenced the School. Many must still look back and feel that these words have influenced their outlook and work, even though the years have taken them far across the world.

"We covered our gymn. dresses with a long skirt, very full, which we took off in the gymnasium and put on again before we left. The gymnasium was in the present library, and there was a sergeant to teach us to struggle with clubs and staves and a round bar.

"After Mrs. McDowall died, Miss Belcher was our head mistress. She had a wonderful outlook, allowing us to play hockey on the gravel playground *in silence*, and to put up our own goal posts—we must not give any worker any trouble.

"The knowledge of flowers and trees, the world of nature, botany walks out of school hours, gave me infinite pleasure, both then and in my world travels of later years.

"Miss Belcher's words of wisdom have lived through the long years. Only the other day, when war was again threatened,

THE SCHOOL

I was in the first Protestant Church in New Zealand, and in my mind's memory I heard her voice singing :

O God, our help in ages past,
Our hope for years to come . . ."

In that same month of November, 1956, Katherine Benson-Hall, who had entered the School (Form I) in September, and whose mother, Elizabeth Bellwood, had entered it in 1933, wrote :

"I remember the first day I was at School, I was very excited. Mummy told me about it, and she had been at the School. I went for a test first. The test was called an exam. At the exam. we did writing and arithmetic. I like the lessons. The first day I was at School Mummy came to prayers. One morning Miss Watkins came into our form room. I do quite a lot of homework. The first day we went into the gymnasium I did not know what to do, and when we were told to climb the wall-bars I scrambled up the bars but I did get down again."

Susan Jefferies, who entered Form I at the same time, wrote :

"My Mother came to the Bedford High School before I did, and of course I came to Harvest Sales, so it did not seem so big to me as to some of the others. When I came to the exam. we had a piece of paper with some sums on it. I think there were about twenty sums altogether. Then we went to Miss Fisher for her to hear our reading. It was not till later that I heard I had passed. I was thankful. My Mother was called Peggy Burton, and as she had been here before she knew that we had a fancy-dress competition and a concert. I wear a mauve tie."

There is something about a school . . .

An additional chapter in the history of the School, contributed by members of the staff who considered the book would be incomplete without it, and edited by Miss Pearl Hackett

EVERYBODY will remember Miss Westaway's brilliant gifts as a raconteur. Sometimes her stories were to illustrate a point (and they always did it superbly) ; sometimes they were told for their sheer fun, revealing her keen sense of humour, of the incongruous and the absurd. Sometimes they were stories "with a moral", and one of these told how, after her appointment as head mistress but before she had taken office, she had overheard in a railway carriage the question : "I wonder what sort of a head that Kate Westaway's going to be ?" Now, thirty-two years later, we are in the fortunate position of knowing the answer, though almost from the beginning that answer was quite clear. At her very first staff meeting, in September, 1924, she impressed every-one deeply by her speed and efficiency in dealing with the business, and when it was over someone said : "I think we have got a very clever young head mistress." The next day at prayers, her dignity and clear voice again made an impression, and it was surely a good omen for a new régime that a small black cat chose that morning to come in at the south door and walk up the hall. (It was nursed by one of the staff and slept peacefully until roused by the loud applause at the end of the speech that followed prayers.) Miss Westaway used to tell how dull and uneventful that first day was, how Miss Chomley dealt with all the letters, Miss Lee with all School affairs, while she sat alone and un-occupied in her room, waiting in vain for something to happen or for someone to come and see her. How different from later days when one wondered how so much activity could possibly be packed into one human day !

For one of her most marked characteristics was the very real interest she took in every single aspect of School life. From the platform she seemed to see into every corner of the hall ; from her office she seemed to know what was going on in every part of the School; if she was standing outside her door, or by Room 5, or at the milk-room corner, you knew long before you arrived that she was there. She would often appear at form-room doors, so that we would see our class suddenly straighten, inexplicably until we saw Miss Westaway's interested face peering through the glass panes. Sometimes she came into lessons, but only after a preliminary note of warning, and she would take part in them so that the ordeal turned out to be no ordeal at all and everybody enjoyed having such an intelligent "pupil" in the class. We never really solved the problem of whether she liked her "class-work" to be corrected, but she certainly liked to ask and be asked questions, and to read aloud if the lesson happened to be French or German, and there was nearly always an apt story or a shrewd comment as she left. She might afterwards query the effectiveness of a newcomer's methods of teaching or keeping order, but she would never authoritatively insist on a change and this freedom was very sincerely appreciated. Once at a cookery lesson she was asked if she would like to toss a pancake, which she did with great aplomb, only afterwards confessing how frightened she had been, especially as she was taking visitors round at the time. In the science block she would be fascinated by all that went on, for she retained in some ways a child's sense of wonder. She would go triumphantly away from a Sixth Form lesson with some biological trophy to be shown off for days to all her visitors. The Preparatory School loved her visits, and there would be groans of disappointment if a message came to say she could not come to read their marks. On one such occasion the children made a book of stories and pictures of rabbits and sent it to her. The next day they received these lines :

Thank you, thank you, dear Form One,
For the lovely book you've done.
I have read it through and through,
Thinking all the time of you,
Till it's quite become a habit
To sit and think about a rabbit.

Later she wrote a song about rabbits for which Dr. Harding

composed some music, and the Juniors sang it at their concert.

She was so sincerely interested in people that she knew instinctively how to hold their attention, one of the marks of a great teacher. Her lessons must have been wonderful, and the one disadvantage of being on her staff was that we were not in a position to attend them. Her services to the classics department were invaluable, for she was a great classical scholar and believed utterly in the value of classical studies. "Everyone who learns Greek", she wrote in *Unwillingly to School*, "contributes, to my mind, to a happier world", and she delighted in teaching it. For years she taught VB Roman history, and how alive and exciting she must have made it! On every possible occasion she would express her conviction that teaching of all kinds is the most wonderful job in the world, once in a symposium on careers when she tried to explain how spiritually satisfying it can be, and that it is the soul as well as the mind that one tries to reach and train. She once addressed the Parents' Association on "Religious Education" (the subject was her own choice), when she expressed her own views simply but forcibly— the importance of straight thinking, of example, of basing all relationships on one's relation to God. After the discussion she summed up by stressing that in all up-bringing and in all education "it is not what you teach that matters but what you are. That is an overwhelming thought which ought to send you to your knees every day of your lives". Her concern for the children's spiritual welfare was always evident, too, in the talks she would give the School in Lent, and in her Confirmation classes. Another career she considered of great worth was nursing, and she was always proud of the large number of nurses that the School had produced. Frequently they were carefully listed in the *Aquila*, and for many years, right up to her last term, there was a nurses' tea party in London or at School, where she would deliver all kinds of School news, and news of nurses who could not be there. Spring flowers used to be picked by the Preparatory School and sent up specially for "Miss Westaway's nurses" to take back to their hospitals.

During the war, Old Girls found themselves doing all kinds of strange and unexpected jobs, and travelled or were interned in very unfamiliar territory. Miss Westaway loved all their letters, and kept a war-time notebook, which she published each term in the *Aquila*. At first it included "Hospitals", "The Services", "Overseas"; later "Husbands, Sons and Brothers", "Home Again", "Bombed Out", and much of the information went into all that was stored in her phenomenal memory. Later it developed into "Old Girls in New Times", where all aspects of their war-work were described. As well as being a record of which any school can be proud, it has the wider value of being a comprehensive picture of what women can do, and do cheerfully and well, at times of crisis. It was followed by an account of all the Old Girls who taught in a great variety of types of schools and conditions. But one did not have to do something outstanding or strange to be remembered by Miss Westaway. She never thought of the School as a collection of children, but as a number of individuals, and she knew an unbelievable amount about every single one. She was deeply interested in each child's welfare, and for them all she battled unceasingly for new buildings, and eventually for "independence", though that was more a question of a courageous decision, made, despite much criticism, because she was convinced of the value of the independent schools and the contribution they could make to the life of the nation, and that a school should be free to experiment (or not to experiment). She felt strongly that the development of the new State system of 1944 would make this more necessary than ever, and many people will remember how in the Great Hall at Bedford School the two heads addressed a joint meeting of parents, after the Governors had decided to apply for independence. She always saw all sides of a question at issue, and her statesmanlike approach to any problem led one to have complete trust in the wisdom of any decision she finally made. During the war a decision might be made quickly, but never hastily, and all who were on the staff in those anxious years felt that she permeated stability and serenity. "At the outbreak of war", writes one of them, "she sat as a rock amidst the storm, a symbol of permanence. There she was fire-watching; in retrospect I see her permanently in a siren-suit with a leopard-skin cape (or was it a coat?) draped over her shoulders, sitting face to the wall at a staff room table, playing bagatelle to herself, intent on beating her own record. I was grateful for her detachment. I remember the first staff meeting after the declaration of war; shelters, safe places, air-raid warnings and first aid were being discussed, everyone was feeling the imminence of disaster, and survival did not seem likely, but she sat like a rock and reminded us that there would be a 'remnant', that we might be that 'remnant' and must be ready to carry on. Her courage was then, and has since been, an inspiration to me." Her addresses to the Guild at that time were heartening and inspiriting, and another member of the staff recalls how when our fortunes were at the lowest ebb she ended her address at prayers one morning by quietly reminding the School that "miracles do still happen".

Miss Westaway was able to rise to any occasion and this showed particularly in her platform manner, adapted so skilfully to all the different kinds of people she addressed. The secret must have been a quick intuitive skill in assessing an audience, even if it consisted entirely of strangers, even of another nationality, and of setting up immediate contact with them. If it was the Preparatory School and "early to bed" was the theme, there was the story of the cows she kept seeing in Austria. "Nobody tells them but they know when it's bed-time—*and they go*." If it was the whole School and there was to be an onslaught against abbreviations, there was the apocryphal story of the child who had been to see her: "I'm worried about my maths., Miss Westaway. I'm in div. four and I'll never get cert. I can do Eng. lit. and Eng. lang. all right, but I get awful marks for maths. prep. and I've had three D.T.s already". More followed, unfortunately unrecorded, but "Bye, bye!" said the "child" on leaving, probably with both hands firmly in both pockets. By mimicking the children's school and roadway manners, or by pointing out that steps had been scientifically measured so that they were just the right height to be mounted *one* at a time, she would get her particular meaning across effectively and unforgettably, and entertained us too. "If you saw yourselves from the back, you'd *never* go upstairs two at a time again!" was the parting shot that morning.

Speech days were always most memorable and were always
looked forward to, because we knew beforehand that she would
depart absolutely from the usual head mistress's account of School
activities, and that her speech would be brilliant. Even so,
somewhere in it she would usually manage to plead for early
bed-time and tidy hats ". . . and I *do* wish you'd sew up their
blazer pockets !" At any function where she was presiding
or introducing a speaker one felt absolutely safe, knowing that
she could handle any situation capably. She inspired confidence, even though she may not always have felt it herself.
She used to tell of a nightmare, in which, as she walked into the
hall for prayers, everyone got up and walked out ! She could
have dreamed of nothing more improbable, for not only was there
the enjoyment of the actual ceremony, but she so often had something of interest to say to the School, always expressed in a unique
and compelling way. There was the "question and answer"
technique to ensure that notices had been assimilated, and once
the School rules, tedious to hear term after term, were repeated
in chorus first from beginning to end and then from the end to
the beginning. There were, too, the short verbal biographies
of Old Girls and former staff, by which she made the School's
past live so vividly for the present generation, and created a
sense of tradition and continuity, so that the children felt they
knew "Hi" and "Ho", and that it was incumbent on them to
live up to the ideals of people like Miss Hiatt and Miss Holmes
and Miss Collie, and treasure the qualities that such people had
admired in the School's early days.

Always Miss Westaway insisted on high standards of behaviour
as well as of work : "If the pavement is full, the place for High
School girls is in the gutter"; and just after independence had
been achieved in 1946, "Don't go rushing across the traffic
lights so that people say '*That*'s what they mean by being independent !'" Punctuality was a favourite theme, and the children
were always told that to be too early was as unpunctual as to be
too late. On introducing O'Maley dinners (reluctantly, because
she disliked the idea of children's homes being places where
they just had "bed and breakfast"), she wanted a "high table"
and civilised conversation. The "high table" was never achieved,

though whenever she came to the meal there was a Latin grace, even for the IIIAs, who used to be very much impressed.

The Preparatory School, too, must have been much impressed when she once gave them a lecture on "Railways", an illustration of her versatility. The children had a firm belief that "Miss Westaway could talk about *anything*!" She would often give the whole School a lantern lecture on the first, otherwise un-occupied, Thursday afternoon of the spring term, usually on a classical subject : Horace ; daily life in ancient Rome ; Greek games. A regular event was her archæological competition, set each summer and covering in turn such subjects as crypts, gargoyles, villages, castles, old kitchens, bench ends, epitaphs, and she would spend many hours judging the sometimes very elaborate and detailed entries. There would be a tea party for all who had entered, or an outing, at her expense, to Cambridge, St. Albans, Peterborough or Ely, and in this way she would transmit her own scholarly enjoyment of such things to those whose interest was just beginning to grow. Nobody knows better what Miss Westaway's stimulating presence could add to an expedition than those who were with her in Rome in April, 1934. "Those of us who were privileged to be of the party will never forget those wonderful days. How lucky we were to have her with us ! She seemed to make the very stones of the Forum teem with the life of ancient Rome, and she never tired of satisfying the curiosity of the less initiated, whether we were gazing at the mosaics on the floor of the baths at Ostia, standing in Cicero's house, climbing up the Appian Way to the little theatre at Tusculum, or even searching for the Cloaca Maxima ! What fun we had—and how untiring was Miss Westaway in her efforts to make this visit to the Eternal City a memorable one for us all !"

She was indefatigable in everything, largely because of the enormous zest she brought to all she did, whether it was playing golf for the staff in matches with the Guild, or driving "Scatter-cash" up to John O'Groats and the Châteaux country and Holland, or playing the double bass in the orchestra for the Guild play, or going fishing, or taking part in the "Village Choir", or the highly amusing duet with Miss C. B. Thomson which opened the performance at the 1942 Jubilee celebrations, or serving soup and sandwiches in the staff room to the exhausted cast of *The Knight of the Burning Pestle*, wearing a gay little embroidered apron brought back from one of her trips abroad. On this, and on more formal occasions, she was always a delightful hostess and an equally delightful guest. She used to plan ingenious whist drives for new staff, in which each game would be played according to a different set of rules ; once it was "Victory Whist" when one hand was played "blind" because the smoke of the bonfires had got into our eyes, and all the other hands would fit appropriately into the story ! The *Aquila* was often enlivened by photographs she had taken, photography being a hobby in which she excels. Sometimes, too, there would be an article obviously from her pen, one in particular, "Those Were the Motor-Cars", a brief history of staff cars and an account of mystery motoring parties which were, in the days of lighter traffic, tremendous fun. Miss Westaway wrote her articles in a vigorous, racy style, and with evident enjoyment, as she had many years before when, as a child in IVc, she had produced a form magazine *The Fly-by-Nights*. (It ran for only one number, and contained the first and only instalment of a hair-raising serial in which the School was flooded and Miss Collie and the staff floated about on blackboards, while the girls rowed round on the tops of their desks !)

Outside the School she worked untiringly. For over twenty years she was a member of the Borough Education Committee, and was a tower of strength to the heads of other local schools in many struggles against officialdom. She founded the Bedford branch of the Soroptimists, believing firmly in its ideals and its importance as a means of bringing together women of all nationalities. It flourished, as most things did under Miss Westaway ; so did the Classical Association which she revived after the war with a splendid inaugural meeting addressed most unforgettably by the Provost of King's, Sir John Sheppard. For several years she helped regularly each Sunday in the canteen for servicemen at the Corn Exchange. With unflagging energy she cut mountains of sandwiches, and all the helpers would be cheered on by her anecdotes and gaiety. She organised wonderful parties for evacuees. The first one was held at the Dujon; many parents came from London for the afternoon and she arranged that each family had its own table for tea. She was in great demand as a speaker by countless women's groups and organisations in Bedford and the surrounding villages, where members would flock to a meeting that she was to address. She was always generously ready to give her time to them, and always knew the right kind of talk for their needs. She would always be delighted to go and open a church bazaar or fête, and would afterwards go round the stalls with her shopping basket in a friendly and business-like way. (Those who were at the 1952 Harvest Sale will know how ingenious her openings could be, for at that she had a tale of how the previous day, returning from Germany and half asleep after travelling all night, she had been asked at the Customs if she had anything to declare. "Yes," she had muttered sleepily, "a Harvest Sale open at Bedford". Very crossly the official had snapped, "Any wines or spirits?" "No, but there'll be lemonade for the children, and coffee in the Country room, and *all sorts* of things on the stalls..." at which she had been hustled through the barrier by the exasperated official who had no more patience. She told the story so convincingly and amusingly that several people said, "Do you think it was true?", and it was one of the most successful openings we had ever had.) For many years she was on the executive of the Head Mistresses' Association, and for a while their representative on the Burnham Committee. She spent many days examining the teaching ability of sister tutors, and was on the Joint Standing Committee of Head Mistresses and Hospital Matrons. By bringing back to us interesting news of these various meetings and of her own experiences, she kept us in touch with educational developments, and of course, there were many entertaining stories to add to her inexhaustible supply.

It was Lady Jaqueta, at the laying of the foundation stone of the science block, who said that Miss Westaway may well be known to the future as the "building head mistress". Not only did she see through the building of the science block and the Susan Collie Wing, but when the new gymnasium was built she shouldered the responsibility of raising enough money to convert the old one into the present library. Nothing was ever "too much trouble", and during the complicated difficulties of erecting the gymnasium, which involved buying up houses in Adelaide Square, she went all the way to Ireland to see the old lady who owned Nos. 38 and 40. Her last acquisition, in 1948, was 3 The Crescent, which became known as O'Maley House, and is used for the cooking and consuming of hot dinners. Equipping this house just at that time was a herculean task, but with parents' co-operation it was managed, and she was so pleased about it all that we held her farewell dinner in its biggest room. This gave the dinner a certain informality and homeliness which was appropriate.

All Miss Westaway's staff knew that they were considered at every turn and at many different levels. "I expect", writes one, "that the nicest things about her are private, the many thoughtful kindnesses she did, often quite unlooked-for and unexpected, but bringing with them a sense of permanence and stability, and the enduring quality of friendship". It was she who introduced "sabbatical terms", and there was never any difficulty about time off for urgent personal affairs. Once when the date of the end of term was altered, and one of the staff remarked that now she could be at her sister's wedding, Miss Westaway said with real surprise : "But surely you would have asked ? We *always* have time off for weddings !" She had great faith in all her staff and would delegate to them, with complete confidence, much responsibility. This was sometimes a difficulty, but the fact that it did happen made a tremendous difference to people in their first post, for one never felt "on trial". They all knew, too, that she would at any time be ready to discuss any problem. No formal appointment had to be made ; whenever her door was open she was there to see anybody about anything, and you knew that if it mattered to you it would matter to her. She would almost certainly have a completely fresh and unexpected way of looking at the problem, and would quickly see the way to solve it. She saw things from the staff's point of view, never forgetting her own early teaching years ; she discussed with us all kinds of plans and problems, heard our views and was some-times guided by them (as in the abolishing of staff hats !), though sometimes it was a case of our *thinking* we had made the decision which had in fact been made before ever the meeting began. It can be no easy task to see things from the point of view of children, staff *and* parents, nor to follow three eminent head mistresses, but with single-minded vision, courage, common sense, kindness, real humility of spirit, and great administrative ability, she proved a worthy successor, inspiring at least twelve staff, at different times, to go off and become head mistresses too ; they could have had no better training than at her hands. She never ceased to consider the staff's comfort and happiness, and she liked to plan surprises for their cheer and entertainment. At the beginning of the 1932 Jubilee celebrations, a short staff meeting was announced, with no agenda other than "to hear a few words from Mrs. Harold Howard". This turned out to be a great surprise, the presentation of a beautiful gold and enamel Jubilee brooch to everyone on behalf of the Governors, but it had, of course, been her idea.

At the end of July, 1948, another short staff meeting was called, also to announce a surprise, but this time a very sad one. When she told us that she had decided to retire the following Easter there was a hush of complete horror. To most people it came as a real shock, and everybody found it quite impossible to visualise the School without her. Some years before, there had been deep consternation when she was invited to be head mistress of a very famous school ; although they had wanted her badly and used all kinds of clever persuasion, she had eventually decided to stay in Bedford and the staff had given her a dinner at the Swan to rejoice and to thank her. But the decision of 1948 was quite final, in spite of a petition signed by all of us, and although nobody could grudge her the leisure and release that retirement would bring, it was a sad blow to us all, whether we had known her for many years or only a few terms.

Fortunately Miss Westaway comes frequently to Bedford, for two years ago she was appointed staff representative on the Harpur Trust ; one always knew that she was ready to back up the staff on every occasion, and no happier choice could possibly have been made. It is not surprising to hear that her life in Yorkshire is still full of activity, carried out with as much vigour and enthusiasm as ever, whether it is a matter of blowing up eight dozen balloons for coronation decorations, taking the W.I. for a two-day trip to London, or filling and addressing five hundred envelopes which is only a fraction of the staggering amount of work she did for the 1955 election campaign in Carlton. In fact, Miss Westaway's varied occupations in the village prove what we have always known, that she has boundless versatility and energy and the gift of enjoying every minute of life, whatever it brings. ("We *did* enjoy it !" is a phrase one instinctively connects with her.) During the post-war years she has been several times to Germany and to Austria, to take part in courses sponsored by the British Council and the Foreign Office, and intended to promote friendship between teachers of different countries. In *Cloudy Summits* she tells of some of her experiences there, amongst German and Austrian teachers, "who, after such an incredibly hard time, are being so heroic and so faithful in what all teachers know to be the finest work of all". It is a book that gives a clear idea of their many, sometimes tragic, problems, but it is spiced with humour and delightful incidents. Knowing Miss Westaway, we can well imagine her holding the children of Essen enthralled with the "Dick Whittington" story of William Harpur.

What a very understanding person they must find her, for everyone talks of her human qualities, though "superhuman" would perhaps be the more appropriate word when one thinks of all she did and still does. It is difficult to know how she managed to achieve so much and yet never seem rushed or flustered ; it must have been partly the gift she has for distinguishing between the essential and the non-essential, so that no time gets wasted, and the ability she has to plan her time and *keep to the plan*, which is where so many of us fail. But when all is said, it is for her humanity and kindness that she is remembered gratefully by the many staff who learned so much from, and owe so much to, a remarkable woman and a great head mistress.

STAFF

Exclusive of those who were on the staff for less than a year

	Appointed	Left
Mrs. McDowall	Feb. 1882	d. Oct. 1882
Head mistress		
Miss Carter	1882	Dec. 1882
Acting head mistress, Oct.-Dec., 1882		
Miss M. E. Roberts	1882	1894
Miss Kenny	1882	1883
Madame Valero	1882	1885
Miss Harcourt (Frau Dörr)	1882	1885
Mr. Bond Andrews	1882	1889
Mr. Diemer	1882	1909
Mr. Ford	1882	1890
Miss Cooper	1882	1886
Sergeant Campbell	1882	1887
Mr. Denyer	1882	1893
Miss M. Belcher	1883	d.1898
Head mistress		
Miss L. Thomas	1883	1886
Mademoiselle Truchet (Madame Pondepeyre)	1883	1904
Miss van Diest	1883	1886
Miss Eveleigh	1883	1884
Miss Baker (Mrs. John Lewis)	1883	1884
Miss Hely (Mrs. Stanley)	1883	1885
Miss Hiatt	1883	1913
Fräulein Nolden	1883	1888
Miss Craig	1884	1887
Miss A. M. Robbins	1884	1922
Miss A. Irvine (Mrs. Gordon)	1884	1887
Miss Birch	1884	1886
Miss Emerson	1884	1890
Miss Burgess	1884	1901
Miss Clements	1884	1886
Mademoiselle Lutz	1885	1923
Miss Richardson	1885	1889
Miss Findlay	1885	1886
Miss Muriel (Mrs. Hole)	1885	1891
Miss Collie	1885	1919
Head mistress from 1899		

	Appointed	*Left*
Miss Taylor	1885	1887
Miss Poole (Mrs. J. de C. Treffry, C.B.E.)	1886	1899
Miss E. Roberts	1886	1920
Miss Turing	1886	1920
Miss Brown (Mrs. Herman)	1886	1887
Madame de Nolhac	1886	1896
Miss Holmes	1886	1913
Second mistress from 1909		
Miss L. J. Irvine	1886	1911
Miss Michel	1886	1887
Miss Stuart Snell	1886	1898
Miss White	1886	1893
Miss Diack (Mrs. Wattie)	1887	1899
Miss Trentham	1887	1916
Miss Baynes (Mrs. Mortimer Wheeler)	1887	1888
Miss Gardner	1887	1902
Miss Stansfeld	1887	1918
Miss Dymond	1887	1888
Miss Slater	1888	1889
Miss Pleydell Bouverie	1888	1889
Mademoiselle Thirion	1888	1896
Miss Morant	1888	1890
Miss M. Craig (Mrs. Wragge)	1888	1889
Miss Arblaster	1888	1923
Miss Lloyd	1888	1892
Dr. Harding	1888	d.1930
Miss Davey	1888	d.1911
Miss Janson	1889	1903
Miss Lee	1889	1929
Second mistress from 1913		
Miss Jackson (Mrs. Edwards)	1889	1896
Fräulein Lippert	1889	1891
Miss Henley	1889	1901
Miss Edith Henley	1889	1900
Miss Shekelton	1889	1894
Miss Hibbert Ware	1889	1896
Madame Archambault	1890	1920
Miss Hartley	1890	1918
Miss Plow-Smith	1890	1926
Miss Robertson	1890	1893
Fräulein Zeise	1891	1894
Fräulein Bünde	1891	1900
Mademoiselle de Nolhac	1891	1920
Mr. Nightingale	1891	1928
Miss Pocock	1891	1901

	Appointed	*Left*
Miss Spackman	1892	1913
Miss L. Matson	1892	1922
Miss Hutchinson (Mrs. Elliot)	1892	1894
Miss Rickard (Mrs. Goldsmith)	1892	1912
Miss Heppel (Mrs. Purdon)	1893	1900
Miss Manning	1893	1926
Miss Scott	1893	1909
Second mistress from 1899		
Miss Windsor	1893	1925
Herr Woltmann	1893	1914
Miss Ebbutt	1894	1902
Miss Luard	1894	1895
Miss Poynder	1894	1899
Miss Footman	1894	1895
Miss Duigan (Mrs. Wallace)	1895	1905
Miss Hart-Smith (Mrs. Parsons)	1895	1904
Miss Slator (Mrs. Nangle)	1895	1900
Miss Oldrey	1896	1899
Miss Spencer	1896	1897
Miss Stone	1896	1919
Miss Felkin	1897	1904
Mademoiselle Bordes	1897	1915
Miss Taylor	1897	1899
Miss Jeffries Davis	1898	1904
Miss Allen	1898	1899
Miss Morland (Mrs. Ransome)	1898	1899
Miss Sander	1899	1903
Miss E. M. Robbins	1899	1930
Miss Lea	1899	1901
Miss Rogers	1899	1902
Miss Moon	1900	1922
Miss Hawson	1900	1903
Mr. Werg	1900	1904
Miss G. Edwards	1900	1909
Miss Forbes	1900	1935
Mr. Hamson	1900	1929
Miss McDougall	1900	1902
Fräulein Meyer	1900	1908
Miss Molyneux	1900	1909
Miss Weedon (Mrs. Owen)	1900	1911
Miss E. M. Belcher	1901	1911
Miss Chaldecott (Mrs. Everett)	1901	1906
Miss Macirone	1901	1903
Miss Justice (Mrs. Wells)	1901	1906
Miss Paul	1902	1906

	Appointed	Left
Miss Reeve	1902	1904
Miss Wedderburn	1902	1905
Miss Fuller (Mrs. Mann)	1903	1911
Miss Hart	1903	1911
Miss Wood	1903	1905
Fräulein Stephan	1904	1907
Miss Chomley	1904	1936
Miss Evans	1904	1910
Miss Corbett	1904	1905
Miss Faulkner	1904	1913
Miss Leach	1904	1908
Miss Leeson	1904	1909
Miss F. M. Pocock	1904	1907
Miss Bowman (Mrs. Bradford)	1905	1914
Miss Deerr	1905	1911
Miss Edghill	1906	1913
Miss Finlay	1907	1912
Miss Jams	1907	1910
Miss Beverley	1908	1910
Fräulein Dirlinger	1909	1914
Miss Chambers	1909	1917
Miss Waddell	1909	1913
Miss M. Tilney	1910	1916
Miss French (Mrs. Savage)	1910	1912
Miss Furze (Mrs. Buzzard)	1910	1912
Miss Burne	1911	1920
Miss Willett	1911	1928
Miss Maclagan	1911	1912
Miss E. Nicholls	1911	1924
Miss E. Tilney	1911	1913
Miss Wilkinson	1911	1915
Miss Cox (Mrs. Crawfurd)	1912	1913
Miss Lock	1912	1919
Miss Batchellor	1912	1915
Miss Evans	1912	1920
Miss Counsell	1912	1913
Miss N. Neild	1912	1914
Miss Brockway	1913	1919
Miss Cracknell	1913	1946
Second mistress 1929		
Miss Holloway	1913	1915
Miss M. E. Thomson	1914	1940
Miss Campbell Taylor	1914	1915
Miss Dawes (Signora de Lucia)	1914	1915
Miss Simpson	1914	1915

	Appointed	*Left*
Miss Letreille	1915	1916
Miss Lockyer	1915	1940
Miss A. Neild	1915	1920
Miss Pearce	1915	1916
Miss M. Millburn	1915	1926
Miss Ellison	1916	1918
Miss Brown	1916	1919
Miss Drought	1916	1920
Miss B. M. Taylor	1916	1919
Miss Maybrook	1917	1918
Miss Sandys (Mrs. Leys)	1917	1920
Miss Askwith	1918	1946
Miss Colwill	1918	1932
Miss Hadley	1918	1931
Miss King (Mrs. Babbs)	1918	1923
Miss J. Harding	1918	—
Miss Dandridge	1919	1929
Miss Arden	1919	d.1940
Miss Campbell (Mrs. Osborn)	1919	1933
Miss E. M. Thomas	1919	1923
Miss TANNER	1920	1924
Head mistress		
Miss Connor (Mrs. Hassell)	1920	1932
Miss Davis	1920	1926
Miss Glen (Mrs. Stern)	1920	1922
Miss N. Harding	1920	—
Miss Hatch (Mrs. Anger)	1920	1927
Miss Hudson (Mrs. Owen)	1920	1924
Miss Kirkham	1920	1924
Miss Lloyd	1920	1925
Miss M. E. F. Madden	1920	1956
Miss D. I. Madden	1920	1955
Monsieur André Mangeot	1920	1932
Miss R. Matson	1920	1927
Miss Nayler	1920	1925
Miss Osborne	1920	1947
Miss Price	1920	1929
Miss Raley	1920	1952
Miss A. D. L. Wilson	1920	1946
Miss Low	1921	1922
Miss Maris	1921	1923
Miss Nicholson (Mrs. Jackson)	1921	1924
Miss Pearce	1921	1922
Mrs. van Dieren	1921	1922
Miss Whitehead	1921	1922

	Appointed	*Left*
Miss B. J. Fisher (Mrs. Colson)	1922	1930
Mrs. Piper	1922	1923
Miss L. R. Jones	1922	1947
Miss G. Read	1922	1933
Miss C. B. Thomson	1922	d.1941
Miss Collier	1923	1956
Mlle Duclos (Mme Gervois)	1923	1925
Miss James	1923	1924
Miss Shepherd	1923	1924
Miss WESTAWAY	1924	1949
Head mistress		
Miss Duncan	1924	1926
Miss van Raalte	1924	1924
Miss Isaac	1924	1925
Miss Rogers	1924	d.1936
Miss Beck	1924	1937
Miss S. G. Fisher	1924	—
Mrs. Mackenzie	1924	1926
Miss Norman	1924	—
Miss Tydeman	1924	1928
Miss Hippisley Barnes	1925	1932
Mlle Combe	1925	1936
Miss Moseley	1925	1944
Miss Pike (Mrs. Hutchins)	1925	1930
Miss Snelgrove	1925	1930
Miss Wills (Mrs. Erlebach)	1925	1928
Miss Wyatt (Mrs. Garry Hogg)	1925	1927
Miss Gowen	1926	1956
Miss Kelly	1926	1929
Miss Leslie	1926	1928
Miss Mandville	1926	1937
Miss Martin	1926	—
Miss Batley	1927	—
Second mistress, 1947		
Miss Davies (Mrs. London)	1927	1938
Miss Johnson	1927	1931
Miss H. S. Millburn	1927	1950
Miss Newlands	1927	1928
Miss Adams	1928	1929
Miss Blakeley	1928	1929
Miss H. M. Brown	1928	1946
Miss Chadwick	1928	1939
Second mistress		
Miss Macdonald	1928	1933
Miss Sale (Mrs. Parbury)	1928	1950

	Appointed	*Left*
Miss Watkins	1928	1937
Head mistress, 1949		
Mrs. Bailey	1929	1930
Miss Sanders	1929	—
Miss Kay	1929	1930
Miss Burnaby	1930	—
Miss Burnip	1930	—
Miss Baldwin	1930	1924
Miss P. Thomas	1930	1936
Miss Walker	1930	1935
Miss Ashcroft	1931	1935
Miss Moyns	1931	1934
Miss J. Jackson	1931	1934
Miss K. Adams	1931	1934
Miss Edith Clegg	1931	1943
Miss M. H. E. Murray	1932	1939
Miss M. A. Norwood	1932	1937
Miss M. I. Hill	1932	1942
Mr. Louis Blofeld	1933	1937
Miss E. M. C. Belcher (Mrs. Carling)	1934	1949
Miss M. Leggitt	1934	1936
Miss B. D. Pawlett	1934	1936
Miss G. L. McFarlane	1935	1936
Miss M. Peters	1935	1936
Miss C. M. Read	1935	1949
Dr. H. D. Megaw	1936	1939
Miss M. M. C. McCallum	1936	1938
Miss J. C. Lomax	1936	1947
Second mistress, 1946		
Mlle M. L. Métraux	1936	1937
Miss M. Taylor	1936	1937
Miss A. C. R. Affleck	1937	1938
Miss K. C. M. Gent	1937	1942
Miss M. Skinner	1937	1942
Miss M. H. Rogers	1937	1943
Miss O. M. Wilson	1937	1938
Miss J. M. Wigley	1937	1941
Fräulein Drescher	1937	1938
Miss M. H. K. Crump (Mrs. Hillman)	1937	1940
Mlle J. M. C. Pasquasy	1938	1939
Miss U. Pehrson	1938	—
Miss C. M. Pike	1938	1940
Miss H. Cusiter	1938	1943
Miss A. M. S. Hole (Mrs. Rogers)	1938	1940
Miss M. Spielmacher	1938	1939

	Appointed	*Left*
Miss K. Mann	1939	1941
Miss G. M. Holmes (Mrs. Thorpe)	1939	1943
Miss J. M. Summers (Mrs. Collins)	1940	1942
Miss A. F. Locke	1940	1944
Miss E. Romero (Mrs. Fisher)	1940	1941
Miss D. V. Machell	1941	—
Miss M. E. Burchell (Mrs. T. Burchell)	1941	1945
Mlle M. L. Vigo	1941	1943
Miss B. M. Weedon	1941	1944
Miss E. Fleure	1941	1944
Miss D. E. Patch (Mrs. Tucker)	1941	1943
Miss D. M. Wood	1941	—
Miss R. Prosser	1941	—
Miss A. Couch	1942	—
Miss C. Clayden	1942	1944
Dr. C. E. Fraenkel	1942	—
Mrs. M. K. Minns	1942	1944
Miss E. D. Stoye	1942	1945
Miss J. M. Gibbs	1943	1946
Miss M. E. Ayre	1943	1947
Miss N. K. Jones	1943	—
Mrs. M. H. Bunton	1943	1945
Miss M. W. D. Wilson	1943	1945
Mrs. P. M. B. Mason	1944	1945
Miss J. M. Nicholls	1944	—
Miss B. B. Laurie	1944	—
Miss E. M. Saunders	1944	—
Miss M. J. Cunningham	1944	1947
Miss G. M. Croker	1944	1945
Mrs. I. J. R. Gardner	1945	1948
Miss G. Bartell	1945	—
Miss P. Hackett	1945	—
Miss G. M. Pearson	1945	1950
Miss D. J. White	1945	1949
Miss E. Fessel	1945	1947
Miss M. A. Pope	1945	1953
Miss M. M. C. Cameron	1945	1947
Miss A. E. Mansfield	1946	1947
Miss R. Hewetson	1946	—
Miss E. E. Addis	1946	—
Miss M. E. Lloyd Smith	1947	—
Miss J. Gibson	1947	—
Miss P. M. Britton	1947	1955
Miss I. E. Charman	1947	1952
Miss B. A. W. Morton	1947	1950

P

	Appointed	Left
Miss R. S. C. Sykes	1947	1951
Miss J. O. Oakley	1947	1950
Miss R. M. Hedges	1947	1952
Miss P. M. Collingwood	1947	1955
Mrs. D. Marriott	1947	1948
Miss E. J. Shettle	1947	1949
Miss M. E. Moore	1948	1952
Miss M. Pullman	1948	1949
Miss C. O. Coates (Mrs. Rose)	1948	1951
Miss S. Harvey	1949	1953
Miss H. M. Nicholson	1949	1950
Miss P. Garton	1949	1956
Miss B. I. Van der Straaten	1950	1952
Miss S. U. J. Findlay	1950	—
Miss J. E. Hunter	1950	1952
Mrs. M. C. Paling	1950	1951
Mrs. V. Johnston	1950	—
Mrs. H. A. E. Brookes	1950	1956
Miss M. Croxford	1950	1952
Miss D. E. Rodd (Mrs. Foster)	1951	1953
Miss H. D. Whale	1951	1955
Mrs. A. M. Ison	1951	1956
Miss E. M. Harrison	1951	—
Miss J. B. Peacock	1952	1957
Miss S. M. Hodgkinson (Mrs. Robinson)	1952	1954
Miss M. E. Bateman (Mrs. Harpur)	1952	1953
Miss R. D. Hill	1952	—
Miss P. L. Wilkes (Mrs. Valentine)	1952	1955
Mlle S. R. Nassivet	1952	1953
Dr. J. Cattermole	1952	1957
Miss M. J. Thompson	1952	—
Miss S. M. Baker	1952	—
Miss F. C. Howard	1952	1957
Mrs. I. A. H. Lea	1952	1953
Miss A. M. Morris	1953	—
Miss J. M. Brown	1953	—
Miss M. E. Grainger (Mrs. Galley)	1953	—
Miss M. K. N. Circuit	1953	—
Miss J. Wallis	1954	—
Miss P. M. C. Bain	1954	—
Miss R. M. Chalk	1954	—
Miss V. A. Wylie	1954	—
Miss M. Blower	1955	—
Miss C. E. Tristram	1955	—
Miss S. Cubitt	1955	—

	Appointed	*Left*
Miss P. H. Goldie	1955	—
Miss E. Edgecombe	1956	—
Mrs. M. C. G. Dickey	1956	—
Miss J. Flood	1956	—
Miss S. R. J. Gaselee	1956	—
Miss L. W. Iggulden	1956	—

OLD GIRLS WHO HAVE BEEN SCHOOL SECRETARY

	Appointed	*Left*
Henrietta Lloyd	1887	1891
Eva Hutchinson (Mrs. Elliott)	1891	1894
Mary Footman	1894	1895
Sybil Slator (Mrs. Nangle)	1895	1900
Fanny Forbes	1900	1936
Pamela Orr	1935	1937
Dorothy Kitchener	1937	—

Assistant School Secretary		
Betty Hockin	1940	1949
Rhoda West	1949	1952
Connie Darrington	1952	—

Bursar		
Betty Hockin	1946	1949
Nancy Garrett	1949	—

HEAD GIRLS

1882	Louie Carter	1894	Hilda Grosspelius
1883	Louie Carter	1895	Elsie Dyson
1884	Louie Carter		(Mrs. J. T. Chamberlain)
1885	Lotti de Fenzi	1896	Elsie Dyson
1886	Flora de Fenzi		(Mrs. J. T. Chamberlain)
1887	Flora de Fenzi	1897	Margaret Thompson
1888	Martie Sampson		(Mrs. Vernon Garratt)
1889	Eva Hutchison	1898	Margaret Thompson
	(Mrs. R. H. Elliot)		(Mrs. Vernon Garratt)
1890	Eva Hutchinson	Jan. 1899	Ella Edghill
	(Mrs. R. H. Elliot)	Sept. 1899	Ella Edghill
1891	Ismay O'Maley	1900	Ella Edghill
1892	May Billson	1901	Violet Apthorp
1893	Agnes Winkfield	1902	Joan Holland

	1903	Kathleen Field	Sept. 1933	Rosalind Wise

1903 Kathleen Field
1904 Kathleen Field
May 1905 Gwen Maitland Watkins
Sept. 1905 Dora Coate
1906 Ruth Peel
1907 Ruth Hall
1908 Ruth Hall
1909 Gertrude Fishwick
1910 Evelyn Askwith
1911 Kate Westaway
1912 Muriel Lloyd
1913 Madeline Oakley-Hill
1914 Madge Ward
1915 Sydney Little
1916 Elizabeth Kaye
    (Mrs. Gordon)
May 1917 May Prickett
Sept. 1917 Kathleen Tulloch
1918 Janet Brown
    (Mrs. Mathews)
1919 Mary Tulloch
1920 Irene Williams
    (Mrs. Pollock)
1921 Sheila Hardie
1922 Joyce Ashmore
1923 Enid West (Mrs. Oatley)
1924 Winifred Lucas
    (Mrs. Roe)
1925 Winsome Barradale
    (Mrs. Saddler)
1926 Esther Hodge
1927 Margaret Foster
    (Mrs. Jackson)
1928 Marjorie Meldrum
1929 Brenda Watson
    (Mrs. Carter)
May 1930 Barbara Garrard
    (Mrs. Solandt)
Sept. 1930 Winifred Hopkinson
1931 Mary Hewitt
May 1932 Elsie Worley
    (Mrs. Quarrie)
Sept. 1932 Joy Theobald
Jan. 1933 Kathleen Neely
    (Mrs. Brown)

Sept. 1933 Rosalind Wise
    (Mrs. Brain)
Sept. 1934 Barbara Harding
    (Mrs. Cocks)
Sept. 1935 Elspeth Corry-Smith
Sept. 1936 Leslie Faulkner
    (Mrs. King)
Sept. 1937 Elspeth Gifford
    (Mrs. Hugentobler)
Sept. 1938 Pamela Seabridge
Sept. 1939 Mary Moller
    (Mrs. Miller)
May 1940 Pat Course
    (Mrs. Fagg)
Sept. 1940 Margaret Rogers
    (Mrs. Rossell)
Sept. 1941 Jane Chappel
Sept. 1942 Marianne Hill
Sept. 1943 Pamela Halsey
Jan. 1944 Ruth Whitley
    (Mrs. Staniland)
Sept. 1944 Janet Hacking
    (Mrs. James)
Jan. 1945 Christine Davison
    (Mrs. Maxwell)
Sept. 1945 Anne Ranken
Sept. 1946 Mary Janes
    (Mrs. Sinclair)
May 1947 Megan Williams
Sept. 1947 Rachel Baldwin
Sept. 1948 Catherine Daughtry
May 1949 Barbara Hayward
Sept. 1949 Margaret Belcher
    (Mrs. Parkes)
Sept. 1950 Olive Rogers
Sept. 1951 Pat Crowsley
Sept. 1952 Mary Webb
Sept. 1953 Rachel Thompson
Sept. 1954 Margaret Craig
May 1955 Josephine Houghton
Sept. 1955 Janet Mabbott
Jan. 1956 Valerie Alsop
May 1956 Candida Parrish
Sept. 1956 Cathrin Thomas

OLD GIRLS WHO HAVE BECOME HEAD MISTRESSES

Name	At B.H.S.	School or College	Date Appointed
I. M. Sampson	1884-89	St. Denys School, Muree	1900
		Doveton Girls' High School, Madras	1906
			1928
A. T. Scott, B.A.	1888-89	Girls' Grammar School, Bingley, Yorks.	1904
A. M. Stephenson, M.A.	1884-89	High School, Preston	1906
		Francis Holland School, Baker Street, London	1912
K. Wragge, HONS. HIST.	1884-91	Girls' County School, Peterborough	1907
H. M. Footman, HONS. MODS. CLASS.	1883-90	City and County School for Girls, Chester	1911
M. A. Grant, HONS. MOD. HIST.	1889-95	Withington Girls' School, Manchester	1908
Deaconess Sybil Turing, B.A.	1884-94	Auckland House School, Simla	1908
		Cathedral High School, Lahore	1919
M. Spurling, B.A.	1888-97	Alice Ottley School, Worcester	1912
E. M. Columbine, B.SC. (Mrs. W. A. D. Russell)	1896-02	Collegiate School, Pietermaritzburg, Natal	1913
E. M. Belcher, M.A.	1887-97	High School, Crediton	1914
E. I. Sutton, B.A.	1901-11	James Allen's Girls' School, Dulwich	1920
F. Sutton	1895-00	High School, Carmarthen	1914
E. M. Edghill, M.A.	1896-01	Mather Kindergarten T.C., Manchester	1914
	1906-13	King's High School, Warwick	1914
		Redland High School, Bristol	1921
		St. Felix School, Southwold	1926
E. Lowde, B.A.	1891-97	County Secondary School, Petersfield	1919
M. L. Hall, M.A.	1898-06	Higher Tranmere High School, Birkenhead	1921
D. Coate, B.A.	1897-06	High School, Truro	1922
K. M. Westaway, M.A., D.LIT.	1902-12	High School, Bedford	1924
M. Norris, M.A.	1893-05	County High School, Walthamstow	1924

219

Name	At B.H.S.	School or College	Date Appointed
C. Stewart, M.A.	1903-08	Training College, Lincoln	1924
W. Coate	1902-10	Girls' High School, Cairo	1924
		Girls' College, Jerusalem	1928
D. Carruthers, M.SC.	1894-05	The Green Secondary School, Isleworth	1925
E. Wainwright, M.A.	1911-14	Jersey Ladies' College	1926
		Penrhos College, Colwyn Bay	1928
M. Spence	1897-00	Kindergarten Training College, Bedford	1927
M. Salmond, B.A.	1905-11	Craighead School, Timaru, New Zealand	1927
M. Malim	1903-05	School for the Deaf, Stockton-on-Tees	1929
A. Langley (Sister Adriene)	1901-09	Old Polar School, Croydon	1930
May Prickett, M.A.	1906-17	Framlingham High School	1933
M. Oakley-Hill, M.A.	1904-14	Royal Naval School, Twickenham	1933
W. Appleton, M.A.	1906-14	Norwich Secondary School	1934
F. Skerman	1907-14	Queen's Park Girls' School	
D. Stokes	1920-26	Kempston Junior School	1942
C. Smith, M.A.	1916-23	Penrhos College, Colwyn Bay	1938
E. Goodman, M.A.	1921-29	Crossley and Porter Girls' School, Halifax	1954
D. Smith	1925-31	Bulawayo Junior School	

220

UNIVERSITY SUCCESSES

Year	Name	University	Subject	Class
1888	F. Douglas de Fenzi	London	Reid Scholarship, Bedford College	I
1889	L. Carter	London	B.A.	I
	C. Douglas de Fenzi	London	B.A.	II
1890	E. Houliston	Cambridge, N.	History	II
	A. Scott	London	B.A.	

Year	Name	University	Subject	Class
1891	V. Beaman	London	B.A., Hons. in French	I
	F. Douglas de Fenzi	London	B.A.	I
	G. Ready	London, R.H.C.	Nat. Sci. Scholarship	
1892	M. Sampson	Cambridge, N.	Mathematics	III
	M. Stephenson	Cambridge, N.	History	II
	J. Best	London, R.H.C.	Bursary for Classics for two years	
1893	M. Richardson	Cambridge, N.	Cobden Scholarship for three years	
	E. Thompson (Mrs. Seymer Hankin)		Exhibition at Aberystwyth College	
1894	E. Wood (Dame Ethel Shakespear)	Cambridge, N.	Natural Science, Part I	II
	H. Fraser	Oxford, L.M.H.	Mod. Hist. Hon. Sch.	II
	M. Footman	Oxford, L.M.H.	Hon. Classical Moderations	
	J. Best	London, R.H.C.	B.A.	II
	E. Thompson (Mrs. Seymer Hankin)	London	B.A.	II
	E. Dyson (Mrs. J. T. Chamberlain) E. Clough	London	Reid Scholarships for two years at Bedford College	I
1895	E. Wood (Dame Ethel Shakespear)	Cambridge, N.	Natural Science, Part II	
	M. Richardson	Cambridge, N.	Bathurst Studentship	
	I. O'Maley	Oxford, L.M.H.	History	II
	B. Dibblee	Oxford, S.	Mod. Hist. Hon. Sch.	III
	M. Thompson (Mrs. Vernon Garratt)	London	Mod. Hist. Hon. Sch. Reid Scholarship at Bedford College	II
	M. Billson	London, Aberystwyth	B.A.	II
	A. Harrison	London, Aberystwyth	B.A.	II

Year	Name	University	Subject	Class
1895	G. Ready	London, R.H.C.	B.Sc.	Hons.
	E. Dyson (Mrs. J. T. Chamberlain)	London	Matriculation (first woman candidate) Gilchrist Scholarship and University London Exhibition	
	M. Fraser	Oxford, L.M.H.	Mod. Hist. Hon. Sch.	III
	M. Grant	Oxford, St. Hugh's	Hist. Scholarship for three years	
	S. Turing	London	B.A.	I
	A. Winkfield	London, R.H.C.	B.A.	II
	I. Winkfield	London, R.H.C.	Open Scholarship for three years	
1897	K. Sampson (Mrs. McKillop Young)	Edinburgh	Second Professional Examination	
	M. Baylay	Oxford, L.M.H.	Mod. Hist. Hon. Sch.	II
	K. Wragge	Oxford, S.	Mod. Hist. Hon. Sch.	II
	A. Winkfield	Oxford, R.H.C.	Mathematical Hon. Mods.	I
	E. Belcher	London	B.A.	I
	E. Clough	London	B.A.	I
	E. Whitworth	London	B.A., Hons. in German	II
	M. Spurling	London	B.A.	I
	E. Dyson (Mrs. J. T. Chamberlain)	Cambridge	Gilchrist Scholarship for three years	
1898	M. C. Holland	Cambridge, N.	Mathematics, Part I	III
	E. Belcher	Oxford, L.M.H.	Classics Scholarship for three years	
	J. Winkfield	London, R.H.C.	B.A.	I
	M. Norman	London, Bedford College	B.A.	II
1899	E. Lowde	Aberystwyth	Scholarship for one year	
	M. Grant	Oxford, St. Hugh's	Mod. Hist. Hon. Sch.	
	F. Livesey	New Zealand	B.A.	II

Year	Name	University	Subject	Class
1899	E. Lowde	London, Aberystwyth	B.A.	II
	G. Dyson	London	B.A.	II
	E. Young	London	B.A.	II
	M. Thompson (Mrs. Vernon Garratt)	Cambridge, G.	Classics Scholarship for three years	
1900	E. Dyson (Mrs. J. T. Chamberlain)	Cambridge, N.	Classics, Part I	II
	F. Poyser	Cambridge, N.	History	II
	E. Rowan Hamilton	Oxford, S.	Mod. Hist. Hon. Sch.	I
	E. Edghill	London	B.A.	I
	M. Smith	London	B.A., Hons. in English	I
	D. Inman	London	B.A.	II
	M. Kilvert	London	B.A.	II
	N. Sutton	London	B.A.	II
1901	E. Belcher	Oxford, L.M.H.	Classical Hon. Mods.	II
	E. Edghill	Cambridge, N.	Classical Scholarship for three years	
	E. Edghill	Cambridge, N.	Gilchrist Scholarship for three years and C.H.L. Prize	
1902	C. Wordsworth	Oxford, L.M.H.	Classical Scholarship	I
	B. Hogg	London	B.A.	II
	M. Thompson (Mrs. Vernon Garratt)	Cambridge, G.	Classics, Part I	Div. I
	C. Malim	London	B.A.	I
	C. Prescott	London	B.A.	I
	J. Northcote (Lady Jaqueta Williams)	Cambridge, N.	History, Part I	II
1903	Mary Stewart	Cambridge, N.	Winkworth Scholarship	
	J. Holland	London, Westfield	Bursary for two years	

Year	Name	University	Subject	Class
1903	M. Dyott	London, R.H.C.	Bursary for three years	
	G. Parker	London, R.H.C.	Bursary for three years	
	E. Edghill	London	M.A. Classics, with special distinction	
	G. Parker	London	B.A.	
	A. Ebden (Mrs. Newton)	Edinburgh	M.B., Ch.B.	II
	V. McLaren (Mrs. T. N. Kelynack)	Edinburgh	M.B., Ch.B.	
1904	E. Landon	Edinburgh	Edgware Gold Medal for Practical Anatomy	
	E. Edghill	Cambridge, N.	Classics, Part I, Arthur Hugh Clough Scholarship	I
	C. Wordsworth	Cambridge, N.	Classics, Part I	II
	J. Northcote (Lady Jaqueta Williams)	Cambridge, N.	History, Part II	III
	A. Trethewy	Oxford	Mod. Hist. Hon. Sch.	III
	G. Maitland-Watkins	Cambridge, N.	Scholarship for Classics	
	E. Edghill	Cambridge, N.	Classics, Part II, special distinction in Philosophy	I
1905	C. Wordsworth	Cambridge, N.	History, Part II	II
	D. Portway (Mrs. Dobson Hinton)	Cambridge, N.	History, Part I	II
	D. Valentine	Cambridge, N.	Med. and Mod. Languages	II
	M. Wilson	Oxford, St. Hugh's	Mod. Hist. Hon. Sch.	II
	E. Landon	Edinburgh	M.B., Ch.B.	
	N. Sutton	London	B.A., Hons. in Classics	I
	K. Field	London	B.A.	I
	J. Langley	London, Bedford College	B.A.	II

Year	Name	University	Subject	Class
1905	D. Ryder	London, University College	Andrews Scholarship for Classics	
	D. Carruthers	London, R.H.C.	Science Scholarship for three years	
			University of London Exhibition for two years	
1906	G. Parker	Cambridge, G.	Mathematics	III
	D. Portway (Mrs. Dobson Hinton)	Cambridge, N.	History, Part II	II
	G. Rose	Cambridge, G.	History, Part I	II
	D. Murray	Cambridge	Scholarship for three years	
	G. Broughton (Lady Chatterjee)	London, University College	Gilchrist Scholarship for two years	
			University Scholarship for Psychology and Logic	
	E. Bazeley	Oxford, St. Hugh's	Nat. Sci. Hon. Sch.	III
	M. Warner	Oxford, L.M.H.	Mod. Hist. Hon. Sch.	III
	M. Norris	London, University College	Andrews Scholarship for Classics and Prize of £30 for Greek	
	D. Ryder	London, University College	Extension of Andrews Scholarship for Classics	
	M. Forrester Brown	London, School of Medicine.	Entrance Scholarship for one year	
1907	D. Maltby (Lady Wells)		Open Studentship at Royal Academy Schools	
	G. Rose	Cambridge, G.	History, Part II	III
	V. Cosier	Cambridge, N.	Med. and Mod. Languages	III
	G. Broughton (Lady Chatterjee)	London, University College	B.A. Hons. in Philosophy, Prizes for Philosophy and Psychology	

Year	Name	University	Subject	Class
1907	D. Ryder	London, University College	Malden Medal and Scholarship for Classics	
	R. Peel	Oxford, L.M.H.	History Scholarship for three years	
	J. Holland	London, Westfield College	B.A. Hons. in Classics	
1908	E. Gordon-Cranmer	London	B.A. Hons. in English	
	K. Field	Cambridge, G.	Mathematics, Part I, Fourth Year Exhibition	II
	G. Maitland-Watkins	Cambridge, N.	Classics, Part I	II, Div. I
	R. Peel	Oxford, L.M.H.	Margaret Evans Prize for History	
	G. Broughton (Lady Chatterjee)	London, University College	John Stuart Mill Scholarship for Philosophy and Pfeiffer Fellowship, with residence at College Hall	
	M. Norris	London, University College	Malden Medal and Scholarship for Classics and Higher Senior Greek Prize	I
	C. Stewart	Cambridge, N.	Cobden Scholarship for three years	
	W. Marks (Mrs. Le Sueur)	London	B.A. Hons. in French	
	W. Stewart (Mrs. Cranko)	London, Bedford College	B.A.	I
	E. Williamson	London		
1909	G. Maitland-Watkins	Cambridge, N.	B.A.	I
	M. Hall	Cambridge, N.	Classics, Part II	II
	K. Field	Cambridge, G.	Classics, Part I	II
	D. Murray	Cambridge, N.	Nat. Sci., Part II (Physics)	II
	M. Milne	Oxford, L.M.H.	Med. and Mod. Languages	II
	R. Warner (Mrs. W. H. B. Somerset)	Oxford, L.M.H.	Eng. Lit. Hon. Sch.	III
			Eng. Lit. Hon. Sch.	III

Year	Name	University	Subject	Class
1909	G. Broughton (Lady Chatterjee)	London, School of Economics	Scholarship for three years for Sociology	
	M. Norris	London, University College	M.A. Classics	
	D. Carruthers	London, R.H.C.	B.Sc. Hons. in Botany	II
	L. Blakiston (Mrs. Milroy)	London	B.A.	I
1910	A. Langley	London	B.A.	II
	C. Stewart	Cambridge, N.	History, Part I	I
	W. Ward (Mrs. Saunt)	Cambridge, N.	History, Part I	II
	R. Peel	Oxford, L.M.H.	Mod. Hist. Hon. Sch.	II
	D. Holmes	Oxford, L.M.H.	Mod. Hist. Hon. Sch.	III
	A. Sandys (Mrs. Leys)	Oxford, St. Hilda's	Open History Scholarship for three years	
1911	G. Fishwick	London	B.A.	II
	C. Stewart	Cambridge, N.	History, Part II	II
	W. Ward (Mrs. Saunt)	Cambridge, N.	History, Part II	II
	Z. Scruby	Cambridge	Diploma of Public Health	
	G. Thomas	Cambridge, N.	Moral Sciences Tripos, Part I	II
	E. Lippett	Oxford, L.M.H.	Mod. Hist. Hon. Sch.	II
	M. Vassall	Oxford, L.M.H.	Mod. Hist. Hon. Sch.	II
	M. Forrester-Brown	London, School of Medicine	M.B., B.S. Hons. in Pathology and Forensic Medicine	
	M. Johnston	London	B.A. Hons. in History	I
	I. Tisdall (Mrs. W. T. Gray)	London	B.A.	I

Year	Name	University	Subject	Class
1911	E. Askwith	London	B.A.	II
	M. Goodman	London	B.A.	II
	D. Greene	London	B.A.	II
	H. Hiley (Mrs. Evans)	London	B.A.	II
	M. Partridge	London, Bedford College	Arnott Scholarship for three years for Science and Mathematics	
1912	K. Westaway	Cambridge, N.	Open Classical Scholarship for three years	II
	M. Madden	London	B.A.	II
	M. Marsden	London	B.A.	
	D. Carrington	London, Slade School of Art	Scholarship for two years and Scott Melville Prize for Sketches	
1913	O. Littledale	Cambridge, N.	History, Part I	II
	K. Stevens (Mrs. E. Routh)	Cambridge, N.	History, Part I	III
	M. Bisdée (Mrs. Trenchard)	Oxford, St. Hilda's	Eng. Lit. Hon. Sch.	II
	J. Pym	Oxford, St. Hugh's	Eng. Lit. Hon. Sch.	III
	R. Dismorr	Oxford, S.	Theology Hon. Sch.	II
	M. Lloyd	Cambridge, N.	Open Classical Scholarship for three years	
	K. Westaway	London	B.A. Hons. in Classics	II
	M. Rainey	London, Bedford College	B.A.	
	M. Salmond	London, Bedford College	B.A.	
	S. Wells	London, Bedford College	B.A.	
	M. Morris	London	B.A.	

Year	Name	University	Subject	Class
1913	M. Forrester-Brown	London, School of Medicine	Gilchrist Studentship	
	E. Craig	London, Royal Academy Schools	Open Studentship for seven years	
1914	K. Stevens (Mrs. E. Routh)	Cambridge, N.	History, Part II	II
	W. Appleton	Cambridge, N.	Med. and Mod. Languages	II
	O. Littledale	Cambridge, N.	History, Part II	III
	A. Sandys (Mrs. Leys)	Oxford, St. Hilda's	Mod. Hist. Hon. Sch.	II
	A. Sandys (Mrs. Leys)	Manchester	Research Studentship	
	S. Haggard	Oxford, L.M.H.	English Hon. Sch.	III
	F. Hodges	Oxford, S.	Nat. Sci. Hon. Sch.	III
	M. Forrester-Brown	London	M.D. (Gynæcology)	
	W. Marks (Mrs. Le Sueur)	London, Bedford College	M.A. (French)	
	M. Partridge	London, Bedford College	B.Sc. Hons. in Mathematics	II
1915	K. Westaway	Cambridge, N.	Classics, Part I	II
	M. Coate	Oxford, St. Hilda's	Mod. Hist. Hon. Sch.	I
	E. Macaulay	Oxford, L.M.H.	Pass Moderations	
1916	K. Westaway	Cambridge, N.	Classics, Part II	I
	M. Lloyd	Cambridge, N.	Classics, Part II	I
	M. Lloyd	Cambridge, N.	"Arthur Hugh Clough" Scholarship (fourth year)	
	L. Jackson	Cambridge, N.	Med. and Mod. Lang.	I
	E. Swire	Cambridge, N.	History, Part I	II

Year	Name	University	Subject	Class
1916	S. Little	Cambridge, G.	"Jane Agnes Chessar" Classical Scholarship for four years	
	K. Westaway	London	M.A. Classics	I
	E. Wainwright	London, Bedford College	B.A. Eng. and French Hons.	III
1917	M. Lloyd	Cambridge, N.	Classics, Part II	
	E. Swire	Cambridge, N.	History, Part II	
	J. Partridge (Mrs. Wenham)	London, School of Medicine	M.R.C.S., L.R.C.P.	
	M. Strachan	Oxford	Mod. Hist. Hon. Sch.	II
1918	M. Gyde	Cambridge, N.	Med. and Mod. Lang.	II
	M. Oakley Hill	Oxford, Home Student	Mod. Hist. Hon. Sch.	II
	K. Field	London, School of Medicine	M.R.C.S., L.R.C.P., Dean's Medal for Clinical Medicine	
	A. Collie (Mrs. Wareham)	London, School of Medicine	M.R.C.S., L.R.C.P.	
	F. Hodges	London, School of Medicine	Second M.B., Part II	
1919	K. Westaway	Cambridge, N.	Marion Kennedy Research Studentship	
	A. Sandys (Mrs. K. Leys)	Oxford	Gilchrist Studentship from British School at Rome for Historical Research	
	M. McKisack	Oxford, S.	Mary Ewart Scholarship for three years for History	
	A. Radice (Mrs. Barrington-Ward)	Oxford, L.M.H.	Mod. Hist. Hon. Sch.	III
	H. Lacey (Mrs. Madden-Gaskell)	Oxford, L.M.H.	Eng. Lit. Hon. Sch.	IV

230

Year	Name	University	Subject	Class
1919	S. Little	Cambridge, G.	Classics, Part I	I
	D. E. Kaye (Mrs. Gordon)	Cambridge, N.	English, Part I	II
	D. Ellis (Mrs. Norman Field)	Cambridge, N.	Mod. and Med. Lang.	III
	K. Housden	Cambridge, N.	Mod. and Med. Lang.	III
	J. Partridge (Mrs. Wenham)	London	F.R.C.S.	
	K. Field	London	M.B., B.S.	
	M. Macgown	Edinburgh	M.B., Ch.B.	
1920	S. Little	Cambridge, G.	Moral Sciences, Part II	II
	D. E. Kaye (Mrs. Gordon)	Cambridge, N.	English Tripos, Part II	II
	D. Ellis (Mrs. Norman Field)	Cambridge, N.	English Tripos, Part I	III
	D. Fishwick (Mrs. Barnes)	Cambridge, N.	Economics, Part I	II Div. I
	R. White	London, Westfield C.	Scholarship for Science for three years	
	I. Williams (Mrs. Pollock)	O. and C. Higher Certificate	State Scholarship for History	
1921	M. Forrester-Brown	London	M.S.	
	K. Westaway	London	Doctor of Literature	
	D. Fishwick	Cambridge, N.	Economics, Part II	II
	K. Tulloch	Oxford	Theology Hon. Sch.	II
1922	M. McKisack	Oxford, S.	Mod. Hist. Hon. Sch.	II
	M. McKisack	Oxford, S.	History Research Scholarship	
1922	E. Birch	Oxford, Home Student	Pass Moderations	

Q

Year	Name	University	Subject	Class
1922	M. Preston (Mrs. Keppel-Compton)	Cambridge, N.	Mathematics, Part I	III
	V. Miles	Cambridge, N.	Agriculture, Part II	I
	L. Ilif (Mrs. A. J. May)	London, School of Medicine	M.B., B.S. with Honours, Distinction in Forensic Medicine	
1923	E. Ramsay	Cambridge, N.	History, Part I	II
	D. Bradshaw	Oxford, Home Student	Pass Moderations	
	M. Forrester-Brown	London	William Gibson Medical Research Scholarship of £250 a year for three years	
	J. Brown (Mrs. Mathews)	London, Bedford College	B.Sc. Hons. in Chemistry	
	M. Bennett	London, Bedford College	B.Sc. Hons. in Botany	
	C. Appleton	London, School of Medicine	M.R.C.S., L.R.C.P.	
	J. Ashmore	Oxford, L.M.H.	History Scholarship	
	C. Smith	Cambridge, N.	Classical Scholarship for three years	
1924	M. Preston (Mrs. Keppel-Compton)	Cambridge, N.	Mathematics, Part II	III
	E. Ramsay	Cambridge, N.	History, Part II	II
	M. McKisack	Oxford, S.	B.Litt., Lothian Essay Prize	II
	M. Brown (Mrs. Clark Mock)	Oxford, L.M.H.	Mod. Hist. Hon. Sch.	II
	A. Deeley	Oxford, St. Hilda's	Mod. Hist. Hon. Sch.	II
	I. Williams (Mrs. Pollock)	Oxford, L.M.H.	Mod. Hist. Hon. Sch.	III

232

Year	Name	University	Subject	Class
1924	E. Birch	Oxford, Home Student	Eng. Lang. and Lit. Hon. Sch.	III
	C. Lucas	London, Bedford College	B.Sc Hons. in Zoology	
	R. White	London, Westfield College	B.Sc. Hons. in Botany	
	L. Ilif (Mrs. A. J. May)	London	Diploma of Tropical Medicine and Hygiene	
	F. Nichol	London, School of Medicine	M.B., B.S.	
	E. West (Mrs. Oatley)	Cambridge, G.	Higgins Scholarship for three years for French and German	
	L. Stonebridge	London, Westfield College	Exhibition for three years for French	
	N. Martin (Mrs. Wooster)	O. and C. Higher Certificate	State Scholarship for Science	
1925	C. Smith	Cambridge, N.	Classics, Part I	I
	E. Carruthers	Cambridge, G.	Classics, Part I	II
	M. McKisack	Oxford, S.	Mary Somerville Research Fellowship	II
	D. Bradshaw	Oxford, Home Student	French Hon. Sch.	
	S. Hardie	Oxford, S.	Mod. Hist. Hon. Sch.	II
	V. Lasbrey	London, Bedford College	B.Sc. Hons. in Botany	
	M. Mitter (Mrs. Hensman)	London, Westfield College	B.A. Hons. in English	
	J. Godber	Oxford, St. Hilda's	History Scholarship for three years	

Year	Name	University	Subject	Class
1926	C. Lucas	London	Univ. Post-Graduate Travelling Studentship for Research at John Hopkins University, Baltimore	
	J. Cotton	Oxford	Research Studentship for History at Wisconsin University, U.S.A.	
	A. Deeley	Oxford	Research Studentship for History at Manchester University	
	C. Smith	Cambridge, N.	Classics, Part II	I
	E. Carruthers	Cambridge, G.	Classics, Part II	III
	E. West (Mrs. Oatley)	Cambridge, G.	Mod. and Med. Lang., Part I	I
	E. Byrde (Mrs. Hargreaves)	Cambridge, G.	First M.B, Parts I and II	
	J. Ashmore	Oxford, L.M.H.	Mod. Hist. Hon. Sch.	II
	G. Tyte (Mrs. Caldwell)	Oxford, Home Student	Eng. Lang. and Lit. Hon. Sch.	III
	B. Lucas	London	M.D.	
	I. Uttley	London	B.A. Hons. in English	
	M. Cave (Mrs. Pilliner)	London, R.H.C.	Classical Scholarship for three years	
	E. Hodge	O. and C. Higher Certificate	State Scholarship for History	
1927	E. West (Mrs. Oatley)	Cambridge, G.	Mod. and Med. Lang., Part II	II
	N. Martin (Mrs. Wooster)	Cambridge, G.	Nat. Science, Part I	II
	M. Landon (Mrs. Johnson Smyth)	Oxford, Home Student	Classics Pass School	

Year	Name	University	Subject	Class
1927	J. Brown (Mrs. Mathews)	London	Ph.D.	
	M. Davies	London, R.H.C.	B.Sc. Hons. in Botany	II
	E. Gilliatt	London, R.H.C.	B.A. Hons. in French	II
	M. Davies	London, R.H.C.	Driver Scholarship for Botany for three years	
	J. Cotton	Wisconsin, U.S.A.	M.A.	
	J. Cormack	Oxford, St. Hilda's	Pass Moderations	
	K. Wooding	Oxford, St. Hilda's	Pass Moderations	
	U. Cormack	Oxford, S.	Exhibition for English	
	E. Traill (Mrs. Oldrith)	Cambridge, G.	Higgens Scholarship for Mod. Lang.	
1928	M. Ellis	O. and C. Higher	State Scholarship for Botany	
	E. Byrde (Mrs. Hargreaves)	Cambridge, G.	Goldsmid Exhibition to University College Hospital	
	N. Martin (Mrs. Wooster)	Cambridge, G.	Nat. Science, Part II, Yarrow Science Research Studentship	II
	W. Lucas (Mrs. Roe)	Cambridge, N.	Nat. Science, Part I	III
	E. Traill (Mrs. Oldrith)	Cambridge, G.	Med. and Mod. Lang. (French), Part I	II
	S. Ewart (Mrs. Emberton)	Oxford, L.M.H.	French Hon. Sch., Distinction in Colloquial French	III
	J. Godber	Oxford, St. Hilda's	Mod. Hist. Hon. Sch.	II
	W. Barradale (Mrs. Saddler)	Oxford, St. Hilda's	Classical Honour Moderations	II
	Mabel Bennett	Oxford, St. Hilda's	Pass Moderations	
	J. Cooke	London, Bedford College	B.A. Hons. in History	II

Year	Name	University	Subject	Class
1928	M. Roberts	London	B.A. Hons. in History	II
	L. Stonebridge	London, Westfield College	B.A. Hons. in French	II
	M. Mackenzie	London, Bedford College	B.Sc. General	
	M. Foster (Mrs. Jackson)	Cambridge, N.	First M.B. Exhibition for Science	
	E. Goodman	O. and C. Higher Certificate	State Scholarship for Mathematics and Physics	
	L. Cooke	O. and C. Higher Certificate	State Scholarship for Botany	
1929	N. Martin (Mrs. Wooster)	Cambridge, G.	Yarrow Science Research Studentship, second year	
	E. Byrde (Mrs. Hargreaves)	Cambridge, G.	Nat. Science, Part II	II
	E. Traill (Mrs. Oldrith)	Cambridge, G.	Mod. and Med. Lang. (Spanish), Fanny Metcalfe Prize	
	M. Prickett	Lille	Licence-es-Lettres	
	J. Cormack	Oxford, St. Hilda's	French Hon. Sch.	II
	K. Wooding	Oxford, St. Hilda's	French Hon. Sch.	III
	E. Snodgrass	Oxford, S.	"Madeleine Shaw Lefevre" Scholarship and a third of Coombs' Prize for History	
	M. Cave (Mrs. Pilliner)	London, R.H.C.	B.A. Hons. in Classics	I
	M. Mackenzie	London, Bedford College	B.Sc. Hons. in Chemistry	II
	K. Mackenzie	London, School of Economics	Social Science Certificate	

Year	Name	University	Subject	Class
1929	M. Baird	Liverpool, School of Architecture	Intermediate Examination of the R.I.B.A.	
	K. Lucas (Mrs. Parry)	Cambridge, N.	Exhibition for Classics	
	M. Meldrum (Mrs. Moore)	O. and C. Higher Certificate	State Scholarship for Botany	
	M. Morton	Edinburgh	Bursary for five years to Royal College of Surgeons	
1930	N. Martin (Mrs. Wooster)	Cambridge, G.	Yarrow Science Research Studentship for third year	
	E. Traill (Mrs. Oldrith)	Cambridge, G.	Med. and Mod. Lang., Part II	II
	E. Goodman	Cambridge, N.	Mathematics, Part I	II
	E. Hodge	Oxford, St. Hilda's	Mod. Hist. Hon. Sch.	II
	E. Hodge	Manchester	Roscoe Research Studentship	
	V. Carruthers	Oxford, St. Hilda's	Mod. Hist. Hon. Sch.	III
	E. Snodgrass	Oxford, S.	Mod. Hist. Hon. Sch.	III
	U. Cormack	Oxford, S.	Philosophy Hon. Sch.	II
			Shaw Lefevre Research Scholarship	
	Mabel Bennett	Oxford, St. Hilda's	Eng. Lang. and Lit. Hon. Sch.	III
	E. Everett	Oxford, Home Student	Eng. Lang. and Lit. Hon. Sch.	III
	M. Hamilton	Oxford, Home Student	French Hon. Sch.	III
	A. Deeley	London	Diploma in Librarianship	
	E. Morton	London, Bedford College	B.Sc. General Honours	II
	V. Robson	Liverpool	B.A.	

Year	Name	University	Subject	Class
1930	N. Cattell	Reading	B.A.	
	B. Le Fanu	O. and C. Higher Certificate	State Scholarship for Science	
1931	B. Le Fanu	Oxford, St. Hugh's	Science Exhibition for three years	
	W. Hopkinson	Cambridge, N.	Major Scholarship for Classics	
	K. Lucas (Mrs. Parry)	Cambridge, N.	Classics, Part I	II
	M. Foster (Mrs. Jackson)	Cambridge, N.	Nat. Science, Part I	II
	L. Cooke	Cambridge, G.	Nat. Science, Part I	II
	B. Watson (Mrs. Carter)	Cambridge, N.	Mathematics, Part I	III
	P. Jarratt (Mrs. Maclennan)	Oxford, St. Hilda's	Honour Moderations	III
	M. Ellis	Oxford, St. Hugh's	Botany Hon. Sch.	II
	W. Young (Mrs. Handley)	London, School of Economics	B.Sc. (Economics)	II
	P. Davies	London, R.H.C.	B.A. Hons. History	II
	C. Doggett	London, Bedford College	B.A. Hons. English	II
	P. Robinson	London, R.H.C.	B.A. Hons. Classics	III
	P. Jones	O. and C. Higher Certificate	State Scholarship for Botany	
1932	M. Hewitt	Oxford, St. Hilda's	Exhibition for Classics	
	N. Martin (Mrs. Wooster)		D.Phil.	
	M. Meldrum (Mrs. Moore)	Cambridge	Nat. Science, Part I	II

Year	Name	University	Subject	Class
1932	E. Goodman	Cambridge	Mathematics, Part II	II
	K. Lucas (Mrs. Parry)	Cambridge	Anthropology	II
	B. fforde (Mrs. Cherrington)	Cambridge	Mod. Languages, Part I	I
	E. Byrde (Mrs. Hargreaves)	London	M.B., B.Clin., Tule Medal for Clinical Pathology	
	Sadie North	Bristol	B.Sc. (Botany)	II(A)
	Cicely James	London	Minor Scholarship to K.C.H.S.Sc.	
1933	G. Broughton (Lady Chatterjee)		Barrister-at-Law	
	E. Hodge	Manchester	D.Phil.	
	M. Pocock	Cape Town	D.Phil.	
	B. Garrard (Mrs. Solandt)	Cambridge	Nat. Science, Part I	I
	B. Watson (Mrs. Carter)	Cambridge	Mathematics, Part II	III
	W. Hopkinson	Cambridge	Classics, Part I	II
	C. Smith	Cambridge	Creighton Memorial Prize	
	B. Le Fanu	Oxford	Botany	III
	M. Prickett	London	M.A. (French)	
	A. Collie (Mrs. Wareham)	London	Diploma of Ophthalmological Medicine and Surgery	
	A. Kelynack	London	M.B., B.S.	
	A. Bryning	London	B.Sc.	
	D. Venour	London	Academic Diploma in Biology	
	D. Herne	London	Bursary at Bedford College	
	D. Murray	Manchester	B.D.	

Year	Name	University	Subject	Class
1932	W. Nicholson	Bristol	B.Sc.	
1933	F. Joyce	Bristol	B.Sc.	
	M. Morton	Edinburgh	Dr. Burnett's Medal and Dr. Robertson's Prize	
	K. Hemmings	Cambridge, N.	Major Scholarship for Mathematics	
	W. Hardy	London, Westfield College	Exhibition for French	
1934	W. Hopkinson	Cambridge	Classics, Part II	III
	K. Hemmings	Cambridge	Mathematics, Part I	II
	M. Hewitt	Oxford	Honour Moderations	II
	J. Brown (Mrs. Matthews)	London	Research Scholarship at Imperial College of Science and Technology	
	N. Bates	London	B.Sc., Chemistry	I
	E. Gray	London	B.Sc., Chemistry	II
	M. Hargreaves (Mrs. Morton)	London	B.A., English	II
	M. Hoppe (Mrs. Washbourne)	London	B.Sc., Economics	II
	K. Neely (Mrs. Brown)	London	University Scholarship in French	
	M. Foster (Mrs. Jackson)	London	M.R.C.S., L.R.C.P.	
	M. Frank	Bristol	B.Sc. (Physics and Geology)	
	V. Foote	Reading	B.Sc., Botany	
	O. Vernon Briggs		Silver Medal awarded by Royal Institute of British Architects	II
	B. Baston	London	Exhibition for Classics	
1935	D. Kitchener	Oxford	Mod. Hist. Hon. Sch.	III

Year	Name	University	Subject	Class
1935	E. Worley (Mrs. Quarrie)	Oxford	Mod. Hist. Hon. Sch.	II
	J. Flood	London	B.Sc., Chemistry	II
	P. Jones	London	B.Sc., Botany	II
	C. James	London	B.Sc., Social Science	
	M. Tate	London	B.Sc., Economics	
	V. Carruthers		Fellow of the Library Association	
	E. Tysoe (Mrs. Ryder)	Bristol	B.Sc., Mathematics and Chemistry	
	M. Morton	Edinburgh	L.R.C.S., L.R.C.P.	
		Glasgow	M.R.F.P. and S.	
	L. Cooke	Edinburgh	Silver Medal for Chemistry, J. A. Carlyle Bursary for Chemistry	
1936	B. Le Fanu	Oxford	B.Sc. (for thesis)	IV
	M. Hewitt	Oxford	Literæ Humaniores	III
	J. Theobald	Oxford	History	II
	K. Hemmings	Cambridge	Mathematics, Part II	II(A)
	J. Baty	London	B.A., English	II(A)
	K. Neely (Mrs. Brown)	London	B.A., French	
	W. Hardy	London	B.A., French	II(B)
	J. Wootton	London	B.Sc., Social Science	
	D. Johnston (Mrs. Aldis)	London	Prize and Scholarship at L.S.M.W.	
	C. Cooke	Edinburgh	Vans Dunlop Prize of £50	
	D. Braggins		Lafontaine Prize from Royal College of Organists	

Year	Name	University	Subject	Class
1936	M. Baird	Cambridge	Associate of Royal Institute of British Architects	
	E. Hargreaves (Mrs. Capstick)		Exhibition for Classics	
	E. Corry-Smith			
	W. Reynolds	London	Exhibition for French	III
	B. Gibbon	Oxford	Eng. Hon. Sch.	II
	J. Thring (Mrs. Mackworth)	Cambridge	Economics, Part I	
		Cambridge	Alma Blakeman Jones	
	D. Braggins	Cambridge	Turle Scholarship of £88 for Music at Girton	
1937	K. Neely (Mrs. Brown)	London	B.A., German	II
	B. Baston	London	B.A., Classics	II
	T. Rustomji (Mrs. Bilimoria)	London	B.A.	
	A. Cliff	London	B.A.	
	M. Carlton-Smith	London	B.Sc., Economics	II(A)
	A. Kelynack	London	M.D.	
	M. Acaster	Oxford	Mod. Lang. Hon. Sch.	II
	E. Hargreaves (Mrs. Capstick)	Cambridge	Classics, Part I	III
1938	C. Watson	Cambridge	English, Part I	III
	D. Braggins	Cambridge	M.B., F.R.C.O.	I
	J. Thring (Mrs. Mackworth)	Cambridge	Alma Blakeman Jones Scholarship	
	L. Forrest	London	B.Sc., Chemistry	II
	J. Williamson	London	B.Sc., Economics	II
	R. Wright	London	B.Sc., Botany	II

Year	Name	University	Subject	Class
1938	M. Rayns-Smith	London	B.Sc., Social Science	III
	R. Wise (Mrs. Brain)	London	B.Sc., Classics	
1939	L. Cooke	Edinburgh	Maclagan Prize for Forensic Medicine	
	J. Thring (Mrs. Mackworth)	Cambridge	Nat. Sci., Part I	I
			Rigby Scholarship	
	C. Johnson (Mrs. Gaunt)	Cambridge	Nat. Sci., Part I	III
	P. Stroud (Mrs. Humphries)	Cambridge	Nat. Sci., Part I	III
	B. Gibbon	Cambridge	Economics, Part II	II
	C. Watson	Cambridge	English, Part II	III
	F. Mettam	Oxford	English	II
	P. Pope (Mrs. Moore)	Oxford	Modern History	III
	E. Corry-Smith	London	B.A., French	
	J. Maunder	London	B.A., Classics	II(A)
	P. Pinfold	London	B.Sc.	III
	D. Ayre	Bristol	M.B., Ch.B.	
	L. Cooke	Edinburgh	M.B., Ch.B.	
			Scottish Association for Medical Education of Women Prize	
			M.R.C.S., L.R.C.P.	
	D. Johnston (Mrs. Aldis)	Cambridge	Exhibition for Classics	
1940	P. Seabridge	Cambridge	Nat. Sci., Part II	I
	J. Thring (Mrs. Mackworth)	Cambridge	Research Scholarship at Newnham	
	D. Braggins	Cambridge	Mus. Bach.	

Year	Name	University	Subject	Class
1940	B. York (Mrs. Stokes)	Oxford	Mod. Lang. Hon. Sch.	II
	E. Wardle	London	B.A., English	II
	S. Gadsden (Mrs. Costin)	London	R. Owens Scholarship of £75	
	L. Meredith Davies			
	M. Moller (Mrs. Miller)	Cambridge	M.R.C.S., L.R.C.P. Minor Scholarship for Science	
	S. Chappel (Mrs. Sloper)	Cambridge	Minor Scholarship for Science	
	I. Kuhlicke	Cambridge	Minor Scholarship for Geography	
	B. Gordon	London	Exhibition for French	
	P. Seabridge	Cambridge	Classics, Part I	II
	M. Davison (Mrs. Maxwell)	Cambridge	Classics, Part I	III
1941	P. Course (Mrs. Fagg)	Cambridge	Modern Languages, Part I	II
	M. Shaw	Oxford	Philosophy and Economics	IV
	M. Turnbull	London	B.Sc., Chemistry	
	V. Lowings	London	B.Sc.	
	J. Findlay	London	B.A., English	
	B. Shaw	London	B.A.	
	L. Meredith-Davies	London	M.B., B.S.	
	D. Pledge (Mrs. O'Hagan)	Durham	M.B., B.S.	
	E. Gifford (Mrs. Hugentobler)	Edinburgh	Andrew Grant Travelling Scholarship for Architecture	
	E. Dangerfield		Final Bar Examination	

Year	Name	University	Subject	Class
1942	M. Davison (Mrs. Maxwell)	Cambridge	Classics, Part II	II
	P. Seabridge	Cambridge	Classics, Part II	III
	S. Chappel (Mrs. Sloper)	Cambridge	Nat. Sci., Part I	II
	M. Moller (Mrs. Miller)	Cambridge	Nat. Sci., Part I	II
	I. Kuhlicke	Cambridge	Geography, Part I	II
	O. Wootton	London	B.Sc.	
	M. Foote	London	B.A., French	II(A)
	B. West	London	B.Sc., Chemistry	
	E. Gifford (Mrs. Hugentobler)	Edinburgh	Associate of Royal Institute of Scottish Architects	
	J. Chappel (Mrs. Russell)	Cambridge	Exhibition for Science	
1943	P. Course (Mrs. Fagg)	Cambridge	Mod. Lang., Part II	II(A)
	I. Kuhlicke	Cambridge	Geography, Part II	I
	M. Fisher	Cambridge	Classics, Part I	II
	M. Rowan	Oxford	Hist. Final Hon. Sch.	II
	J. Hartley	Oxford	Mathematics	III
	B. Gordon	London	B.A., French	III
	P. Sears	London	B.A., French	III
	E. Gifford (Mrs. Hugentobler)		Associate of Royal Institute of British Architects. Scholarship of £120 for Town Planning	
	S. Gadsden (Mrs. Costin)		M.R.C.S., L.R.C.P.	

Year	Name	University	Subject	Class
1944	M. Fisher	Cambridge	Classics, Part II	I
			The Alice Gardner Prize	
	M. Sherwood (Mrs. V. Martin)	Cambridge	Mod. Lang., Part I	II(1)
	J. Kirke (Mrs. Miles)	Cambridge	Mod. Lang., Part I	II(1)
	M. Williams	Cambridge	Mod. Lang., Part I	II
	J. Allison	Cambridge	Mary Ewart Scholarship of £100	
	M. Suggett	Oxford	Classics	II
	M. Abbiss (Mrs. Farrant)	London	B.Sc., Chemistry	III
	H. Campbell	Edinburgh	M.A.	I
	A. Atherstone (Mrs. Fielden)	Melbourne	B.A.	
	Eileen Keventer		M.R.C.S., L.R.C.P.	
1945	M. Sherwood (Mrs. V. Martin)	Cambridge	Mod. Lang., Part II	II(1)
	J. Allison	Cambridge	Nat. Sci., Part I	II
	J. Fisher	Cambridge	Geography, Part I	II(2)
	A. Singer	Cambridge	Mod. Lang., Part I	I
	M. Moller (Mrs. Miller)	Cambridge	Newnham College Prize of £10	
	S. Chappel (Mrs. Sloper)		M.B., M.R.C.S., L.R.C.P., Lagg Prize, Cheyne Prize	
			M.R.C.S., L.R.C.P., Almond Prize	
	P. Halsey	Oxford	Classics	
	G. Leigh	London	Hare Prize for Geology	
	M. Clements	London	B.Sc. (Household Science)	IV

Year	Name	University	Subject	Class
1945	M. Cameron (Mrs. McNair)	Edinburgh	M.B.	
	C. Davison (Mrs. Maxwell)	Cambridge	Exhibition for Science	
	V. Douet	Edinburgh	Andrew Grant Scholarship of £60 for Art	
1946	M. Coate	Oxford	Suzette Taylor Fellowship	
	R. Hawkins	Oxford	Janet Watson Bursary of £100	
	B. Wadia	Oxford	English	II
	J. Fisher	Cambridge	Geography, Part II	II
	B. Human	London	B.A., French	II(A)
	J. Beveridge	Edinburgh	Scholarship of £120 for Art	
	L. Cooke	Edinburgh	Fellow of the Royal College of Surgeons	
1947	J. Allison	Cambridge	Science, Part II	II(1)
	M. Hill	Cambridge	Science, Part I	II
	N. Nicholson	Cambridge	English, Part I	II(2)
	A. Singer	Cambridge	Mod. Lang., Part II	II(2)
	M. Williams	Cambridge	Mod. Lang., Part II	II(2)
	H. Peatfield	Cambridge	Mod. Lang., Part I	II(2)
	R. Whitley (Mrs. Staniland)	Oxford	History	IV
	M. Smylie	London	B.A., Greek	III
	A. Smallwood	London	Ll.B.	II
	S. Jacobs	London	B.Sc., Economics	
	M. Dawe	Edinburgh	M.B, B.Ch.	
	D. Woodward	Edinburgh	M.A.	
1948	C. Davison (Mrs. Maxwell)	Cambridge	Science, Part II	II
	N. Nicholson	Cambridge	Travelling Scholarship to Denmark English, Part II	II(2)

R

Year	Name	University	Subject	Class
1948	B. Elphick	Cambridge	Classics, Part I	II
	H. Peatfield	Cambridge	Mod. Lang., Part II	II
	R. Bates	London	B.A., Classics	II(A)
	A. Chandler	London	B.A., History	II
	G. Fairey	London	B.A., German	II
	M. Pearson	London	B.Sc., Economics	
1949	B. Elphick	Cambridge	Classics, Part II	II(2)
	H. Peatfield	Cambridge	Mod. Lang., Part I	II(2)
	M. Williams	Cambridge	Classics, Part I	II(1)
	E. Baldwin	Oxford	History	II
	G. Roberts	London	B.Sc., Economics	
	M. Beveridge	Edinburgh	L.R.C.P., L.R.C.S.	
	C. Messinger (Mrs. Rose)	Edinburgh	B.Sc.	
	A. MacBean	St. Andrews	M.B., Ch.B.	
	D. Woodford	Manchester	B.A.	
	K. Hardy (Mrs. Sampson)	Sheffield	M.B.	
1950	S. McCullagh	Leeds	M.A. (with distinction)	
	D. Hacking	Reading	B.Sc., Agriculture	
	S. Booth	Reading	B.A., Fine Arts	
	E. Skinner	Cambridge	Minor Scholarship for Classics	
	P. Galley	Cambridge	Theology, Part I	
	R. Bach	London	B.A., Spanish	II(2)
	G. Hoskins	London	B.A., English	II
	A. Martin	Edinburgh	M.A.	II(2)
	J. Chappel (Mrs. Russell)	Edinburgh	B.Sc.	

Year	Name	University	Subject	Class
1950	J. Eastop	Reading	B.Sc., Horticulture	
1951	D. Braggins	Dublin	Doctor of Music	
	C. Vasey (Mrs. Holmes)	Oxford	Honour Moderations	II
	P. Galley	Cambridge	Theology, Part II	II
	C. Messinger (Mrs. Rose)	Cambridge	Science, Part II	III
	E. Skinner	Cambridge	Classics, Part I	II(2)
	M. Williams	Cambridge	Classics, Part II	III
	T. Hankey	London	B.A., History	II(1)
			Annette Ackroyd Research Scholarship	
	P. Arnold	London	B.A., Spanish	II(2)
	F. Parkin	London	B.A., History	II(2)
	J. Woodin	London	B.A.	
	M. Viner	London	B.Sc., Social Science	
	S. Watson	London	B.A.	
	J. Kirk	St. Andrews	M.A.	
	R. Bryant	Edinburgh	M.A.	II
	J. Smedley	N. Wales	B.A., English and Philosophy	II(2)
1952	E. Skinner	Cambridge	Classics, Part II	
	C. Davison (Mrs. Maxwell)	Cambridge	M.B., B.Chir.	
	M. Belcher (Mrs. Parkes)	Oxford	Mathematics	II
	E. Parr	Oxford	Mathematics	
	N. Marsden (Mrs. Maguire)	London	M.B.	III
	A. Ranken	London	M.B.	

Year	Name	University	Subject	Class
1952	R. Baldwin	Edinburgh	M.A.	III
	J. Smallwood (Mrs. Macklin)	Edinburgh	M.A.	II
	B. Hayward	Leeds	B.Sc.	
	M. Blundell	London	B.Sc., Horticulture	
	P. Crowsley	Oxford	Exhibition for Classics	
	J. Innes	Cambridge	Exhibition for Modern Languages	
	F. Clark		Diploma du Cours de Civilisation Française	
1953	C. Vasey (Mrs. Holmes)	Oxford	Literæ Humaniores	II
	J. Innes	Cambridge	Mod. Lang., Part I	II
	A. Braybrooke	London	B.A., French	III
	J. Cooper	London	B.A., English	III
	M. French	London	B.A., French	II(B)
	H. Marshall	London	B.A., Latin	III
	A. Bagshaw (Mrs. Hall)	Bristol	B.A.	II(B)
	D. Daniel	Liverpool	M.B., B.Ch.	
	M. Bagot	Cambridge	Open Scholarship	
1954	M. Belcher (Mrs. Parkes)	Oxford	Mathematics	III
	E. Parr	Oxford	Mathematics	IV
	A. Young	Oxford	Literæ Humaniores	II
	K. Bird	London	Mathematics	III
	A. Gray	London	B.Sc.	
	P. Shortland	London	B.A., French	
	S. Cartwright	London	B.Sc.	
	T. Christie	Edinburgh	M.A.	III

Year	Name	University	Subject	Class
1954	R. Thompson	Oxford	Open Exhibition	II
	M. Entwistle	Cambridge	Open Exhibition	
	P. Farr	London	Open Exhibition	
	R. Srinivasan	London	Open Exhibition	
1955	T. Hankey	London	Ph.D.	
	S. Green	Oxford	Mathematics	III
	P. Crowsley	Oxford	Gladstone Travelling Scholarship	III
	D. Braggins	Cambridge	B.A., English and Music	II(1)
	S. Booth	Cambridge	Archaeology, Part I	II(1)
	M. Bagot	Cambridge	Science, Part I	III
	M. Webb	Cambridge	Science, Part I	II(2)
	J. Innes	Cambridge	Mod. Lang., Part II	
	H. Baxter	Cambridge	English, Part I	II
	J. Lawrie (Mrs. Birkett)	London	B.Sc., Science	III
	F. Houghton	London	B.A., English	II
	G. Orme	London	B.Sc.	III
	R. Pursehouse	London	B.A., History	II
	J. Stobbs	Nottingham	B.A.	
	M. Fensome	Cambridge	Open Exhibition	
	J. Wynn Williams	Oxford	Open Exhibition	
	J. Boddy	London	Open Exhibition	
1956	P. Crowsley	Oxford	Literæ Humaniores	II
	R. Thompson	Oxford	Honour Moderations	III
	M. Bagot	Cambridge	Science, Part II	II
	M. Webb	Cambridge	Science, Part II	I
	H. Baxter	Cambridge	English, Part II	II(2)
	D. Hall	London	B.A., Spanish	II

Year	Name	University	Subject	Class
1956	R. Milner	London	B.A., French	II
	E. Fairey	London	B.Sc., Zoology	II
	J. Bennie	Durham	B.Sc.	II
	R. Hawker	Cambridge	Open Exhibition	

INDEX